DIMENSIONS
OF BAHÁ'Í LAW

DIMENSIONS
OF BHARAT LAW

DIMENSIONS
OF BAHÁ'Í LAW

**ROSHAN
DANESH**

BAHÁ'Í
PUBLISHING

WILMETTE, ILLINOIS

Bahá'í Publishing
401 Greenleaf Avenue, Wilmette, Illinois 60091

22   21   20   19   4   3   2   1

ISBN 978-1-61851-151-5

Cover design by Jamie Hanrahan
Book design by Patrick Falso

For Cathy

Contents

CONTENTS

CONTENTS

Contents

Acknowledgments

The articles in this book represent some of the outcomes of dialogue, research, and writing that took place over a period of two decades. Because of this, there are so many people to thank that it is almost too many to keep track of. Names will be missed, as there are so many who provided assistance, insight, and comments on each of these articles, who inspired and refined my thinking, and who made my relatively incoherent thoughts and words readable and meaningful.

As such, I will not try to name everyone. I thank those mentors, teachers, and students who guided and inspired the ideas in this volume. I thank the institutions and publications that supported my teaching, research, and writing, and the encouragement they gave me to explore areas that were unexplored. And most of all I thank my dear family and friends, who made all aspects of this a reality. You all know who you are.

Foreword

This volume brings together articles written by Dr. Roshan Danesh following the publication in 1992 of the English translation of the Kitáb-i-Aqdas, the central legal text of Bahá'u'lláh's revelation. These articles explore fundamental dimensions of Bahá'u'lláh's laws within the theological context of Bahá'í teachings for the betterment of the world. While the essence of the law constitutes, or is related to, the divine will, these essays show that Bahá'u'lláh's "epistemic vision" of social change—and the role of divine law in effecting normative, structural, legal, political, economic, and other social changes toward the unification of peoples and nations—enables one to explore why His law operates in a transformative manner that is distinct from common conceptions of divine law. The articles collectively illustrate—each with its own dimensional focus—that the Bahá'í teachings offer the most comprehensive and expansive revelation thus far in human history of that staggering phenomenon in which God communicates, periodically and successively, His laws and teachings to humanity through His chosen Prophets. As shared in this volume, Bahá'í literature, particularly the Kitáb-i-Aqdas, offers the reader abundant opportunities to acquire knowledge of the scope and character of divinely-revealed law and how its standards may be realized on earth. Additionally, these essays explore the most effective ways and circumstances for assimilating and telling the great story of Bahá'í law.

Over many years, an international community of scholars has witnessed the prolific yield of Roshan Danesh's enthralling engagement in gaining insights into the legal dimensions of Bahá'í teachings for social change. These articles originally appeared in prominent academic and professional publications, including the prestigious *Journal of Law and Religion*, distinguished for its publications of cutting-edge research on the relationship between law and religion. Their publication now, within the covers of this single volume, makes the multidimensional character of the legal teachings more readily accessible to individuals from all backgrounds. Discussions are presented, for example, on the concept of Bahá'í law; on the structure of the Kitáb-i-Aqdas; on specific laws, principles, and processes; on internationalism and divine law; and on the relationship between law, governance and religion, and the motivating factors for obeying Bahá'í law. Readers will also be able to explore discussions on social and political dimensions, which involve the principle of the oneness of humanity for a new world order.

The volume as a whole raises our consciousness that law—and especially divine law—has a distinctive educational function, a distinct transformative purpose and force, and a unique position in the spiritual and material evolution of humankind. The inclusions of enlightening commentaries by 'Abdu'l-Bahá, Shoghi Effendi, and the Universal House of Justice—particularly extracts from the latter's introduction to the English translation of the Kitáb-i-Aqdas—are a striking feature of this volume, and in it readers will find descriptions of the unique status of the Kitáb-i-Aqdas and how, as the Universal House of Justice has noted, its translation into English "extends the sphere of its influence, opening wider the door to a vast process of individual and community development."* *Dimensions of Bahá'í Law* also allows readers the opportunity to, as the Supreme Body has encouraged, "recite its [the Kitáb-i-Aqdas's] verses; study its contents; adhere to its exhortations; and thus transform their lives in accordance with its divine standard."**

---

* Universal House of Justice, *Messages from the Universal House of Justice, 1986–2001: The Fourth Epoch of the Formative Age*, no. 150.4.

** Universal House of Justice, *Messages from the Universal House of Justice, 1986–2001: The Fourth Epoch of the Formative Age*, no. 150.5.

As Dr. Danesh points out in the essay "Some Reflections on the Concept of Law in the Bahá'í Faith," the Bahá'í legal approach is not a "legalistic, rule-oriented, and fear-based one." Rather, Dr. Danesh continues, it reflects "His [Bahá'u'lláh's] concept of the spiritual reality of human existence . . . [and] articulates a vision of religion and law in which the operation and applicability of the law must evidence, reinforce, and cultivate the central human capacities of love and knowledge." The careful review of trends and approaches of scholarship on Bahá'í law is a thoughtful initiative. In some places, achievements and misunderstandings are considered.

A mention here of the author's engagement with national and cultural legal studies; his practical experiences with the administration of law is also illustrative, as these achievements are integral parts of his striving to advance an appreciation of Bahá'u'lláh's revelation. Dr. Danesh completed his legal studies at the University of Victoria and Harvard Law School, where he earned a Doctor of Juridical Science (S.J.D.). He has lectured at the University of British Columbia, University of Victoria, European Peace University, Landegg International University, and the Justice Institute of British Columbia. He has also taught courses in law and religion, constitutional law, indigenous rights, and conflict resolution. A practicing attorney specializing in constitutional law and the rights of indigenous peoples, he recently served as the special counsel on Indigenous reconciliation to the Minister of Justice and Attorney General of Canada.

Another influence on the writing of this foreword, in addition to Dr. Danesh's clarity of expressions, are impressions that may be drawn from what he calls "my own journey through writing about Bahá'í law." This journey is a remarkable story of his learning and taking action—not only as a scholar, an educator, a lawyer, and a member of the Bahá'í Faith, but also as a human being with spiritual and intellectual aspirations to assist others. His story is a source of encouragement for all of us, and it has certainly increased my admiration for his labors.

I have had occasions to participate in discussions about Bahá'í law in different parts of the world—in auditoriums, lecture halls, a variety of neighborhoods, and remote village gatherings. Educated participants, and those uneducated or poorly educated, hesitantly expressed—and understandably so—what they sensed could be said for themselves, and for their fellow human beings, about the accessibility of the Kitáb-i-Aqdas and its exalted rank. Some expressed the searching, preliminary, and tentative character of their impressions. It did not matter. Everyone present always spoke and listened with courtesy, without any thought that our efforts to understand Bahá'í law would succeed overnight. We understood, too, as best we all could, that our undertakings at gaining and sharing insights about the "Most Holy Book" were valuable and worthwhile. Most of all, I remember the wonder in people's voices and on their faces.

With feelings of admiration for this publication, I think I cannot do better than close with words written by Dr. Danesh himself. He observes that it is likely the Bahá'í community will continue to "transform its understanding of Bahá'í law . . . in the decades and centuries to come." He continues, "It is hoped that by bringing this volume together, a contribution will be made to the expansion and advancement of understanding of Bahá'í law. In twenty-five years of engaging the subject, the main insight gained, if any, is how infinitesimal our understanding is of the legal dimensions of Bahá'u'lláh's revelation. I expect generations in the future will look back with bemusement about what we thought and how we got there. But, of course, this incessant human search for knowledge helps enable generations to look back and generate lessons and meanings that can be used to propel humanity forward. It is hoped that this volume, and all of those studying and writing about Bahá'í law in these early years, may make one tiny contribution in that regard."

Kiser Barnes
Raleigh, North Carolina, U.S.A.

Introduction

In 1993, at the age of twenty-one and having completed studies in film at McGill University, I somehow ended up beginning law school in Victoria on Canada's Pacific coast. Why I moved from the study of film to the study of law is a transition for which I have yet to find a reasonable explanation.

However, from my earliest days at law school, it became increasingly clear to me what my focus would be. Ultimately, my goal was to gain knowledge that would be helpful in thinking and learning about Bahá'í law, as well as the central Bahá'í legal text, the Kitáb-i-Aqdas.

Bahá'u'lláh's Kitáb-i-Aqdas occupies a distinct place within the corpus of Bahá'í literature. As the "Most Holy Book," the "Mother Book," as well as His book of laws, the Kitáb-i-Aqdas is the central scriptural text of the Bahá'í revelation, and it is a work of unparalleled importance and standing (Universal House of Justice, Introduction to the Kitáb-i-Aqdas, 1). Shoghi Effendi describes the Kitáb-i-Aqdas as being "unique and incomparable among the world's sacred Scriptures" (Shoghi Effendi, "A Description of the Kitáb-i-Aqdas by Shoghi Effendi" in the Kitáb-i-Aqdas, 14). The Universal House of Justice emphasizes its pivotal importance to the coming of age of humanity as the repository of laws "designed to carry humanity forward into a world civilization the splendors of which can as yet be scarcely imagined" (Universal House of Justice, Introduction to the Kitáb-i-Aqdas, 2). In 1992, the first authorized English translation of the Kitáb-i-Aqdas was published.

Prior to 1992, the book was not broadly accessible outside of its original Arabic language. One effect of this delay—which is wholly consistent with Bahá'u'lláh's own vision and intent regarding the nature and use of the sacred texts and the development of Bahá'í community life—was that the relationship of the worldwide Bahá'í community to the text was at once intimate and distant. Even before its publication in 1992, the standing of the Kitáb-i-Aqdas was well understood, and certain passages from the Most Holy Book were used in Bahá'í communities for study and dialogue. Bahá'ís always treated the study of such passages with the same reverence one finds toward sacred texts in other religious systems. However, passages from the Kitáb-i-Aqdas were not the only source of study for Bahá'í communities, and at various times, other scriptural sources and areas of focus were more pivotal at shaping individual and community life.

The release of the authorized translation of the Kitáb-i-Aqdas was a source of anticipation and excitement for Bahá'ís. In 1992, prior to my decision to attend law school, my small Bahá'í community in a Montreal neighborhood—like Bahá'í communities around the world—began a focused study in preparation for the release of the authorized translation. I also recall that in 1993, at the annual conference of the Association for Bahá'í Studies, a special symposium was held at McGill University on the Kitáb-i-Aqdas, and this symposium helped launch a new era of English-language scholarship on this sacred text, at a time when it would be more widely accessible.

Some of these experiences prior to the release of the Kitáb-i-Aqdas also spurred significant questions and inquiry on my part. I remember attending, prior to the release of the book, a multiday course on the Kitáb-i-Aqdas, at the De Poort Bahá'í School. While the course was rich in many aspects, I remember being puzzled by the strictly doctrinal and rules-oriented mode of discourse throughout the session. I also doubted whether comparing the rules in the Kitáb-i-Aqdas to those that might be found in canon law or the Qur'án would be particularly useful to

understanding the role and relevance of Bahá'u'lláh's laws in the contemporary world. I had questions for which I sought answers.

Of course, law school itself had nothing to say to me about Bahá'í
law specifically, and I doubted there was any other person in the law
school building who had ever even come across such a term. Indeed, at
the time, there was little if any interest in discussing the relationship
between law and religion within Canadian law schools (something that
has changed only marginally in the last two decades).

Even though I was uncertain at first whether I had chosen wisely to
attend law school, a few positive signs began to appear. One day while I
was perusing books in the library, I stumbled across a small, beaten-up
copy of Harold J. Berman's *The Interaction of Law and Religion*. Often
credited with reinvigorating the study of law and religion in the United
States, Berman's short work raised questions about the spiritual foundations of law, the revolutionary dynamics of legal history, the relationship between religion and the legitimacy of legal systems, and the
pressures on global legal systems resulting from a rapidly changing and
increasingly integrated humanity. For me, the book was a first glimpse
at how the study of law, social change, and humanity's religious and
spiritual heritage were inextricably intertwined.

A far more important development, however, in my study of religion
and law was the guidance and mentorship of Professor John McLaren.
A former dean and prominent legal historian, Professor McLaren was
keenly interested in the relationship between law and religion, both
historically and in today's world, and he had brought his vast intellect to
researching and writing on how small religious communities interacted
with State legal orders.

Professor McLaren's encouragement that I begin exploring the
dimensions of Bahá'í law was the beginning of a journey. From Victoria, with various detours, I moved on to Harvard Law School and
began five years of master's and doctoral studies—all with the express
purpose of studying Bahá'í law. In addition to specifically studying the

Bahá'í Faith, my research included the study of Islamic law and legal systems, the historical relationship between law and religion in Europe and North America, and treatment of religion in contemporary constitutional orders.

The decision to approach the study of Bahá'í law, as well as the Kitáb-i-Aqdas, through advanced studies in law, as distinct from religious studies or Islamic or Middle Eastern studies, was a purposeful one. My particular interest was and remains, understanding the relevance of the legal dimensions of Bahá'u'lláh's teachings for the processes of social change and the advancement of social justice. In searching for a deeper understanding of these topics, I studied the dynamic role law plays in society and how Bahá'u'lláh foresees a role for law in general, as well as laws He revealed, for achieving a better world. During my research, I also looked at the operation of Bahá'í law in practice—both how it operates and how it is experienced by individuals and communities.

This approach differs from primarily focusing on the relationship between Bahá'í law and theology, categorizing or delineating Bahá'í laws, comparing Bahá'í law and other scriptural laws, or writing an exegesis of the Kitáb-i-Aqdas. Indeed, a predominant tendency in the study of Bahá'í law—which is unsurprising given the early stage we are in—is to focus on the categorization, delineation, and description of what are understood to be the laws or rules Bahá'u'lláh promulgated. Quite consciously, I have sought to pursue a different approach to the subject matter.

All of the articles in this volume reflect this focus on the application and use of Bahá'u'lláh's laws and legal teachings in the world and the life of humanity. They explore four main areas of focus.

The first area is Bahá'u'lláh's conception of law itself, which is presented as being a radical break from both the Bahá'í Faith's Islamic legal heritage as well as predominant conventional understandings of law. In this way, understanding Bahá'í law challenges us to question, and ultimately abandon, our taken-for-granted ways of thinking, talking about, and using law.

This radical conception of law is explored through the analysis of Bahá'u'lláh's legal language and the very structure of the Kitáb-i-Aqdas itself. A deeper understanding of this new legal conception is also revealed in the historical treatment of Bahá'í law and its peculiar pattern of delay and backgrounding in the use and application of Bahá'í law.

The second area includes constitutional dimensions of the Bahá'í Faith, including Bahá'u'lláh's teachings regarding the relationship between legal and religious institutions and authorities, and the Bahá'í concept of world order. Of course, throughout history and across the globe, this relationship has been a pivotal one and has often been a subject of tensions and controversies. These tensions and controversies continue to exist in the contemporary world, where in varying ways, struggles over the relationship between law and religion contribute to struggles between—among other things—social order, governance, human rights, gender equality, social justice, and war and security.

Perhaps unsurprisingly, therefore, the relationship between religious and legal institutions in the Bahá'í Faith has been one area related to Bahá'í law where there has been some scholarly debate. The articles in this volume suggest that Bahá'u'lláh proposes a fluid and contingent vision of the relationship between legal and religious institutions and that this vision rejects many of the predominant assumptions about the relationship of law and religion that are typically made.

The third area comprises Bahá'u'lláh's theory of social change and the role of law in effecting change. Bahá'u'lláh's vision of how social change can occur in a manner that supports and advances the centrality of unity in human life and affairs is a subject with which the worldwide Bahá'í community is increasingly engaged. The current focus of the Bahá'í community on social action and contributions to the discourses of society reflects this orientation.

As the articles discuss, Bahá'u'lláh's vision of social change is primarily an epistemic one, where changes in social meanings are understood as the doorway to broader normative, legal, and structural changes in ways that are aligned with the necessity of unity. This vision of social change informs us why Bahá'í law operates in a distinct way from common conceptions of divine law.

The fourth area involves the examination of Bahá'í community discourse and scholarship about Bahá'í law. With the publication of the authorized English translation of the Kitáb-i-Aqdas in 1992, there has been a growth in both the Bahá'í community's study and understanding of its Most Holy Book, as well as scholarship examining the text and the nature of Bahá'í law.

What has emerged over this quarter century are certain patterns and trends, which collectively reflect the early stages of the development of a Bahá'í legal tradition. As the articles demonstrate, there are many ways in which we can expect to see the Bahá'í community continue to challenge, question, refine, and transform its understanding of Bahá'í law and ways of reading the Kitáb-i-Aqdas in the decades and centuries to come.

The articles represent an effort to explore the dimensions of Bahá'í law—beginning from the time of the release of the authorized English translation of the Kitáb-i-Aqdas until today—and they have been organized thematically rather than chronologically throughout this volume. Indeed, one of the most interesting aspects of my own journey in writing about Bahá'í law is that my ideas regarding more foundational and core aspects of Bahá'í law developed only after more than two decades of study. While the earlier essays allude to Bahá'u'lláh's radical and new conception of law, they are, in a sense, preoccupied with more specific and sometimes tangential issues and areas of focus. It took time for me to fully recognize that in order to engage in meaningful discourse about Bahá'í law, one must deepen on what is actually meant by this term. Without striving to do this—which is an ongoing and lifelong undertaking—we will be ever more prone to the lazy conflation of our own assumptions and beliefs about law and about Bahá'u'lláh's unique conception of law.

Finally, it is worthwhile to note that the articles in this volume originally appeared in a diverse range of publications.

Two of the most recent articles—"Some Reflections on the Concept of Law in the Bahá'í Faith" (2014) and "Some Reflections on the Structure of the Kitáb-i-Aqdas" (2015)—appeared in the *Journal of Bahá'í Studies* and were written at the same time as companion pieces. They are considered to be entry points to the study of Bahá'í law. Alongside "Imagining Bahá'í Law" (2007) in *Bahá'í Studies Review* and "The Politics of Delay—Social Meanings and the Historical Treatment of Bahá'í Law" (2004) in *World Order,* these two articles present an argument for a particular approach to understanding the nature of Bahá'í law. This argument challenges some of the contemporary patterns that have been common in scholarly discourse.

Three of the articles originally appeared in publications with no connection to the Bahá'í Faith. Two of them—"Internationalism and Divine Law: A Bahá'í Perspective" (2004) and "Church and State in the Bahá'í Faith: An Epistemic Approach" (2008)—appeared in the *Journal of Law and Religion,* the most prominent journal of the relationship between law and religion. These articles focus on the Bahá'í conception of the relationship between law, governance, and religion. Along with Udo Schaefer's "An Introduction to Bahá'í Law: Doctrinal Foundations, Principles, and Structures" (2002), these articles represent the only articles on Bahá'í law that have been published in the *Journal of Law and Religion.* The third, "Hegemony and Revelation: A Bahá'í Perspective on World Order" (2010), which was published in *Religious Studies and Theology,* reinforces key themes of the articles in the *Journal of Law and Religion* by specifically discussing the Bahá'í concept of world order.

The remaining articles—"Some Reflections on Bahá'í Approaches to Social Change" (coauthor Lex Musta, 2012, *Bahá'í Inspired Perspective on Human Rights,* volume 2, Juxta Publishing) and "Themes in the Study of Bahá'u'lláh's Kitáb-i-Aqdas: Emerging Approaches to Scholarship on Bahá'í Law" (*Journal of Bahá'í Studies,* 2018)—explore our patterns of thinking and talking. The first offers a specific Bahá'í theory of social change based on the relationship between social meanings, social norms, and social forms. The second examines how scholars have talked about Bahá'í law, and it examines where we may be headed in the future in the study of Bahá'í law. In a sense, it is an attempt to summarize the quarter century of scholarship since the release of the authorized translation of the Kitáb-i-Aqdas in 1992.

It is hoped that by bringing this volume together, a contribution will be made in the expansion and advancement of understandings of Bahá'í law. In twenty-five years of pursuing this subject, the main insight gained, if any, is how infinitesimal our understanding is of the legal dimensions of Bahá'u'lláh's revelation. I expect generations in the future will look back with bemusement about what we thought and how we got there. But, of course, this incessant human search for knowledge will help enable generations to look back and generate lessons and meanings that can be used to propel humanity forward. It is hoped that this volume, and all of those individuals studying and writing about Bahá'í law during these early years, may make one tiny contribution in that regard.

PART 1

Foundations for
Understanding Bahá'í Law

1 / Some Reflections on the Concept of Law in the Bahá'í Faith

[FIRST PUBLISHED IN *JOURNAL OF BAHÁ'Í STUDIES*, VOL. 24, NO.1/2, 2014.]

Abstract

This article examines the concept of law in the Bahá'í Faith through aspects of the Islamic context within which Bahá'u'lláh promulgated laws as well as the nature of legal language and discourse in Bahá'u'lláh's writings. What emerges is a portrait of Bahá'u'lláh's concept of law that indicates a sharp and radical break from conceptions of law extant at the time. He revealed laws and, more broadly, a distinct concept of religious law rooted in conscious knowledge and the dynamics of love that rejects rigid and legalistic preoccupations with rules.

Setting out to identify the concept of law within the Bahá'í Faith is an act of hubris, for both general and specific reasons. Trying to identify the conception of law in any particular legal order is by its very nature fraught with problems. It implies, at the outset, that there is an essential concept of law to be identified—an almost objective meaning to be discovered that reflects facts about that order itself. By its very nature, however, law is relatively incapable of definition in this way because of its innate subjective dimensions. Understanding conceptions of law will require looking at how individuals and groups interact with, use, respond to, and understand phenomena of a legal character. In this respect, conceptions of law in any particular context are inevitably varied and dynamic.

Exploring a conception of "Bahá'í law" is particularly complicated. The Bahá'í Faith is a relatively young religious system, and—reflecting its age and particular pattern of growth—very little legal architecture has emerged.[1] Further, throughout Bahá'í history, the significance of law—and Bahá'í laws in particular—has been consciously, and quite consistently, back-grounded—including, for example, the very gradual distribution and translation of legal texts and the limited application of laws.[2] While discussion of law and the propagation of laws have a central place in Bahá'í scripture, they have not been central in the ways one might expect to the lives of individual Bahá'ís or Bahá'í communities. For example, unlike predominant Islamic traditions, discourses on law, while important, have not been a primary lens through which Bahá'í identity has been defined. What might be called "Bahá'í law" is not a central item of discussion or preoccupation among the community at large, nor is it a widespread subject of scholarly study.[3]

Nonetheless, it is still timely and appropriate, for two reasons, to put forward a few observations about the theory of law in the Bahá'í Faith. First, the Bahá'í Faith represents an interesting case study of a nineteenth-century independent religious movement that was born in the Middle East out of Islamic roots; that has strong commitments to pluralism, equality, participatory democracy, and social justice; and that includes prescriptions for change and reform. At a time of massive change and upheaval throughout the Muslim world, such a case study reveals some of the diverse and dynamic strands of reformist thought that have long been present. Second, the Bahá'í Faith represents an interesting example of a relatively new religion engaging with issues of diversity on a global scale. The capacity of religious law to manage and to be responsive to such diversity is a challenge facing all major religious systems, and the Bahá'í Faith is of interest in its explicit effort to grapple with this issue through the very nature and understanding of law itself and how this understanding might be applied in a diverse world.

This article offers reflections and observations that are preliminary in nature and meant to be nothing other than markers that might be taken into account by future scholars as they consider and advance the study of the Bahá'í Faith, including its legal dimensions. Collectively, these reflections highlight the sharp break that Bahá'u'lláh's writings and ideas about law represent from the orthodox conceptions of the Shi'i context in which He was immersed. They also reflect an orientation to religious law that is dynamic and contextual and necessitate viewing the law as practice in order to gain insight into its meaning and operation. Finally, these reflections illustrate how, in Bahá'u'lláh's writings, there is a necessary relationship between the spiritual and the social and how processes of spiritualization are intimately connected to the purpose, meaning, and application of His laws.

Bahá'u'lláh's Break with the Islamic Legal Imagination

Gaining insight into the conception of law in the Bahá'í Faith requires some understanding of the attitude and orientation toward law in predominant Islamic worldviews and of the legal context within which Bahá'u'lláh lived. Broadly, three core elements of this legal imagination are important: the necessity for obedience to legal rules on the path to salvation, an emphasis on rules covering all aspects of human life, and the practice of imitation (*taqlíd*) as a legitimate method of demonstrating obedience.

Whether one is speaking of orthodox Shi'i or Sunni traditions, the predominant legal imagination views law, and obedience to the law, as crucial on the path toward salvation and to meeting religious obligations and requirements.[4] Individual believers need to follow religious rules if their purpose in life is to be fulfilled. Further, all dimensions of life—all choices and actions—have legal value attached to them. On this spectrum, every act, no matter how private and personal or public and general, may be categorized as forbidden, discouraged, tolerated, encouraged, or required. Nothing falls outside of this spectrum.

How is one to know what the rules (*ahkam*) are? In the classical theory, and ideally, gaining knowledge of the law is a text-based endeavor—the process of divining the intent of God through turning to the Qur'án and to a narrow and prescribed set of other sources. The method of sincere striving to discover God's legal intent, or *ijtihád*, is, in theory, an endeavor that all pious individuals can and should undertake for themselves. In practice, however, interpretation through *ijtihád* remains the domain of the few, while legitimate rationales have emerged over time for the masses of people to practice imitation, or *taqlíd*, of those who are learned (whether living or dead). As such, demonstrating fidelity to the religious law in practice has often become more a function of power and hierarchy than of individual intent, striving, and knowledge. So at once, obedience to rules is essential and necessary in all aspects of life, and obedience can be demonstrated by following those designated to possess knowledge and power.[5]

In the Shi'i world, the evolution of *ijtihád* and *taqlíd* are layered with a somewhat different orientation to legal authority than in the Sunni world. Shi'ism revolves around the concept of the Imamate, which cultivates an understanding that an authoritative lawgiver remains other than the Prophet Muhammad and the Imams who followed Him. This notion of an Imamate authority—an authority figure who was understood to be inaccessible after the occultation of the twelfth Imam—bred some degree of resignation and political quietism among Shi'i adherents, given the inevitable illegitimacy of all temporal rulers other than the Imam (who had disappeared from human view).[6] In this context, the practices of *ijtihád* and *taqlíd* emerged on a somewhat different timetable than in the Sunni world and with some differences in principles and roles. In particular, some distinctions concerning the role of the clerics were practiced in the Shi'i world, which in the contemporary world contribute to clerics holding temporal political power since the creation of the Islamic Republic of Iran.[7]

This legal imagination was one of extreme constraints. In predominant forms, it reflected a sharp rule orientation that privileged adherence to rules based on the perceived authority of those in the clerical hierarchy, whether living or dead. In practice, one could follow the rules not out of a conscious engagement with them and the texts that supported them, or seeking an understanding of their import, or out of recognition of their morality, but because they were the rules adopted and legitimized by a particular cleric who was worthy of following.

In this framework, little space exists between law and its operation and the requirements and necessity to travel the path to salvation. In order to lead the good life and confirm a place in the afterlife, one needed to follow the duties and obligations of the law. In effect, rigid obedience to the law and securing one's spiritual health were intertwined endeavors. For this reason, detailed rules covering minute aspects of life were spelled out and articulated. Little was to be left to chance when the well-being of the soul was on the line.

Against such a backdrop, Bahá'u'lláh's treatment of the legal content of His revelation must be seen as a sharp and radical break with the predominant Shi'i view within which He was born. Indeed, every central aspect of the Shi'i legal imagination would appear to be completely upended.

At first glance, Bahá'u'lláh's radicalism is not obvious. In the canon of His writings, the book most closely associated with His laws—the Kitáb-i-Aqdas—holds a superior place, which suggests that law possesses a similar central role as in Islam.[8] The Kitáb-i-Aqdas is unquestionably considered the most significant of His writings (a fact given away by its title, which translates as "Most Holy Book"), and Bahá'u'lláh repeatedly called people to recognize this singular significance. He referred to it as His "weightiest testimony," noted that "blessed are those who peruse it" and "ponder its meaning," and cautioned that "such is the majesty of what hath been revealed therein, and so tremendous the revelation of its veiled allusions that the loins of utterance shake when attempting their description." In addition, the context of the revelation of the Kitáb-i-Aqdas in many respects would appear to mirror the dynamics and preoccupations of the prevailing Shi'i legal imagination. Beginning in 1863 (the time of His declaration as the bearer of a new revelation from God), Bahá'u'lláh began to receive requests for the new Faith's laws from converts. One can fathom the consternation that might have preoccupied these new adherents who, after choosing to abandon the orthodoxy of the time and accept that a new revelation had been bestowed upon humanity, were nonetheless eager to know the new rules that had to be followed in order to ensure fidelity to the requirements of the new age. And indeed, around 1873, after receiving many such requests, Bahá'u'lláh finally decided it was timely to respond, which He did by revealing the Kitáb-i-Aqdas.[9]

But Bahá'u'lláh's revelation of the Kitáb-i-Aqdas was not in continuity with the expectations concerning the role of law in the Shi'i world. Prior to the revelation of the Kitáb-i-Aqdas, Bahá'u'lláh had already denied the validity of orthodox conceptions of law, and His own attitude toward the revelation of new laws actually epitomizes the radical nature of this break.

Before His declaration in 1863, Bahá'u'lláh had already effectively condemned the role of clerics and religious authorities (regardless of religious persuasion) in perverting the direct connection between human beings and their Creator. In the Kitáb-i-Íqán, Bahá'u'lláh mercilessly places blame for humanity's poor track record of heaping suffering and condemnation on Bearers of new revelations from God—and generally the public's failure to recognize these Messengers—on the distortions and deceptions of an insincere and power-hungry clerical class. Reflecting this theme, Bahá'u'lláh writes in the Kitáb-i-Íqán, "Leaders of religion, in every age, have hindered their people from attaining the shores of eternal salvation, inasmuch as they held the reins of authority in their mighty grasp. Some for the lust of leadership, others through want of knowledge and understanding, have been the cause of the deprivation of the people. By their sanction and authority, every Prophet of God hath drunk from the chalice of sacrifice."[10]

Bahá'u'lláh's discourse in the Kitáb-i-Íqán is comprehensive and expansive, not merely pointing to the legal role of clerical authority in

Islam. Rather, His discourse is a direct attack on this role and on similar ones in other religions. Indeed, a core precept of Bahá'u'lláh's teachings—and a legal principle within the Bahá'í Faith—is the elimination of clergy and clerical authority in general, and the power typically associated with them. From early on it was clear that one pivot of the Shi'i legal imagination—imitation of a learned religious authority—was now rejected. There would be no such authority to imitate, nor a class of clerics authorized, as spiritual authorities in legal matters in the Bahá'í Faith.[11]

Even more striking as a radical departure from the legal context that constructed the background in which Bahá'u'lláh revealed law is His orientation toward the revelation of laws and His own treatment of His laws. It is significant that Bahá'u'lláh waited a decade before revealing the compilation of His laws in the Kitáb-i-Aqdas. However, as has been discussed in significant detail elsewhere,[12] this delay was only one expression of a far broader principle of gradualism in the dissemination and application of His laws. In addition to a delay in the revelation of laws, there was only gradual dissemination and translation of the Kitáb-i-Aqdas. Indeed, about one hundred years passed before authoritative compilations of the laws were produced, and 120 years before the Kitáb-i-Aqdas was formally and authoritatively translated from Arabic.[13] Parallel to these delays in revelation, dissemination, and translation is a principle of gradualism in the application of Bahá'u'lláh's laws. The notion that the laws should only be applied gradually began in Bahá'u'lláh's time and continues today. Official Bahá'í statements have specifically noted that this gradualism is a purposeful tenet of the Bahá'í understanding of law: "there is . . . divine wisdom in a gradual, rather than immediate, application of all the laws."[14]

Such delay and gradualism clearly upends the orthodox expectation that there should be no space between the path to salvation and rigid adherence to legal duties and obligations. In fact, in real ways, converts to the new religion were being directly told that the new religion demanded a very different orientation toward fulfilling their spiritual destinies. Of course, such shifts in orientation and consciousness are neither easy nor immediate. Indeed, the uprooting of such deeply entrenched ideas often takes multiple generations, as new understandings and contexts begin to emerge. From the earliest days of Bahá'u'lláh's explicating His law, one can see Him laying the groundwork to cultivate this new understanding, in complete contradiction to the expectations and preoccupations of the orthodox mindset held by the vast majority of His early followers.

For example, one notable aspect of the Kitáb-i-Aqdas is that it explicitly calls individuals into a knowing relationship with the laws revealed and into a stance of consciously striving to understand them. This theme is present throughout the work. In the opening paragraphs, Bahá'u'lláh speaks of the people of "insight"—a station that anyone can attain—who will see in His laws the "highest means for the maintenance of order in the world and the security of its peoples." He calls to individuals and praises those who have "apprehended the meaning of His decisive decree." In critiquing those who may claim special or distinct knowledge, He universally urges all individuals, "Read ye the Tablets that ye may know what hath been purposed in the Books of God, the All-Glorious, the Ever-Bounteous." In undertaking the search for knowledge, He argues for sincere striving and cautions, "make not your deeds as snares wherewith to entrap the object of your aspiration."[15]

Consistent with this theme of seeking knowledge, Bahá'u'lláh allowed His followers to ask Him questions about the Kitáb-i-Aqdas. The questions, which came from many individuals but were compiled into one collection, are striking in how they reveal the legal context within which Bahá'u'lláh appeared. Almost without exception, the questions are preoccupied with ritual and personal legal matters and are largely focused on trying to clarify specific details of particular rules. Even though Bahá'u'lláh had warned early in the Kitáb-i-Aqdas, "think not that We have revealed unto you a mere code of laws,"[16] the yearning for a specific code of laws is apparent from the questions Bahá'u'lláh was asked. While His allowing questions alone signifies a break from the past, the nature of the questions themselves shows that the concerns of the past were still very apparent in the present.

The condemnation and outlawing of the clergy; the delay in the revelation, dissemination, and application of His laws; the call to individuals to knowingly engage the laws for themselves; and the explicit admonishment that He was not revealing a "mere code of laws" all demonstrate that Bahá'u'lláh was actively undermining the pillars of the Shi'i legal imagination.

This important departure from orthodoxy is reinforced by later writings and evidence. A startling example is *The Secret of Divine Civilization*, which Bahá'u'lláh asked His son 'Abdu'l-Bahá to write during the same period of time that the Kitáb-i-Aqdas was revealed. It was a time of upheaval in Iranian political and social life, and Bahá'u'lláh requested that His son write a work "on the means and the cause of development and underdevelopment of the world in order to reduce the prejudices of the dogmatic conservatives."[17]

Taking up that challenge, in a clear broadside against the power and control held by the *'ulamá* (Islamic scholars), 'Abdu'l-Bahá opens *The Secret of Divine Civilization* with an essentialist statement about human consciousness, praises God for endowing human beings with the powers of "intellect" (*'aql*), and links these powers to the traditions of Islamic philosophy and the role of Islam in the evolution of civilization. He directs His message of political and social reform to all people, because God has endowed everyone with the intellectual capacity to participate in political and social matters.

In His ranking of intellect as the "supreme emblem of God [which] stands first in the order of creation and first in rank" and with His broad appeals to the Persian people to use their intellect for change—"how long shall we spend our days like barbarians in the depths of ignorance and abomination?"—'Abdu'l-Bahá is overturning the power structures that upheld the clerics and articulating His vision of a world in which all people use rational thought to order and structure their individual and collective lives. Building on this theme, 'Abdu'l-Bahá reminds people that the Prophet Muhammad Himself commanded His followers to seek out knowledge "even in the furthermost reaches of China."[18]

To challenge the view of some orthodox 'ulamá that adopting Western ideas and practices amounts to a forbidden form of imitation, 'Abdu'l-Bahá points out that if "the incompetent and caviling doctors forbid this [the adoption of Western ideas or practices], offering as their justification the saying 'He who imitates a people is one of them,'" they are thus in violation of the Prophet's teachings. In effect, 'Abdu'l-Bahá has turned the tradition of *taqlíd* on its head, demonstrating that imitation—a cornerstone of the operation of law—is inconsistent with the teachings of Muhammad and, rather than being the source of salvation, is the cause of oppression: "O People of Persia! Open your eyes! Pay heed! Release yourselves from this blind following of the bigots, this senseless imitation which is the principal reason why men fall away into paths of ignorance and degradation. See the true state of things. Rise up; seize hold of such means as will bring you life and happiness and greatness and glory among all the nations of the world."[19]

Bahá'u'lláh's Legal Language

An important element for beginning to identify some additional aspects of Bahá'u'lláh's conception of law is the exploration of His legal language. Bahá'u'lláh employs a number of different terms in the Kitáb-i-Aqdas that have connotations of and potentially translate as *law* or a synonym of *law,* such as *decree, precept, ordinance,* or *commandment.* While in the English translation of the Kitáb-i-Aqdas Arabic terms for law (or its equivalents) are translated in multiple ways, reflecting a range of contextual and stylistic considerations, it is helpful to look at how these Arabic terms are employed in the opening paragraphs of the Kitáb-i-Aqdas, where Bahá'u'lláh introduces key aspects of His discourse around law.

In the opening paragraph of the Kitáb-i-Aqdas, Bahá'u'lláh discusses the "twin duties" that all human beings have—to recognize the Manifestation of God and to "observe every ordinance" revealed by that Manifestation.[20] This discussion of duties is concomitant with a definition of the essential human purpose: to know and worship God, the very reason for which we have been created. This preamble describes the ontological order of the universe and how, in this contingent world, the human being has been created to fulfill these duties.

Hudúd is the term translated as "ordinance" in this paragraph. In literal meaning *hudúd* refers to "limits," "restrictions," or "boundaries." In Islam, the term came to be associated with the core class of punishments for serious crimes that have explicit discussion in the Qur'án. These include theft, sexual intercourse in certain contexts, drinking alcohol, and apostasy. This class of punishments in Islamic penal law is effectively understood as fixed and required to be implemented if the crime is proven.

In this sense, *hudúd* comes to be associated with the external use of power by the sovereign to mete out punishment to those who have committed such a crime. Additionally, reference to the *hudúd* in Islamic legal traditions comes to be associated with laws that are explicitly revealed and stated within the Qur'án. These ordinances might be contrasted with rules that are instead derived from other legitimate sources which, depending on tradition or school of thought, may include recorded traditions (*hadíth*), consensus of scholars, various types of reasoning, and certain principles of utility.[21]

Bahá'u'lláh recasts the notion of *hudúd* away from the narrow Islamic category of specific penal punishments and links it instead to a teleological conception of human nature in which humans are seen as having been created with certain potentialities and purposes to be achieved. In effect, Bahá'u'lláh offers an internalization and spiritualization of the concept of *hudúd* in which achieving our spiritual destiny (which is at the heart of human purpose) requires and involves striving to live within certain parameters that are most conducive to our spiritual growth and well-being. The restrictions (*hudúd*) are not punishments to be applied by an external force; rather, they delineate the boundaries within which our spiritual health and purpose can best be achieved.

Bahá'u'lláh points to this spiritualization of the meaning of *hudúd* in the second paragraph of the Kitáb-i-Aqdas, where He speaks of individual recognition of the significance of the *hudúd* and individual intention to strive to observe them. In emphasizing the importance of individual knowledge, He states, "They whom God hath endued with insight will readily recognize that the precepts [*hudúd*] laid down by God constitute the highest means for the maintenance of order in the world and the security of its peoples." He then goes on to emphasize that individuals have been commanded to "refuse the dictates of [their] evil passions and corrupt desires, and not to transgress the bounds (*hudúd*)," which have been fixed—thus locating discourse about *hudúd* at the level of human nature and the various tendencies that may be present in it. Reflecting the notion that spiritual fulfillment emerges out of striving to recognize and implement certain limits in our choices in life, Bahá'u'lláh explains that these limits are the "breath of life unto all created things."[22]

This meaning of *hudúd*, grounded in the notion of fulfilling our human purpose, is contrasted with Bahá'u'lláh's use of the term *ahkam* (the plural of *hukm*). In paragraph 5 of the Kitáb-i-Aqdas, adopting a critical stance, He writes, "think not that we have revealed unto you a mere code of laws."[23] In Islam, *ahkam* is associated with the numerous and detailed bodies of specific rules developed by the clerics through application of the sources and principles of Islamic jurisprudence. In theory, as noted earlier, the method of developing these rules is through conscious individual striving (*ijtihád*), though in practice the masses of people practiced imitation (*taqlíd*).

Having already reoriented the notion of *hudúd*, Bahá'u'lláh then pushes aside the central position that the derivation of rules of right conduct has had in defining the path to salvation in orthodox Islamic traditions. In His reduction of the significance of "mere" codes of law, and in His caution to recognize that the development of codes is not the enterprise in which He is engaged, Bahá'u'lláh emphasizes that He has "unsealed the choice Wine."[24]

The metaphor of the "choice Wine" is significant for a number of reasons. First, it further separates Bahá'u'lláh's discourse on law from the Islamic tradition by using a term typically associated with the *hudúd* (drinking alcohol being one of the punishable crimes) as a positive reference to something unique and of the highest order. Secondly, rather than associating law with the rigid application of a code and rules, this metaphor encourages an orientation to seeing how law can be a source of freedom from constraints and oppression. The language used encourages, in particular, a view of law as guiding one on the pathway to spiritual fulfillment and ecstasy. Reflecting His concept of human nature, Bahá'u'lláh links the achievement of human freedom and happiness with living in such a way that one consciously strives to recognize one's spiritual reality and purpose, and structures one's life to reflect that reality and meet that purpose. As opposed to a paradigm of law being associated with the application of external temporal power, in this instance the "fingers of might and power" have unsealed the "choice Wine" that can help us meet our spiritual destiny.[25]

As these few illustrations show, Bahá'u'lláh appears to upend the legalistic rule orientation that traditionally accompanied the meanings of *hudúd* and *ahkam* in Islamic traditions. Further, however, He also shifted His discourse of law from a narrow and prescriptive focus on the application of temporal rules to reflecting on law in terms of the nature of human purpose and spiritual reality.

This is not to say that Bahá'u'lláh does not reveal rules, but a focus is placed on the role of law in relation to a human being's spiritual consciousness and the fulfillment of its spiritual purpose. This adds another dimension to the significance of the pattern of delay, as well as the outlawing of spiritual clerical authorities which were identified earlier as core aspects of Bahá'u'lláh's profound break with Islamic traditions. The inward turn, the focus on positioning His discourse of law in terms of the spiritual well-being of individuals, and the emphasis on individual (as opposed to clerical) responsibility for one's spiritual state establishes yet another logical basis for the reason that Bahá'u'lláh does not emphasize the importance of identifying rules and rigidly enforcing them. Rather—as is discussed in more detail in the next section—consistent with the Bahá'í concept of the human soul as expressive of the human capacities of knowledge, love, and will, conscious knowledge and acting out of love for one's Creator become the prime legitimate motive forces for obeying the law.

A last note about Bahá'u'lláh's legal language in these opening paragraphs relates not to His actual terminology of law but rather to the form in which He enunciates His laws. While His caution against seeing His laws as a code could not be clearer, at the same time it must be recognized that He does articulate certain provisions that appear clearly as rules. These rules, while not extensive in number, do appear to cover a wide range of subjects. Yet, even this apparent form of rules has other purposes. Bahá'u'lláh's language in articulating laws has been referred to as having "a certain fluidity and imprecision inherent in the very language." One reason for this is its "observable tendency to deal with whole areas of legislative concern by reference to a single representative example or illustrative instance." In this "elliptical" model, the statement of rules may be understood as indicating certain themes, directions, and areas that Bahá'u'lláh views as important in future legal development, as well as certain principles that may be relevant to the development of that area of law. In other words, the purpose of an apparent "rule," in some cases, may not be to articulate a specific directive but to act as a proxy for drawing out a particular theme, principle, or concept of import. At the same time, this means that the apparent rules should not be read as standing on their own apart from how they function "integrally within the Bahá'í system as a whole," as is well explained in the following example: "Thus, although in paragraph 34 Bahá'u'lláh appears to restrict Himself to prohibiting the kissing of hands, the fact that it is not so much the action in itself about which He is concerned, as the condition of self-abasement that it represents, is demonstrated by His having elsewhere in His Writings expanded the prohibition to cover the display of all such forms of obsequious reverence and undue veneration towards one's fellow mortals."[26]

Bahá'u'lláh's Rationale for Obedience to the Law

Another term that Bahá'u'lláh employs in paragraph 3 of the Kitáb-i-Aqdas is *avamir* (plural of *amr*), translated as "commandments." This term is used more specifically to refer to the things that God commands. Bahá'u'lláh employs the term in the context of articulating an answer to the age-old question in the philosophy of law of why individuals should observe the law.

Regardless of which legal order one may be discussing, the issue of what compels obedience to law is a window into deciphering aspects of the meaning and operation of law in that context. The range of answers is immense and can involve looking at questions of power and institutional structures, the dynamics of the threat of force and fear, perceptions and understandings of the law, the relationship between law and morality, and the role of social relationships and the structuring of social norms.

When speaking about the demonstration of obedience to His own laws, Bahá'u'lláh grounds His answer to this age-old question in the concept of love, positioning love as the motive force for an individual striving to follow the laws of God. He states "My commandments are the lamps of My loving providence" and exhorts His followers, "Observe My commandments, for the love of My beauty."[27]

In the Bahá'í understanding of the universe, love is the fundamental universal law. 'Abdu'l-Bahá states that "love is the most great law . . . the unique power that bindeth together the divers elements of this material world, the supreme magnetic force that directeth the movements of the spheres in the celestial realms." 'Abdu'l-Bahá further writes that love is the "establisher of true civilization in this mortal world, and the shedder

DIMENSIONS OF BAHÁ'Í LAW

of imperishable glory upon every high-aiming race and nation." God's revelation of laws to humanity is an act of love, and the legitimate reason for them to be applied and followed is as an expression of love.[28]

This particular construction of the interaction between law and love is notable in how it grounds adherence to religious law within the particular spiritual dynamics of each individual and the state and position of that individual's own spiritual journey. Love, in this context, is a conscious state of individual recognition of one's Creator and, relatedly, of one's reciprocal love relationship with that Creator. God has created the human being out of love, and through learning to reciprocate that love and acting out of love, our potential and purpose in life can be fulfilled. Obedience to the law is a conscious choice that one must make out of that experience of love; it is not the arbitrary imposition of will by an external power. Bahá'u'lláh makes it clear that "[h]appy" will be one who has understood the importance of observing God's commandments out of love, and that when one is moving toward such a state one will "circle around [His] commandments." He also suggests that the laws themselves are an expression of God's love for humanity: "Say: True liberty consisteth in man's submission unto My commandments, little as ye know it. Were men to observe that which We have sent down unto them from the Heaven of Revelation, they would, of a certainty, attain unto perfect liberty. Happy is the man that hath apprehended the Purpose of God in whatever He hath revealed from the Heaven of His Will that pervadeth all created things. Say: The liberty that profiteth you is to be found nowhere except in complete servitude unto God, the Eternal Truth. Whoso hath tasted of its sweetness will refuse to barter it for all the dominion of earth and heaven."[29]

This concept is completely in contrast to notions that laws should be followed out of imitation, blind obedience, ignorance, or fear. As Bahá'u'lláh Himself says in the Kitáb-i-Aqdas, "we have assigned to every end a means for its accomplishment." This connection between "means" and "ends" is also true in the legal realm. The end (obedience) requires the means (love)—the combination of which derives from a sincere, conscious desire to strive to manifest obedience in one's own life. Further, through obedience, our love may be deepened and one of our ultimate ends—love of our Creator—advanced.[30]

The implications of this relationship between law and love add a whole range of other dimensions to our understanding of Bahá'í law. Intimate individual contexts become a primary (though not exclusive) arena within which the religious law operates on a number of levels. For example, adherence to certain laws identified within the Kitáb-i-Aqdas is purely private and personal—laws such as those governing prayer, fasting, or the payment of a particular tax on certain categories of savings.[31]

On the one hand, this notion of personal and private compliance obviously highlights how Bahá'í laws are not to be imposed on individuals who are not adherents of the Bahá'í Faith. But more far-reaching than this, individual contexts, mindsets, states of learning, of being, and of consciousness generally are relevant to the question of how Bahá'í laws are used and applied. This understanding introduces a dynamic concept into the operation and application of Bahá'í law, which is linked to, but distinct from, the concept of delay discussed earlier. Law, in this conception, is most meaningfully operative when it functions in a context in which individual consciousness has striven to understand the reason and purpose for that law and is motivated to follow that law as part of the process of individual spiritual growth and fulfillment. This fact presents another rationale for the delay in the applicability of the law, since creating communities of individuals with the orientation and opportunity to engage the law with such knowledge and love is a multigenerational project. Bahá'u'lláh's instruction that the application of the law was not really timely reflects the idea that certain contexts and orientations must emerge so that the actual meaning and intent of the law—to be an agent of positive spiritual progression and development—can, in turn, emerge and evolve.

This dynamic nature of the law is reflected in a whole series of features of how Bahá'í law has been used and applied. For example, in addition to the general pattern of delay, it is also the case that, generally speaking, among those laws that do apply, more of them apply to individuals from historic Bahá'í communities than to individuals in new Bahá'í communities.[32] Similarly, a number of areas of conduct that one would typically expect to be regulated by religious law are left, at this time, to "individual conscience," with individuals being encouraged to strive to review relevant guidance, examine their own motivations, and choose the path they feel is right for them.[33]

Reflecting this dynamic nature, Bahá'u'lláh's laws have been called "evolutionary and organic in conception." This evolutionary nature reflects the need to enable them to "develop, progress, and burgeon" over time, through the passing of legislation by the Universal House of Justice. Even more so, the connection between context, spiritual processes, and knowledge and love of the law orient one toward the necessity of understanding the laws "according to their informing spirit, and not the letter of the law."[34]

Following the laws of Bahá'u'lláh out of love and according to their "informing spirit" demands conscious effort. In Bahá'u'lláh's words, it demands sincere striving of the mind to "apprehend" the meaning of His laws. It also demands striving to view His laws within their own terms of reference so that their spirit and meaning can be revealed. As Bahá'u'lláh exhorts in the Kitáb-i-Aqdas, "Weigh not the Book of God with such standards and sciences as are current amongst you, for the Book itself is the unerring balance established amongst men. In this most perfect balance whatsoever the peoples and kindreds of the earth possess must be weighed, while the measure of its weight should be tested according to its own standard, did ye but know it."[35]

In this essential linkage between love and knowledge of the laws as the rationale for obedience, the relationship between Bahá'u'lláh's laws and human purpose is again drawn. In the Bahá'í teachings, the central capacities of our soul—the essential attributes all human beings have—are our capacities of mind (knowledge) and heart (love). The highest expression of those capacities—their greatest refinement—is found in conscious knowledge and love of our Creator and in actions that reflect that knowledge and love. This statement of human capacity and purpose is encapsulated in one of the obligatory prayers of the Bahá'í Faith:

> I bear witness, O my God, that Thou hast created me to know Thee and to worship Thee. I testify, at this moment, to my powerlessness and to Thy might, to my poverty and to Thy wealth.
>
> There is none other God but Thee, the Help in Peril, the Self-Subsisting."[36]

Failure to strive to understand the laws of the Kitáb-i-Aqdas in accordance with their spirit can lead to quick and massive confusion. To use one illustrative example, in the Kitáb-i-Aqdas Bahá'u'lláh appears to spend an unusual amount of time on rules that relate to issues of personal appearance, cleanliness, and refinement. While some of these rules would make sense in specific cultural contexts—and would be somewhat reformist in nature—for many readers they are quite confounding.

But when viewed in the context of Bahá'u'lláh's writings and teachings as a whole, one sees that, far from being a disparate set of distinct rules that are of specific significance, they are expressions of a comprehensive and overarching principle of refinement (latafah). Latafah, which is translated in various places as "cleanliness" or "refinement," is an overarching principle that reflects the notion of the highest spiritual and physical expression of the human being. As is explained in the notes to the Kitáb-i-Aqdas, latafah "has a wide range of meanings with both spiritual and physical implications, such as elegance, gracefulness, cleanliness, civility, politeness, gentleness, delicacy and graciousness, as well as being subtle, refined, sanctified and pure."[37]

With this principle in mind, Bahá'u'lláh's references to mundane and basic physical expressions of latafah takes on a new character and meaning. The emphasis and import is not on rules about length of hair or purity of water for washing or any other mundane detail; rather, it is on the principle that every aspect of life, even the most mundane, engages our spiritual reality and that with every action, no matter how seemingly insignificant, we should endeavor to honor that spiritual reality by striving for refinement.

Physical and spiritual reality cannot be separated and divorced from one another and, as such, in all our actions we should be aiming for excellence, beauty, and refinement. In this context, rules about cleanliness are not intended to develop rigid and strict guidelines for our physical appearance; rather, they inform our consciousness of how all of our actions have spiritual implications and dimensions and suggest that we should move beyond any false dichotomies between our daily lives and our spiritual journey.

As a final note, a lot of emphasis has been placed in the previous discussion on the individual and individual rationales for obedience to the law. It should be noted, however, that there are also collective imperatives and principles that provide insight into Bahá'u'lláh's views of how laws should be applied and used. Central to this is the Bahá'í concept of unity or oneness, and the idea that certain contexts and conditions conducive to unity are necessary before certain specific laws can be followed, applied, or enforced. As Bahá'u'lláh states, "in observing [the laws] one must exercise tact and wisdom. . . . Since most people are feeble and far-removed from the purpose of God, therefore one must observe tact and prudence under all conditions, so that nothing might happen that could cause disturbance and dissension or raise clamor among the heedless."[38]

He goes on to state that "one must guide mankind to the ocean of true understanding in a spirit of love and tolerance."[39] In this linking between the applicability and enforceability of laws and social context, one sees a whole other set of rationale for the pattern of delay and another set of rationale for why and when Bahá'í law might be followed. This second rationale links to the particular constructs of Bahá'í social and political theory.

Bahá'í Legal Imagination

As these few examples illustrate, the Bahá'í legal imagination, as revealed in Bahá'u'lláh's writings, is not a legalistic, rule-oriented, and fear-based one. It also rejects an emphasis on the relationship between power and the application of rules. Reflecting His concept of the spiritual reality of human existence, Bahá'u'lláh articulates a vision of religious law in which the operation and applicability of the law must evidence, reinforce, and cultivate the central human capacities of love and knowledge. In these aspects of the Bahá'í teachings, Bahá'u'lláh's vision of law is not only a fundamental departure from the Islamic traditions into which He was born, but it is also a stark challenge to how law is conventionally and typically thought about in many other contexts, including in Europe and North America. To date, there is little sign that studies of Bahá'í law have grappled meaningfully with these novel aspects of Bahá'u'lláh's approach to law; the emphasis still appears to remain on the primacy of examining rules[40] as distinct from viewing the legal imagination Bahá'u'lláh challenges His followers to have, and the related implications for law in practice. Hopefully, future scholars of Bahá'í law, reflecting on the distinct dynamics of Bahá'í legal history and the legal content of Bahá'u'lláh's writings, will chart new pathways for the study of Bahá'í law.

PART 2:

Reading the Kitáb-i-Aqdas

2 / Some Reflections on the Structure of the Kitáb-i-Aqdas

[FIRST PUBLISHED *JOURNAL OF BAHA'I STUDIES*, VOL. 25, NO. 3, 2015.]

Abstract

Secondary literature on the Kitáb-i-Aqdas has tended to comment that the book is relatively unstructured—that it is a mix of topics without any logical or discernible order. This short article challenges the assumption that the Kitáb-i-Aqdas is unstructured and suggests there is value to our understanding of the book and of Bahá'í law by exploring further elements of structure. Particular emphasis is placed on the first nineteen paragraphs of the Kitáb-i-Aqdas and how they state in most concise form the pivotal constructs of Bahá'í spiritual and social teachings.

Very little has been written about the structure of the Kitáb-i-Aqdas, the "Most Holy Book" of the Bahá'í Faith, which is also often referred to as Bahá'u'lláh's book of laws. With a few notable exceptions,[1] the bulk of the comments on the structure of the Kitáb-i-Aqdas suggests that the work is in various ways unstructured. For example, the Kitáb-i-Aqdas has been compared to the Qur'án as a work "in which legislation is often alluded to rather than expounded and in which disparate topics are placed together without obvious logic."[2] Similarly, it has been observed that in the Kitáb-i-Aqdas, there are "no *numerus clausus*: legal norms (like moral instructions) are scattered throughout the revealed scripture. They do not form a consistent system; instead, they constitute supreme norms (as in the case of legal provisions in the Qur'án) that require systematization and specification."[3] As another prominent scholar observes, "Bahá'u'lláh, after expounding some of His choicest teachings or revealing some of His counsels and exhortations, abruptly changes the subject and gives one or more laws which outwardly seem not to have any relevance to the previous subject."[4]

Such observations about the structure of the Kitáb-i-Aqdas are sometimes advanced in support of arguments about the nature of Bahá'í law and elements of the Bahá'í teachings. By advancing expectations that law be written, systematized, and organized—that it have a "rigid outline"[5]—and by suggesting that Bahá'u'lláh did not reflect these expectations, we open a door to certain assertions or arguments about the legal aspects of Bahá'u'lláh's revelation of laws and their importance. For example, the suggestion that the Kitáb-i-Aqdas is unstructured and does not meet our norms of legal texts might be used to justify the view that the precepts contained in it are not meant to be statements of legal rules, but should be understood primarily as ethical norms and principles.

As I have discussed elsewhere,[6] Bahá'u'lláh does offer a distinct and quite radical concept of law—one that represents a sharp break from the Shi'ite legal context in which the Bahá'í Faith was born, and that challenges formalist and positivist conceptions of religious law. The concept of law in Bahá'u'lláh's writings does not fall into established Qur'ánic or other scriptural categories, nor does it conform to Eurocentric assumptions about the form and nature of law. Rather, Bahá'u'lláh articulates a concept of law grounded in a particular understanding of the human being, as well as the role of law in social change, which at once accepts the social construction of law in action while maintaining fidelity to a teleological understanding of human nature.

In this article, I develop further arguments about Bahá'u'lláh's legal vision and challenge assertions about the ostensibly unstructured format of the Kitáb-i-Aqdas. I pay particular attention to its paragraph 19 and how it contributes to our understanding of the book's structure.

The Arcs of Ascent and Descent

In some respects, it might be surprising to the reader who first opens the Kitáb-i-Aqdas to hear the commonly expressed view that the book is unstructured; the opening paragraphs appear to have a relatively clear thematic structure.

The first five paragraphs of the Kitáb-i-Aqdas stand together as a statement of the central elements of Bahá'í ontology and locate Bahá'u'lláh's concept of law within that ontology. Bahá'u'lláh refers, in various ways, to God, the Primal Will, the Manifestation, and humanity, as well as to the relationships among them. The primary responsibility of the individual human being is recognition of the Manifestation "Who representeth the Godhead in both the Kingdom of His Cause and the world of creation," and the individual is exhorted "to observe every ordinance" the Manifestation reveals.[7]

Bahá'u'lláh continues in the first five paragraphs to provide a series of observations about the nature of His laws and ordinances and to develop the meaning and concept of law He is propounding. In this regard, He both grounds His concept of law (*hudúd*) in a particular vision of human nature and the purpose of human existence and distinguishes it from mere rules (*ahkam*). This distinction reflects His conception of the human soul as well as His vision of the relationship between unity and diversity as the metanarrative of human history and the force and purpose of social change.[8] He thereby highlights the role of knowledge and love as the rationale and the foundation for choosing to obey His laws.

These opening paragraphs might be said to reflect the metaphor of a circle that is sometimes used to describe Bahá'u'lláh's teachings about the structure of reality—that there is an arc of descent and an arc of ascent. 'Abdu'l-Bahá describes the relationship between God, the Manifestation of God, and humanity; and between material and spiritual reality through reference to the arcs of descent and ascent.[9]

The arc of descent expresses the movement from God (at the peak or apex) to creation, symbolized as a downward arc. It is an expression of how human beings are from God and of the order of things in creation. The arc of ascent speaks to a movement upward, of how we return unto God. 'Abdu'l-Bahá describes the place of humanity in this scheme in the following terms: "For the inner reality of man is a demarcation line between the shadow and the light, a place where the two seas meet; it is the lowest point on the arc of descent, and therefore is it capable of gaining all the grades above. With education it can achieve all excellence; devoid of education it will stay on, at the lowest point of imperfection."[10]

If we understand the first five paragraphs as expressing the arc of descent, and recognition and obedience as the key to a human being's ascent, we see a shift in paragraph 6. In paragraphs 6 through 18, Bahá'u'lláh identifies the fundamental spiritual obligations of the individual human being—obligatory prayer, fasting, and repetition of "Allah-u-Abhá."[11] While paragraphs 1 through 5 explain the principles of descent and ascent at a metaphysical level, paragraph 6 transitions to discussing the dynamics of ascent in the physical world, in how we lead our daily lives. The spiritual obligations that are identified, beginning in paragraph 6, are the fundamental architecture of ascent—they are the practices that individuals perform to focus their mind and body on their spiritual reality, and on their relationship with their Creator.

Taken together, therefore, we see that in paragraphs 1 through 18, Bahá'u'lláh is moving us on the arcs of descent and ascent. He moves us quickly to that "demarcation line" on which humanity resides and speaks about the fundamentals needed for a human being's ascent.

It should be acknowledged that a few scholars have noted, in various ways, the relationship between the theme, or metaphor, of ascent and descent and the structure of the Kitáb-i-Aqdas. For example, Adib Taherzadeh uses the same metaphor to describe the structure of the

Kitáb-i-Aqdas but employs the terms in a different way, in which ascent refers to the revelation of spiritual principles and descent refers to the proclamation of laws to be obeyed by humanity:

> In revealing the *Kitáb-i-Aqdas,* Bahá'u'lláh may be likened to a celestial bird whose habitation is in the realm of the spirit far above the ken of men, soaring in the spiritual heights of glory. In that station, Bahá'u'lláh speaks about spiritual matters, reveals the verities of His Cause and unveils the glory of His Revelation to mankind. From such a lofty horizon this immortal Bird of the Spirit suddenly and unexpectedly descends upon the world of dust. In this station, Bahá'u'lláh announces and expounds laws. Then the Bird takes its flight back into the spiritual domains. Here the Tongue of Grandeur speaks again with majesty and authority, revealing some of the choicest passages treasured in the *Kitáb-i-Aqdas.* . . . This ascent and descent, the revelation of spiritual teachings on the one hand, and the giving of laws on the other, follow one another throughout the Book.[12]

In his article "Unsealing the Choice Wine at the Family Reunion," Bahá'í author John S. Hatcher provides one of the most systematic and scholarly analyses of the concept of the arcs of ascent and descent, including the relationship of the Kitáb-i-Aqdas to this theme in Bahá'u'lláh's writings. Hatcher has developed his analysis in a range of works—including *The Arc of Ascent*—that provide detailed discussion of the Kitáb-i-Aqdas as identifying the dynamics of the ascent of humanity's individual and collective life and of the relationship between physical and spiritual reality and how they relate to the role of the laws of the Kitáb-i-Aqdas in our individual lives. Hatcher's work provides important insights into how the structure of the Kitáb-i-Aqdas relates to the complex process of a human being's spiritual ascent, beginning with the importance of the twin duties of "recognition" and "obedience" identified in the opening paragraph of the book as expressing "the two-part paradigm that frames the entire process of divine enlightenment, defines the fundamental properties that distinguish all human activity, and establishes with clarity the unique position and status of *The Kitáb-i-Aqdas* in the evolution of humankind on our planet."[13]

Professor Nader Saiedi—who provides one of the few sustained efforts to identify a structure in the Kitáb-i-Aqdas—focuses on four overarching themes that give structure and coherence to the work. In his book *Logos and Civilization,* Saiedi calls these four principles (1) the removal of the sword, (2) the principle of covenant, (3) the universal revelation, and (4) the principle of heart. He then identifies how these themes are expressed in clusters of paragraphs in the Kitáb-i-Aqdas, including significant shifts at a few points in the book. Similar to the observations above about the arc of descent and arc of ascent, Saiedi identifies how the opening paragraphs provide the fundamentals of Bahá'í "metaphysics" and "social theory" and then move into a discussion about specific laws. As he observes, the first specific laws revealed—obligatory prayer and fasting—are "the means of God through His Manifestation," which can be associated with the dynamics of ascent.[14]

The Centrality of Paragraph 19

Having seen the thematic coherence of paragraphs 1 through 18, one is struck by the apparent shift in paragraph 19. Only one sentence long, paragraph 19 states, "Ye have been forbidden to commit murder or adultery, or to engage in backbiting or calumny; shun ye, then, what hath been prohibited in the holy Books and Tablets."[15]

This paragraph has not been the subject of much scholarly consideration. In popular Bahá'í discourse, it is sometimes the subject of speculation about the apparent relationship Bahá'u'lláh draws between murder, adultery, and backbiting or calumny—and indeed it is often asserted that He is somehow equating these categories of wrongful acts. However, I suggest that paragraph 19 merits much deeper exploration and analysis in terms of both its meaning and content, its pivotal place in the structure of the work, and its relationship to the rest of the work.

The transition from paragraph 18 to paragraph 19 clearly marks a shift from Bahá'u'lláh's discussion of spiritual obligations to a discussion of laws regulating human relations. Paragraph 19 is the first one, in this work, to contain prohibitions or laws that speak to the relationships between human beings and to the elements of social order.

When studying Bahá'u'lláh's writings, one must recognize that certain meta-themes and principles run throughout His teachings, and that He often made use of explicit and implicit interreferences to His other works. The need to recognize the interrelated nature of Bahá'u'lláh's writings is emphasized by the observation that Bahá'u'lláh's laws in the Kitáb-i-Aqdas cannot be read apart and in isolation from the rest of His teachings and writings. In its introduction to the Kitáb-i-Aqdas, the Universal House of Justice highlights the importance of the reader being acquainted with the "interpretive and legislative institutions that Bahá'u'lláh has indissolubly linked with the system of law thus revealed."[16] The Research Department at the Bahá'í World Center comments that "the provisions of the Kitáb-i-Aqdas are not to be regarded as standing on their own, but rather functioning integrally within the Bahá'í system as a whole."[17] This analysis includes, for example, how certain statements in the Kitáb-i-Aqdas are best understood by statements elsewhere in His Writings that give context and clarity.

When discussing prohibitions in the Bahá'í Faith, one needs to note that there is an initial prohibition, enunciated in 1863 by Bahá'u'lláh at the moment when He declared Himself a Manifestation of God, stating that "in this Revelation the use of the sword is prohibited."[18] In a number of His writings, Bahá'u'lláh describes this prohibition both in specific and broad terms. As the statements below illustrate, this prohibition rejects the advancement of Bahá'u'lláh's Faith through force and promotes a broad and constructive principle of inclining our hearts toward others in positive and constructive ways:

Know thou that We have annulled the rule of the sword, as an aid to Our Cause, and substituted for it the power born of the utterance of men. Thus have We irrevocably decreed, by virtue of Our grace. Say: O people! Sow not the seeds of discord among men, and refrain from contending with your neighbor. . . .[19]

Strife and conflict befit the beasts of the wild. It was through the grace of God and with the aid of seemly words and praiseworthy deeds that the unsheathed swords of the Bábí community were returned to their scabbards. Indeed through the power of good words, the righteous have always succeeded in winning command over the meads of the hearts of men. Say, O ye loved ones! Do not forsake prudence. Incline your hearts to the counsels given by the Most Exalted Pen and beware lest your hands or tongues cause harm unto anyone among mankind.[20]

The prohibition of the sword is at once a negative statement about the use of force, coercion, and violence, and an overarching positive statement about the requirement for, and application of, the dynamics of love and unity in all aspects of life, as well as the importance of individuals seeking out knowledge and truth for themselves. It is also an explicit contrast to how previous religions have—over time and in various ways—justified or permitted the use of coercion and force to spread God's message. Bahá'u'lláh exhorts the avoidance of conflict and contention, and the centrality of love and unity among all peoples of the world, throughout His writings:

O contending peoples and kindreds of the earth! Set your faces towards unity, and let the radiance of its light shine upon you. Gather ye together, and for the sake of God resolve to root out whatever is the source of contention amongst you. Then will the effulgence of the world's great Luminary envelop the whole earth, and its inhabitants become the citizens of one city, and the occupants of one and the same throne. This wronged One hath, ever since the early days of His life, cherished none other desire but this, and will continue to entertain no wish except this wish. There can be no doubt whatever that the peoples of the world, of whatever race or religion, derive their inspiration from one heavenly Source, and are the subjects of one God. The difference between the ordinances under which they abide should be attributed to the varying requirements and exigencies of the age in which they were revealed. All of them, except a few which are the outcome of human perversity, were ordained of God, and are a reflection of His Will and Purpose. Arise and, armed with the power of faith, shatter to pieces the gods of your vain imaginings, the sowers of dissension amongst you. Cleave unto that which draweth you together and uniteth you. This, verily, is the most exalted Word which the Mother Book hath sent down and revealed unto you. To this beareth witness the Tongue of Grandeur from His habitation of glory.[21]

In Saiedi's analysis, the prohibition of the sword represents all of the following: "The prohibition of killing, violence, and religious coercion; the promotion of love, unity, and fellowship among peoples; the call for peace among the nations; the condemnation of militarism and of the proliferation of arms; the assertion of the necessity for education and productive employment; the condemnation of sedition; the assertion of the need for religion and social justice."[22] Saiedi states that "all these are presented by Bahá'u'lláh as systematic expressions of the same underlying principle of the removal of the sword."[23]

The prohibition is at once a rejection of conflict, violence, division, oppression, and prejudice, as well as the affirmation of love, equality, justice, unity, and peace. It is the call Bahá'u'lláh makes for the construction of fundamentally new patterns of relationships for all of humanity, and for the ethic of authentic and altruistic love in its most comprehensive form.

Against the backdrop of this initial prohibition by Bahá'u'lláh, the categories of forbidden acts in paragraph 19—murder, adultery, and backbiting or calumny—can all be understood as expressions of the "sword," or the antithesis of love and unity at different levels of human conduct and relations, and the failure to express our spiritual reality in our physical and daily lives. These acts all fundamentally do harm in different ways. They are actions that annihilate elements of our humanity—whether our physical being, our relationships, or our nobility and integrity—and all have spiritual implications for those who perpetrate them. Murder expresses the sword through physical violence and damage to community and order—including, of course, the physical annihilation of another human being. Backbiting and calumny are expressions of the sword through mind and speech—the annihilation of another person's humanity and integrity—and at the same time are acts that devastate the soul of the perpetrator and cause disunity.[24] Adultery expresses the sword through our interpersonal relationships and the institution of marriage, by undermining and violating the bonds of love that bind people together. At the three primary levels of our human relations with others—how we think and talk, our intimate and familial relations, and our social order and community—these acts are the antithesis of the standard to which Bahá'u'lláh calls us. They are the cause of conflict, contention, and disunity—rather than expressions of love and unity—and are acts of annihilation and destruction that have spiritual consequences.[25]

From this perspective, the second half of the verse ("shun ye, then, what hath been prohibited in the holy Books and Tablets") has a number of possible allusions. On the one hand, the reference to "holy Books" appears to indicate the sacred texts of previous religions. As Saiedi observes, "verse 19 recapitulates commandments revealed to Moses."[26] At the same time, Bahá'u'lláh's statement might be said to hearken back to His own prohibition of the sword and to draw an intimate connection between His prohibition at the time of His Declaration and

His revelation of laws in the Kitáb-i-Aqdas a decade later. Further, the statement evokes the Bahá'í view of the fundamental relationship and essential indivisibility between all revelations of God's word, which intimately and intrinsically connects Bahá'u'lláh's revelation—including the Kitáb-i-Aqdas—with all previous sacred texts. As the Universal House of Justice states in its introduction, the provisions of the Kitáb-i-Aqdas "rest squarely on the foundation established by past religions, for, in the words of Bahá'u'lláh, 'This is the changeless Faith of God, eternal in the past, eternal in the future.' In this Revelation the concepts of the past are brought to a new level of understanding, and the social laws, changed to suit the age now dawning, are designed to carry humanity forward into a world civilization the splendours of which can as yet be scarcely imagined."[27]

In the one sentence of paragraph 19, Bahá'u'lláh has connected His laws with those of previous dispensations and reiterated the first over-arching social teaching. He promulgated the prohibition of the sword and illustrated its expression at all levels of individual life and human relationships.

This analysis of paragraph 19 has implications for the structure of the Most Holy Book. The Kitáb-i-Aqdas was not written in the style of a comprehensive code of laws. In its introduction to the Kitáb-i-Aqdas, the Universal House of Justice writes that "in general, the laws of the Kitáb-i-Aqdas are stated succinctly."[28] It further states,

A word should be said about the style of language in which the Kitáb-i-Aqdas has been rendered into English. Bahá'u'lláh enjoyed a superb mastery of Arabic, and preferred to use it in those Tablets and other Writings where its precision of meaning was particularly appropriate to the exposition of basic principle. Beyond the choice of language itself, however, the style employed is of an exalted and emotive character, immensely compelling, particularly to those familiar with the great literary tradition out of which it arose.[29]

The Research Department of the Bahá'í World Center has observed that the Kitáb-i-Aqdas has an "elliptical"[30] style. In simple terms, this description means that Bahá'u'lláh employs a style of extreme economy in which very brief statements—apparently specific in nature—represent broader concepts, even an entire discourse. In the words of the Research Department, the Kitáb-i-Aqdas has an "observable tendency to deal with whole areas of legislative concern by reference to a single representative example, or illustrative instance, from which conclusions can then be drawn about a range of other matters comprised within the category it represents."[31] A related, and equally significant observation is that the provisions of the Kitáb-i-Aqdas "must be understood according to their informing spirit, and not according to the letter of the law,"[32] which echoes Bahá'u'lláh's own statement in paragraph 5 that He has not revealed "a mere code of laws" but rather has "unsealed the choice Wine with the fingers of might and power."[33]

Paragraph 19 can be read as a prime example of this elliptical style that employs "the utmost economy of diction."[34] In a single sentence, Bahá'u'lláh highlights the fundamental teaching underlying all of His interpersonal and social laws—that they are expressions of, and should be understood as, the rejection of the sword and the acceptance of the call to love and unity. The "informing spirit" through all of the laws should be understood, then, as an expression of the pathway through which human beings can learn and reflect their fundamental oneness and what this means regarding how we think about, speak about, and relate to one another.

The structure of the Kitáb-i-Aqdas may now be seen in a new light. Paragraph 19 is not only a transition between Bahá'u'lláh's discussions of spiritual obligations to His discussion of laws of human relationships; indeed, the verse might be said to be, in the most concise way possible, a statement of the entirety of Bahá'u'lláh's laws regarding human relationships. It may even be suggested that the laws that are stated subsequently in the work might be understood as more specific and detailed expressions of the fundamental prohibition of the sword, and a concomitant call to love and unity at the various levels of human individual and collective life. With this orientation in mind, when trying to understand the "informing spirit" of the laws, one is oriented to look at all of them as illustrative of the overarching and fundamental dynamic of the prohibition of the sword in all of its comprehensive meanings.

There is another dimension to these observations about paragraph 19 that further illustrates the complexity, brilliance, and subtlety of the structure of the Kitáb-i-Aqdas. Suggested earlier is the understanding that paragraphs 1 through 5 are a statement of the fundamental metaphysical principles of ascent and descent, including discussion of a statement on the fundamental structure of reality, the descent to the realm of the human being through the categories of God, the Primal Will, and the Manifestation (paragraph 1), and a discussion of the concept, nature, and purpose of law (paragraphs 2 through 5). Paragraphs 6 through 18 begin the journey of ascent in the physical world by articulating the required spiritual practices fundamental for that journey. Paragraph 19, in a statement of "utmost economy of diction," articulates in one sentence the fundamentals of Bahá'u'lláh's interpersonal and social laws. It completes the requisites for a human being on the arc of ascent by speaking to the realm of interpersonal relations and to the social dynamics of ascent.

Taken together, paragraphs 1 through 19 may be seen as complete. They articulate in multiple layers the fundamentals of the structure of reality, our spiritual reality, and the ordering of our social lives. A foundation of Bahá'u'lláh's legal universe is expressed and presented.

While highly speculative, the fact that this is completed in nineteen paragraphs may also have some significance. In the original Arabic there are no paragraph delineations in the Kitáb-i-Aqdas. The book is comprised of verses numbering in the hundreds. However, the authorized translation of the work by the Universal House of Justice organizes the book into 190 paragraphs. The Arabic version released by the Universal House of Justice, while noting verses, is similarly organized into 190 paragraphs. Seemingly, the organization of verses into paragraphs in the authorized versions of the text in Arabic and English apparently reflects topical, thematic, or literary linkages between particular verses. In "Kitáb-i-Aqdas as Described and Glorified by Shoghi Effendi," Dr. Cyrus Alai elaborates:

> The original manuscript of the Aqdas, the numerous subsequent manuscript copies, and the early printed editions are in the form of a continuous text without punctuation or division into verses or paragraphs. Only later did the Persian Bahá'í scholar Ishráq-Kháverí divide the Holy Text into 463 verses, leaving out the opening phrase "In the Name of Him Who is the Supreme Ruler over all that hath been and all that is to be."
>
> In the English edition, the division of the Holy Text into verses has been ignored. Instead, it is divided into 190 paragraphs, each comprising of one or a few of the verses. However, there are exceptions to this rule. For example, verse 366 is divided into two sentences, forming two separate paragraphs 152 and 153 (see page 75), whereas verse 439 is split into two sentences, forming the closing sentence of paragraph 181, and the opening sentence of paragraph 182 (see page 85).
>
> In the newly published Arabic/Persian edition—which is in the same format as the English edition—the verses are separated by the insertion of a star between them, but are not numbered. However, the number of each paragraph is noted in the margin.[35]

The number 19 is commonly known as a holy number in the Bahá'í Faith, with another important symbolic number being nine. In Persian and Arabic, according to the *abjad* system, every letter has a numerical value, meaning that every letter—and thus every word—is equivalent to a number. In Arabic, the word *váhid* (meaning *unity*) has a numerical value of nineteen and symbolizes the unity of God. In the history of the Bahá'í Faith, we see the number 19, and the connotations of unity and wholeness that it symbolizes, in a variety of ways. For example, there were eighteen "Letters of the Living" plus the Báb (nineteen). Nineteen is also the organizing principle for the Badíʿ calendar (established by the Báb in the Kitáb-i-Asmá and later confirmed by Baháʾuʾlláh), which divides the year into nineteen months of nineteen days each.

Also interesting to note is that there are 190 paragraphs in the Kitáb-i-Aqdas in total. After this first unit of nineteen paragraphs is counted, the total remaining paragraphs equal 171, or nineteen times nine. The first nineteen paragraphs may be viewed as a complete unit, a *váhid*, that are then expounded upon in the number of paragraphs equivalent to the multiplication of the two numbers of the Baháʾí Faith that have important symbolic meaning.

Viewing paragraphs 1 through 19 as a unit suggests that aspects of the rest of the work might be read as elucidating or expressing different elements and aspects of the first nineteen paragraphs. These range from mystical and spiritual exhortations about the nature of God, the Manifestation, and humanity, to various individual, interpersonal, and social laws, to calls to kings and rulers to play their role in expressing the principles of recognition and obedience, as well as manifesting the dynamics of unity in the domain of social order.

Conclusion

While the reflections shared in this paper are clearly speculative in nature, they are hopefully illustrative of the utility of exploring and seeking to understand the elements of structure in the Kitáb-i-Aqdas. Assuming that the book does not have a discernible structure, or is mirroring the Qurʾán in its structure, potentially predefines or limits insights we may gain from study of the work. At the same time, care must be taken not to impose a rigid or fixed structure on the book. Baháʾuʾlláh was clear in the Kitáb-i-Aqdas that one should strive to read and understand it from its own context and terms of reference: "Say: O leaders of religion! Weigh not the Book of God with such standards and sciences as are current amongst you, for the Book itself is the unerring

Balance established amongst men. In this most perfect Balance whatsoever the peoples and kindreds of the earth possess must be weighed, while the measure of its weight should be tested according to its own standard, did ye but know it."[36]

As this paper has sought to demonstrate, there are many potential layers of meaning to understanding the structure of the Kitáb-i-Aqdas, and it will take extensive further work and examination to comprehend them. Through further developing our understanding and discourse around structure, our ability to read this complex book will advance, and with it may come new insights and understandings into the nature and operation of Bahá'í law.

3 / The Politics of Delay—
Social Meanings and the Historical Treatment
of Bahá'í Law

[FIRST PUBLISHED IN *WORLD ORDER*, VOL. 35, NO. 3, 2004.]

Of particular note in Bahá'í legal history is the delay of the official translation and distribution of the Kitáb-i-Aqdas, or "The Most Holy Book," which is the central text of Bahá'í scripture and the repository of the basic laws of the Bahá'í Faith. Revealed by Bahá'u'lláh in 1873, the Kitáb-i-Aqdas was not officially translated or released to the worldwide Bahá'í community until 1993. To the outside observer, this delay seems incomprehensible. One might expect that the Kitáb-i-Aqdas—and law generally—would have been at the epicenter of the Bahá'í community from its inception. The Muslim context within which the Bahá'í Faith was born lends itself naturally to a deep attachment to a "Book" or central text. Law and legalism hold a central place within orthodox Muslim belief systems, a focus that was not substantially undermined by the Bábí Faith.[1] Thus one would assume that the Kitáb-i-Aqdas would be a foundational force in shaping the individual and community life of the Bahá'í faithful.

The issue of delay is seized upon by Francesco Ficicchia in *Der Baha-ismus-Weltreligion der Zukunft? Geschichte, Lehre und Organisation in kritischer Anfrage.*[2] Ficicchia, a former Bahá'í, derives from the fact that the Kitáb-i-Aqdas was not made widely accessible in official form to the

Bahá'í community that the book is a "'thorn in the flesh'" of the "'organization,'" that it is not published in its entirety "'for propagandistic reasons'" and that "'the Bahá'í organization is ashamed of its most holy book and knows that publication of the full content would result in an excessive number of withdrawals.'"[3] He goes on to ascribe to the Bahá'í leadership a history of duplicity and pretext in dealing with the Most Holy Book, a pattern which, in effect, calls into question the motives and objects of the entire Bahá'í administration.

In Chapter 5 of *Making the Crooked Straight*, Udo Schaefer offers an extensive response to Ficicchia's allegations that the Bahá'í leadership suppressed the Kitáb-i-Aqdas. In its comprehensiveness and command of Bahá'í law and history, Schaefer's critique is persuasive. Schaefer is, without question, the preeminent Bahá'í jurist, and his treatment of Bahá'í law in responding to Ficicchia illustrates the strength of his scholarship. Engaging Bahá'í law from historical, comparative, theological, and philosophical perspectives, he clarifies important aspects of Bahá'í law as a divine and religious law and exposes Ficicchia's erroneous method and conclusions.

Yet, Schaefer's attempts to account for the delay in the release of the Kitáb-i-Aqdas are not wholly satisfactory. Although he thoroughly documents the historical treatment of the Kitáb-i-Aqdas, as well as formal and substantive challenges to translation, his rationale and justification for the delay are somewhat limited. This brief article argues that by focusing on the political and social dimensions of Bahá'í law, additional rationale for the historical treatment of the Kitáb-i-Aqdas become clear.

Dealing with Delay

In responding to Ficicchia's allegations, Schaefer highlights the following points:

1. Numerous publications and translations of the Kitábi-Aqdas existed prior to 1993. As such, "the laws, which had not yet been

published in an official translation, and which Ficicchia finds so peculiar, were therefore known to many Bahá'ís."[4]

2. The translation of the Kitáb-i-Aqdas was not an easy task. The specific challenges included the style of Arabic in the Kitáb-i-Aqdas;[5] the need to account for the context of late Islamic culture;[6] the need to set translation priorities given the vastness of the Bahá'í revelation;[7] and the fact that many Bahá'í laws were not in force.[8]

3. The special character of divine legislation necessitates a particular and careful process of translation. Unique aspects of divine revelation in the Bahá'í context include the lack of a systematic presentation;[9] the "hidden aesthetics" of the text;[10] the need for authoritative interpretation;[11] and the gradual coming into force of Bahá'í law as part of a historical process, which is illustrated by how the law of monogamy is treated in the Bahá'í Faith.[12] As a result, divine law is characterized by unusual modalities, or dynamics and processes of articulation and application, which necessitates a particular and systematic process of translation.

4. There is no principle of Bahá'í doctrine that legitimizes suppression of the Kitáb-i-Aqdas. Ficicchia asserts that Bahá'u'lláh affirmed a law of *taqíyya* (voluntary dissimulation), that legitmizes the suppression of the Kitáb-i-Aqdas. Yet, Bahá'u'lláh did not affirm *taqíyya* or the novel extension of this law to support the historical treatment of the Kitáb-i-Aqdas.[13]

Taken collectively, Schaefer's points about the publication, translation, and application of the Kitáb-i-Aqdas rebut sufficiently Ficicchia's argument, particularly its ascription of a negative intention to the Bahá'í leadership. Schaefer also illustrates Ficicchia's tenuous and grossly distorted knowledge of Bahá'í history and law. His arguments are not, however, wholly convincing as a justification for the delay in the official translation and dissemination of the Kitáb-i-Aqdas.

While translation of the Kitáb-i-Aqdas was undoubtedly complex and time-consuming, translations of Bahá'í texts—particularly into English—were common beginning in the early 1900s. It is true that priorities had to be set, and there are good reasons—as Schaefer points out—why the legal aspects of the revelation would not have priority. He writes, "Priority was given to those works that informed the world of the theological foundations of the faith, its moral principles and its societal and political goals, i.e. those works that deal with the doctrines concerning God, revelation, the Prophets, the image of man, the divine Covenant, the salvation of the individual and society, as well as the societal and legal structures of a future world and the prerequisites for world peace."[14]

However, if one uses the criteria that Schaefer outlines for deciding which texts should be translated, the Kitáb-i-Aqdas merits priority. As Schaefer points out, the Kitáb-i-Aqdas is not merely a code of laws, but the Mother Book, which includes "elucidations on fundamental theological issues, exhortations, ethical appeals, paranesis and prophecies."[15] Thus Schaefer's argument that the Kitáb-i-Aqdas would not be among translation priorities because of its content is not without its contradictions.

Furthermore, while Schaefer correctly notes that many laws of the Kitáb-i-Aqdas were not in force—thus implying that its translation would not be a priority—the delay in translating the Mother Book only raises more questions. It is not only laws of a public character which have not been and are not in force—this can be pragmatically explained by the historical growth pattern of the Bahá'í Faith and the lack of a Bahá'í state—but, as Schaefer notes, "the majority of the ritual and legal norms are not yet in force."[16] The fact that Bahá'í laws of a public character are not in force can be pragmatically explained by the historical growth pattern of the Bahá'í Faith and the lack of a Bahá'í state. But this does not explain why, for example, there has been a delay in bringing into force such ritual practices as the recitation of specific scriptural phrases. The fact that many ritual norms are not in force raises broader issues concerning the nature and status of Bahá'í law that should necessarily be engaged when trying to account for the delay in translating the Mother Book.

The contradictions in the arguments about the delay in translation and publishing the Kitáb-i-Aqdas do not suggest the lack of validity to the arguments themselves. But they do suggest the need to place such arguments in a broader framework. Indeed, delay concerning Bahá'í law is not merely an issue of when the Kitáb-i-Aqdas finally reached the hands of the Bahá'í community. Rather, the delay in the official translation and widespread dissemination of the Most Holy Book might be seen as part of a consistent historical pattern concerning the release and application of Bahá'í law. Consider the following facts:

- Bahá'u'lláh's revelation of laws occurred ten years after He declared Himself a Manifestation of God.
- Bahá'u'lláh revealed a tablet in Persian laying out a set of laws, but ultimately held it back.[17]
- Bahá'u'lláh did not act on petitions requesting laws before He revealed the Kitáb-i-Aqdas.[18]
- After Bahá'u'lláh penned the Kitáb-i-Aqdas, He delayed its widespread distribution for a period of time before its publication in Bombay (Mumbai).[19]
- Bahá'u'lláh issued cautions about how His laws were to be implemented and followed.[20]
- Numerous laws that could be "in force" have consistently had their application suspended and left as a matter of individual conscience. Moreover the application of Bahá'í law has been consciously inconsistent.[21]
- The publication of the Kitáb-i-Aqdas in 1993 did not result in more laws being applicable to Bahá'ís.[22]
- The Universal House of Justice has been in existence since 1963 with wide legislative powers, yet these powers have remained largely unused.

Given the facts about the delay in revealing, legislating, and applying Bahá'í law, the delay in publishing the Kitáb-i-Aqdas appears as but one expression of a consistent pattern of treatment of Bahá'í law. One explanation of this pattern is found within the logic of progressive revelation. In relation to the revelation of Bahá'í law, the Universal House of Justice has stated there is a "divinely-purposed delay in the revelation of the basic laws of God for this age."[23] Schaefer observes that delay in revealing Bahá'í law illustrates that "revelation has, to a certain extent, the character of a dialogue. This means that the dialectical relationship between revelation and human thought, whereby human capacity is taken into account in the revelation of God's Word—a relationship that is immanent in the principle of progressive revelation—operates not only in the chain of successive outpourings of divine revelation but also during the period of each prophet's mission."[24]

A more mundane explanation for the delay in translating and publishing the Kitáb-i-Aqdas and in applying Bahá'í laws is also available—namely, that the pattern of divinely-purposed delay originates in Bahá'u'lláh's recognition of the inevitably political and social nature of law, given the human hands in which His law would inevitably be placed.

Social and Political Dimensions of Bahá'í Law

Through delay, and the logic underlying it, Bahá'u'lláh aims to prevent the co-optation of His transformative social program by the realities of the contexts, power arrangements, and politics that inherently shape legal regimes.[25] Consider the following statement from Bahá'u'lláh:

Indeed, the laws of God are like unto the ocean and the children of men as fish, did they but know it. However, in observing them one must exercise tact and wisdom. . . . Since most people are feeble and far-removed from the purpose of God, therefore one must observe tact and prudence under all conditions so that nothing might happen that could cause disturbance and dissension or raise clamor among the heedless. Verily, His bounty hath surpassed the whole universe and His bestowals encompassed all that dwell on earth. One must guide mankind to the ocean of true understanding in a spirit of love and tolerance. The Kitáb-i-Aqdas itself beareth eloquent testimony to the loving providence of God.[26]

In this statement, Bahá'u'lláh emphasizes His perspective on the social and political dimensions of His laws in two ways.

The Political Dimensions of Bahá'í Law

First, because law is applied by human beings, it inevitably has a political dimension. It can be applied with "tact and prudence," or it can presumably be applied in an inappropriate manner. It can be imposed and followed in a manner that can cause "disturbance and dissension," or presumably in a manner that is positive and harmonious. The simple observation this reflects is that any law, whether divine or not, is subject to being shaped, used, and applied based on political choices, power structures, and the inherent fallibility of being human. When Bahá'u'lláh comments that "one must guide mankind to the ocean of true understanding in a spirit of love and tolerance," He is also acknowledging the innately coercive nature of legal rules when they are accompanied by enforcement mechanisms supported by social institutions. While one would expect that a divine law would, by its very nature as divine, attract unquestioned legitimacy as a positive law, Bahá'u'lláh largely rejects this position. In His matrix, divine law only appears to gain legitimacy as a positive law when particular social conditions are met, in which the application of Bahá'í law would not be a divisive force.

Bahá'u'lláh's observation of the political dimensions of law is a natural expression of His broader critique of the legal traditions in Muslim societies. Classical Islamic legal theory[27] was intentionalist and textualist,[28] relying on the striving of individual jurists using *ijtihád* (struggle or striving in the process of making an independent judgement) to derive laws from sources—in particular the Qur'án or Sunna (normative customs)—considered pure and pristine in their divine legitimacy. In theory, this system was constructed to present the appearance of achieving the highest possible degree of conformity to divine text and purpose and to be free from issues of power, politics, and the requirements to rule. This striving to maintain the integrity of independent legal judgement and to be as free as possible from human motivations when rendering judgements is exemplified by the fact that the idea of legislation—the promulgation of a generally applicable rule by the ruler—did not have a natural place within classical Islamic legal theory as articulated by medieval jurists. A premise of the classical system was that the derivation of law would be apolitical by being a form of "instance law."[29] The law applicable to a situation would be gleaned through a specific act of *ijtihád* by a learned scholar—and for every situation a new act of *ijtihád* would occur. In other words, a law would be found and applied to a situation; then it would disappear.

The reality within Muslim societies, however, was that the application of the classical Islamic legal theory proved to be quite complex. 'Abdul-Bahá also raises questions about the ability of the classical theory to capture divine purposes and intentions when He writes that the majority of Islamic laws "were devised by the divines of a later age according to the laws of Islamic jurisprudence, and individual divines made conflicting deductions from the original revealed ordinances. All these were enforced."[30]

In contrast to the predominant Islamic legal tradition, the Bahá'í system adopts an explicitly political form: creating institutions (in particular the Universal House of Justice) which have clear legislative powers and political roles. For example, 'Abdul-Bahá writes, "this House of Justice enacteth the laws and the government enforceth them. The legislative body must reinforce the executive, the executive must aid and assist the legislative body so that through the close union and harmony of these two forces, the foundation of fairness and justice may become firm and strong, that all the regions of the world may become even as Paradise itself."[31] Bahá'u'lláh writes that "all matters of state (*umúr-i-siyásiyyih*) should be referred to the House of Justice."[32] By using the term *siyásat*, a term for politics in many Middle Eastern languages including Persian, the political implications are inescapable.[33]

The Social Dimensions of Bahá'í Law

The political dimensions of Bahá'í law are complemented by its social dimensions. Bahá'u'lláh's call for the delay of His laws because He was concerned that they could cause "disturbance or dissension" or "raise clamor," and the general injunction that they be applied with "love and tolerance," are a reflection of the types of social and political action in which Bahá'u'lláh instructed his followers to engage.

There are many methods of action for social change. They often target varying aspects of society. One method, which has been used by some religious communities both historically and in the contemporary world, focuses their aspirations for change on coopting existing political and legal institutions—or more generally assuming a position of public power—in an attempt to use the institutions to implement a particular vision of a sacred social order. One predominant example of this method—but by no means the only one—is the creation of a theocracy, in which religious officials assume positions of political power. But examples of a religious community attempting to coopt existing political institutions to pursue social change is also present in liberal democracies such as the United States, where certain Christian denominations have used a combination of bloc voting and aggressive lobbying to secure the election of politicians who are sympathetic to their religious agenda (though the politicians themselves are not religious officials and often may not even be a member of the same Christian denominations that seek to secure their election).

The current Bahá'í community is subject to several internal limitations to effect social change through efforts to achieve public power to

coopt existing political and legal institutions. While Bahá'ís are permitted to vote, they are currently prohibited from seeking political office.
Bahá'ís also do not seek to have their moral and behavioral values and
precepts adopted by civil governments. For the Universal House of Justice states that "it is not our purpose to impose Bahá'í teachings upon
others by persuading the powers that be to enact laws enforcing Bahá'í
principles, nor to join movements with such legislation as their aim."[34]

Another important locus of action—one which is often used by
governments, organizations, and groups of individuals—is action at
the level of social meanings. Lawrence Lessig, a professor at Harvard
Law School, explains that a social meaning is the "semiotic content
attached to various actions, or inactions, or statuses, within a particular
context."[35] Such meanings are often consciously constructed by governments or other social actors to reinforce a particular set of behaviors,
understandings, or outcomes. The most powerful meanings are those
which appear most natural—or uncontested—and such meanings have
a significant impact on shaping the contexts within which individuals
act and relate. The process of social change necessarily involves a process of contesting predominant social meanings, and in some cases,
advocating for a different social meaning.

The central pivot that Bahá'u'lláh argues should shape the construction of social meanings is oneness or unity. Unity is a *grundnorm*, or the
ultimate or basic norm that forms the basis of commonplace associations
from which Bahá'u'lláh wishes to shape the individual and collective life
of humanity. A recurring metaphor in Bahá'u'lláh's writings is the need
to perceive the world through the eye of unity or oneness. The wayfarer
in the Valley of Unity "looketh on all things with the eye of oneness,
and seeth the brilliant rays of the divine sun shining from the dawning-
point of Essence alike on all created things, and the lights of singleness
reflected over all creation." More generally, He exhorts individuals to
"Shut your eyes to estrangement, then fix your gaze upon unity" and to
"discern with the eye of oneness His glorious handiwork. . . ."[36]

Within Bahá'u'lláh's positioning of unity as the lens through which the phenomenal world should be viewed can be discerned a Bahá'í focus on action at the level of social meanings. One of Bahá'u'lláh's intentions is to move unity into the foreground and to have the essential oneness of humanity frame the basic associations people attach to the social realities around them. Bahá'u'lláh gives us examples of how to perceive social phenomenon through the eye of unity and oneness. For example, in His letter to Queen Victoria, Bahá'u'lláh states that the "representatives of the people" should "regard themselves as the representatives of all that dwell on earth," thus associating with traditional notions of representative democracy a meaning of universalism.[37] Examples can also be seen in the discourse on peace in the Bahá'í writings, in which unity is the key association and harbinger of peace. At the collective level, similar to how individuals should view the world through the eye of unity, the Bahá'í community is an experiment in creating a community life in which unity is foregrounded. Shoghi Effendi writes that the community should "so exemplify that spirit of universal love and fellowship as to evoke in the minds of their associates the vision of that future City of God" and "demonstrate to their fellow Country-men the ennobling reality of a power that shall weld a disrupted world."[38]

As the architecture of social meanings increasingly reflects the unity *grundnorm*, the necessary contexts for the application of Bahá'í law are expanded. For Bahá'í law to be applied in contexts where the architecture of social meanings was not sufficiently engaged with unity would be contradictory and self-defeating. Law tends to dictate, as opposed to educate. It demands, prior to offering justifications and explanations. As such, it is prone to being a source of social disruption and discord in contexts of diversity. If one wishes to avoid the disunity that the Bahá'í emphasis on unity necessitates, then there are two strategies that one might follow. First, one could wait until there is broad social consensus on a subject before legislating on it. This is, however, often impractical, as is made clear by modern liberal constitutionalism in which, because of the impracticality of achieving consensus, appeal is made to legitimated procedures.[39] Second, one can strive to create a context wherein unity becomes part of the foreground of what is considered socially good, and social meanings increasingly reflect the principles of unity. While substantive disagreement may continue to exist, policy and law on a contested topic may not have the same socially disruptive effects. Rather, policy and law become an agent for engaging with the substance of unity within a challenging context.

Simply stated, therefore, the pattern of delay within Bahá'í law is following a particular logic of social constructivism. If unity-centered social meanings increasingly predominate—a reality that Bahá'ís should be working toward—then the possibility for the application of Bahá'í law will and should increase. If such change in social meanings does not take place, then the relevance of Bahá'í law will remain limited both within and outside of the Bahá'í community.

A comment should be made on this last point—the relevance of Bahá'í law outside the Bahá'í community, and more generally the relationship between Bahá'í political institutions and civil institutions. Debate has been increasing on this issue, and this debate is often and distortedly labeled as a debate about the relationship between "Church" and "State" in the Bahá'í Faith. Scholarly points of view have been varied, ranging from an assertion of theocratism,[40] to versions of Christian dualism,[41] to affirmations that Bahá'u'lláh had a separationist, if not secular, worldview.[42] This brief description of the relationship between social meanings and Bahá'í law offers an alternative approach to the church/state issue that moves beyond an attachment to a particular institutional form. Over time, in various contexts, the scope and limits of Bahá'í law, and the role of the institutions that legislate and apply it, will be dependent upon how the architectures of social meanings change. As such, the role of Bahá'í institutions within and without the Bahá'í community is contingent and open-ended. The relationship between Bahá'í institutions and civil institutions, as well as the scope and limits of Bahá'í law, will also vary from context to context. There will be no single, nor any certain, form. Expectations or presumptions of a particular pattern of relationships between Bahá'í institutions and civil political institutions ignore Bahá'u'lláh's sensitivity to the role of social meanings in shaping legitimate uses of institutional power.

Conclusion

As this brief article has attempted to illustrate, Bahá'í law may, in some respects, be seen as articulating themes present in much of contemporary legal thought. The relationship between the application of Bahá'í law and social meanings that one observes in the historical treatment of Bahá'í law is rooted in insights that remain powerful in much of contemporary legal thinking: the rejection of formalism, the emphasis on the political dimensions of law, the contextual application of law, and the mediating of the demands of diversity and unity. Udo Schaefer's powerful response to Ficicchia in *Making the Crooked Straight*—and in particular his thorough treatment of the history of the Kitáb-i-Aqdas—opens the door to exploring these more speculative approaches and theories. By building from the five decades of scholarship Schaefer has produced on Bahá'í law, future generations of Bahá'í legal scholars will, one hopes, begin to explore novel approaches to the subject and to build bridges for legal scholars to begin approaching the legal content of the Bahá'í revelation.

PART 4:

Bahá'í Law, Political Structures, and World Order

4 / Hegemony and Revelation:
A Bahá'í Perspective on World Order

[FIRST PUBLISHED IN *RELIGIOUS STUDIES AND THEOLOGY*, VOLUME 29.1, 2010, © EQUINOX PUBLISHING LTD 2010.]

Abstract

Similar to most world religions, the Bahá'í Faith provides a vision of a promised age of the future. According to Bahá'u'lláh, the Prophet-Founder of the Bahá'í religion, this promised future age is characterized by the progressive spiritualization of the individual and collective life of humanity, global peace, and the explicit recognition of the fundamental oneness of humanity. But the very fact that the Bahá'í Faith provides such a specific model of world order raises an essential question: is Bahá'u'lláh's vision of a new World Order rooted in a power-claim, which will assert the legitimacy of a future Bahá'í political hegemony? This article explores this question and the aspects of Bahá'í theology, doctrine, and political thought that assist in answering it. It concludes that this new World Order is not to claim future temporal power, but to lay out a general architecture for the structuring and exercise of power that strives to reflect the principles of oneness of religion and oneness of humanity. It is not a claim to power, but a claim about power, including its proper uses, manifestations, and limitations in a truly global society.

Introduction

The Bahá'í Faith, like most world religions, provides a vision of a promised age of the future. Referred to by Bahá'u'lláh, the founder of the Bahá'í Faith, by a number of titles including "the Kingdom of God," the "Most Great Peace," and a "Golden Age," this promised future age is characterized by the progressive spiritualization of the individual and collective life of humanity, global peace, and the explicit recognition of the fundamental oneness of humanity. 'Abdu'l-Bahá, Whose writings, along with those of Shoghi Effendi, are considered authoritative interpretations of scripture, describes the coming of the "Most Great Peace" as a "marvelous cycle," when

the earth will become another earth and the world of humanity will be arrayed with perfect composure and adornment. Strife, contention, and bloodshed will give way to peace, sincerity, and harmony. Among the nations, peoples, kindreds, and governments, love and amity will prevail and cooperation and close connection will be firmly established. Ultimately, war will be entirely banned . . . [U]niversal peace will raise its pavilion in the midmost heart of creation and the blessed Tree of Life will so grow and flourish as to stretch its sheltering shade over the East and the West. Strong and weak, rich and poor, contending kindreds and hostile nations—which are like the wolf and the lamb, the leopard and kid, the lion and the calf—will treat one another with the utmost love, unity, justice, and equity. The earth will be filled with knowledge and learning, with the realities and mysteries of creation, and with the knowledge of God.[1]

As 'Abdu'l-Bahá's description illustrates, the Bahá'í vision of the future is indisputably to be established in the contingent world. It by no means signifies an end to human life and organization on this planet. Moreover, while there are extensive allusions in the Bahá'í writings to the ordeals humanity will face on the path to achieving the Most Great

Peace, the future age will come about not as a result of a dramatic cataclysm or apocalyptic events, but rather as the culmination of a long journey of humankind, a journey subject to the uncertainties of human choice and action. "The whole earth is now in a state of pregnancy," Bahá'u'lláh writes, and "the time is approaching when every created thing will have cast its burden."[2] As the "generation of the half-light,"[3] humanity is currently engaged in the inevitably painful struggle of being born into a new age.

Bahá'u'lláh's vision and promise of a future age of fulfillment is accompanied by a detailed discussion of both the steps leading to the achievement of this vision, and institutions and patterns of social and political order that will be established. Writing in 1873, Bahá'u'lláh identified the ramifications of His revelation for systems of order: "The world's equilibrium hath been upset through the vibrating influence of this most great, this new World Order. Mankind's ordered life hath been revolutionized through the agency of this unique, this wondrous System—the like of which mortal eyes have never witnessed."[4]

Shoghi Effendi expounded at some length on the institutional dimensions of a "new World Order." For example, he explains that it includes a "world legislature," a "world executive, backed by an international Force," and a "world tribunal" which "will adjudicate and deliver its compulsory and final verdict in all and any disputes that may arise between the various elements constituting this universal system."[5] The creation of such institutions was explicitly identified as being the result of a gradual process of change, which includes clear stages in which there will be changes to the political structures of humanity. Most notably, there will be a period of "lesser peace,"[6] characterized as a time when "the majority of the world's nation-states formally commit themselves to a global order comprising institutions and laws, and equipped with the means by which collective decisions can be enforced."[7]

The specificity with which the Bahá'í writings engage the political dimensions of the Most Great Peace and the transformations of political institutions which must take place to achieve this vision, as well as the fact that the Bahá'í Faith is a recent religion, offers an interesting challenge to present-day thinkers. The explicit Bahá'í reflections on a system of world order invite speculation concerning the challenges posed by religion to create, through peaceful means, a global and inclusive system of international law and order. To the degree that religious visions and claims are exclusive and universal, it is unclear how, in political terms, they can translate into a global, peaceful, and encompassing system in the absence of coercive methods or the seismic change that might be wrought by acts of divine intervention. The very fact that the Bahá'í Faith provides such a specific model of world order well illustrates these tensions, as it raises an essential question: is Bahá'u'lláh's vision of a new World Order rooted in a power-claim, which will assert the legitimacy of a future Bahá'í political hegemony? By exploring this question, and the aspects of Bahá'í theology, doctrine, and political thought which assist in answering it, the distinctive aspects of the Bahá'í world order model, and indeed of a particular understanding of the relationship between religion and world order, are highlighted.

Dimensions of Bahá'u'lláh's New World Order

Coxian theory provides a helpful lens for unpacking some of the fundamental elements of Bahá'u'lláh's "new World Order." Robert Cox views world order through the matrix of ideas, institutions, and material capabilities that allow for the establishment of hegemony by a state, a set of states, or a civilization at a particular moment in the history of the world.[8] As ideas, institutions, and material capabilities evolve and change, historical structures, including patterns of world order, are altered or even transformed. World order is thus dynamic, and has a long history and advancing future. Hegemons have existed throughout recorded history, even as the various peoples and parts of the globe may have been unaware of one another's existence.

Explicit within Coxian theory is also the contemplation of the possibility of a post-hegemonic world, or a world in which no particular grouping of humanity translates a particular set of ideas, institutions, and material capabilities into a hegemonic pattern. One way of conceptualizing the possibility of a post-hegemonic order is through Cox's understanding of the role of ideas in the transformation of patterns of world order. Cox identifies ideas and understandings with intersubjective meanings, or shared understandings between individuals within any particular historical structure. These intersubjective meanings ultimately "constitute the order itself."[9] In other words, intersubjective meanings are primary agents in the construction of new historical structures.

This focus on intersubjective meanings raises important and challenging questions concerning world order in an age of globalization. As the sharing of information increasingly becomes unmoored from the obstacles of time and space, and the processes of economic and social integration continue to advance, it is to be expected that intersubjective meanings may increasingly form across the limited boundaries of nation, culture, and civilization that have shaped hegemons throughout the history of the world. At the same time, pluralism within nations may increasingly result in intersubjective meanings within those nations, which to some degree parallel and reflect, and at some point may merge with, meanings being formed on a global scale. The possibility of the emergence of intersubjective meanings on a global scale implies that a post-hegemonic world may be attainable, or, in other words, the achievement of a system of world order that is universal in the sense that it is not characterized by the dominance of a particular hegemon. The achievement of such "supraintersubjectivity" may allow for the emergence of some form of truly global society.

To say that Coxian theory entertains the possibility of a post-hegemonic world is not to say that he is advocating or expecting some seamless emergence of a global culture that provides the foundation for an enduring global system of order. It is precisely the challenge of articulating universals that are not borne out of the dominance of a particular tradition or power that is the fundamental and vexing question. Is it truly possible, as is required for a post-hegemonic order, for a global order to derive normative content in a search for common ground among constituent traditions of civilization?[10]

This question is helpful in identifying the foundations of Bahá'u'lláh's vision of a "new World Order." When Bahá'u'lláh writes in 1873 that "the world's equilibrium hath been upset through the vibrating influence of this most great, this new World Order," and that "mankind's ordered life hath been revolutionized through the agency of this unique, this wondrous System—the like of which mortal eyes have never witnessed," He clearly was not referring to any existing system of order in its institutional or political aspects—although the term might later be interpreted to encompass particular institutions and political realities. Rather, Bahá'u'lláh was referring to fundamental premises that He articulated as the foundation for the transformation of the collective, as well as political, life of humanity, and, by implication, the method through which that transformation was to occur.

The first premise is that of progress. Infused with a dynamic and relative understanding of the relationship between God and humanity, the Bahá'í concept of revelation is distinct from that found in most other religious traditions. The process by which the divine is made known to humanity, and thereby provides guidance for how humans should live their lives, is a mediated one. This mediation is not simply the fact that there is a medium for the revelation (i.e., a Prophet). Rather, the mediation is revealed by God in a manner and form relative to the conditions, needs, and state of humanity at a given time in history. Further, mediation occurs because the medium for the revelation—in Bahá'í terminology, the "Manifestation"[11] of God—speaks in the context in which He lives, and exerts control over the social expression of the revelation.

This mediated and relative understanding of revelation expresses the Bahá'í understanding that the human relationship with God is eternal and requires ongoing divine input through the periodic appearance of a Manifestation. As humanity continues to change and progress, there is a continuing need for a rearticulation of God's will in a manner and form responsive to the changing conditions of humanity.[12]

Implicit within this concept of revelation is a commitment to dynamism as both an element of the structure of the world and as a social and historical reality. 'Abdu'l-Bahá writes that "'change is a necessary quality and an essential attribute of this world and of time and place.'"[13] In collective historical terms, humanity may be thought of as being in a process of maturation, and as such is always undergoing change and transformation. At this point in human history, humanity is passing through its stage of collective adolescence, as described by Shoghi Effendi:

> The long ages of infancy and childhood, through which the human race had to pass, have receded into the background. Humanity is now experiencing the commotions invariably associated with the most turbulent stage of its evolution, the stage of adolescence, when the impetuosity of youth and its vehemence reach their climax, and must gradually be superseded by the calmness, the wisdom, and the maturity that characterize the stage of manhood. Then will the human race reach that stature of ripeness which will enable it to acquire all the powers and capacities upon which its ultimate development must depend.[14]

The emphasis in the Bahá'í Faith on dynamism and progress is ultimately an expression of the central norm of the Bahá'í teachings: oneness, which may also be expressed as unity. Shoghi Effendi writes that the "principle of the Oneness of Mankind" is "the pivot round which all the teachings of Bahá'u'lláh revolve."[15] At the individual level, all human beings come into existence through the uniting of spirit and matter, and, while alive in the contingent world, are an integration of the eternal soul and physical body. Oneness is reflected in, as opposed to being a negation of, the differences among human beings:

Consider the flowers of a garden: though differing in kind, color, form and shape, yet, inasmuch as they are refreshed by the waters of one spring, revived by the breath of one wind, invigorated by the rays of one sun, this diversity increaseth their charm, and addeth unto their beauty. . . . How unpleasing to the eye if all the flowers and plants, the leaves and blossoms, the fruits, the branches and the trees of that garden were all of the same shape and color! Diversity of hues, form and shape enricheth and adorneth the garden, and heighteneth the effect thereof. In like manner, when divers shades of thought, temperament and character, are brought together under the power and influence of one central agency, the beauty and glory of human perfection will be revealed and made manifest. Naught but the celestial potency of the Word of God, which ruleth and transcendeth the realities of all things, is capable of harmonizing the divergent thoughts, sentiments, ideas, and convictions of the children of men.[16]

Just as all individual human beings are created through the coming together of diverse entities, and collectively represent diverse expressions of a single human race, Bahá'u'lláh emphasizes that the challenge of political and social life is the development of patterns of unity and diversity at both the social and political level. In emphasizing that the "'Tabernacle of Unity'" has been raised, He speaks to the ethical and globally-minded orientation through which we must view fellow human-beings: "'Of one tree are all ye the fruit and of one bough the leaves;'" "'the earth is one country and mankind its citizens;'" "'Let not a man glory in that he loves his country; let him rather glory in this, that he loves his kind.'"[17]

Thus, when speaking of a "new World Order," Bahá'u'lláh emphasizes the fundamental importance of the commitment to a dynamic vision of social change, particularly a change in the direction of oneness and unity. But how far does this get us in answering the Coxian question as to how the normative foundations for a post-hegemonic world could be developed? Stated more bluntly, even if Bahá'u'lláh's ontological principle of unity in diversity is true, how is it something that may be reified at the social and political level?

It is in this regard that a Bahá'í rendering of Coxian theory is helpful. Within this dynamic and progressive vision, Bahá'u'lláh places revelation—as distinct from religion—at the epicenter of historical progress. Revelation is an animus that contains within it ideas that may stand as the foundations for the transformation of the social life of humanity. "Everything that is hath come to be through His irresistible decree," Bahá'u'lláh declares;[18] and as such, when revelation occurs, the architecture of human life is irresistibly shattered: "No sooner had He revealed Himself than the foundations of the kindreds of the earth shook and trembled, and the learned swooned away, and the wise were bewildered, except such as have, through the power of Thy might, drawn nigh unto Thee. . . ."[19] The new revelation has an impact on the entirety of creation, as characterized by simultaneous forces of decay and regeneration: "No place is there for any one to flee to when once Thy laws have been sent down, and no refuge can be found by any soul after the revelation of Thy commandments. Thou hast inspired the Pen with the mysteries of Thine eternity, and bidden it teach man that which he knoweth not, and caused him to partake of the living waters of truth from the cup of Thy Revelation and Thine inspiration."[20] Ultimately, the purpose and object of every revelation is to effect a total transformation of human affairs: "'And yet, is not the object of every Revelation to effect a transformation in the whole character of mankind, a transformation that shall manifest itself both outwardly and inwardly, that shall affect both its inner life and external conditions? For if the character of mankind be not changed, the futility of God's universal Manifestations would be apparent.'"[21]

This concept of revelation as the centrifugal force in the evolution of humanity's progress must be understood as being distinct in important respects from the particular religious system which reflects each revelation. As a religious system, the Bahá'í Faith strives to embody the revelation of Bahá'u'lláh in as comprehensive and complete a form as possible, and in so doing to exemplify to the fullest extent its teachings, doctrines, and principles. But an effort to reflect comprehensively the content of the revelation does not capture the revelation. Revelation breathes life into every atom, and affects the course of human development and progress in myriad ways dissociated from any particular actions that may be carried out by the community of Bahá'ís. Human beings, having been endowed by God with "the unique distinction and capacity to know Him and love Him"—a capacity "that must needs be regarded as the generating impulse and the primary purpose underlying the whole of creation"—cannot remain unaffected by God's choice to reveal Himself again.[22] Receptivity to the act of revelation is, if you will, "wired" into the human essence.

The meta level at which revelation acts to influence all of humanity—beyond the limiting confines of religious labels and distinctions—is echoed throughout the Bahá'í writings. Bahá'u'lláh breathed a "Spirit" upon the world "which is manifesting itself with varying degrees of intensity through the efforts consciously displayed by his avowed supporters," but also, for example, "indirectly through certain humanitarian organizations."[23] Bahá'u'lláh's concept of revelation also allows the Bahá'í writings to expound and advocate at length for particular social and political reforms, without rationalizing these reforms through advocacy for adoption of the Bahá'í Faith at the individual and collective level.[24] It also explains the laudatory comments made by Bahá'u'lláh, 'Abdu'l-Bahá, and Shoghi Effendi concerning particular social and political developments. If a development was viewed by them as a response to the fundamental challenge and purpose of this revelation, and as such of this age of humanity—such as supporting the creation of patterns of unity in diversity—then it was something to be affirmed and noted. Shoghi Effendi writes that the principle of the oneness of mankind "has its indirect manifestations in the gradual diffusion of the spirit of world solidarity which is spontaneously arising out of the welter of a disorganized society."[25] For example:

> The fierce opposition which greeted the abortive scheme of the Geneva Protocol; the ridicule poured upon the proposal for a United States of Europe which was subsequently advanced, and the failure of the general scheme for the economic union of Europe, may appear as setbacks to the efforts which a handful of foresighted people are earnestly exerting to advance this noble ideal. And yet, are we not justified in deriving fresh encouragement when we observe that the very consideration of such proposals is in itself an evidence of their steady growth in the minds and hearts of men? In the organized attempts that are being made to discredit so exalted a conception are we not witnessing the repetition, on a larger scale, of those stirring struggles and fierce controversies that preceded the birth, and assisted in the reconstruction, of the unified nations of the West?[26]

In other words, Bahá'u'lláh clearly asserts the principle of the hegemony of revelation throughout human history. Revelation, in its progressive and relative nature, and in the fact that it exerts an influence on all of humanity through various mediums and channels, has shaped and will continue to shape ideas over the longue durée. But the principle of the hegemony of revelation goes one step beyond this: it argues that, at the level of ideas, we witness the influence of revelation on the overarching development of historical structures. In other words, the concept of ideas—in Cox's triumvirate of ideas, institutions, and material capabilities—is multilayered. At the meta level, the ideas that may influence and enable the establishment of a particular hegemon are influenced by the fact that God has a continuous relationship with human beings that is progressively announced and regenerated in relative terms. Revelation, in this sense, is a historical framing device that shifts the underlying architecture within which historical structures take shape.

The Principle of Oneness and a New Form of Politics

The question of causality in an assertion of the hegemony of revelation is open to criticism. One might legitimately ask *how* the Bahá'í revelation was causing (or at least influencing), directly or indirectly, social and political developments that take place in complete ignorance of the fact that such a revelation exists. Answers to such a query could be provided through explicit Bahá'í terms of reference—that is, by explaining the Bahá'í concepts of the human soul, creation, and the role of the Manifestation of God. Outside this frame of reference, however, it is worth noting that within the Bahá'í concept of collective maturation, a collective parallel to some of the more intangible aspects of individual growth and development is being drawn. As Shoghi Effendi states, "That mystic, all-pervasive, yet indefinable change, which we associate with the stage of maturity inevitable in the life of the individual and the development of the fruit must, if we would correctly apprehend the utterances of Bahá'u'lláh have its counterpart in the evolution of the organization of human society."[27]

But such answers will not likely satisfy the lay reader, and the question of causality will remain key, as it poses a similar question to that raised by Coxian theory: how will the universal "normative content" to sustain a post-hegemonic order be derived?

To answer this question, it is helpful to look at the methods that Bahá'u'lláh emphasizes as being fundamental to effective movement toward the establishment of the Most Great Peace. The placement of oneness at the epicenter of the Bahá'í revelation results in the principled exclusion of many predominant methods of effecting social and political change. Commenting on the numerous places in the Bahá'í writings that reflect the principle of oneness, Nader Saiedi describes the implications of the comprehensive principle of the "removal of the sword": "The prohibition of killing, violence, and religious coercion; the promotion of love, unity, and fellowship among peoples; the call for peace among the nations; the condemnation of militarism and the proliferation of arms; the assertion of the necessity for education and productive employment; the condemnation of sedition; the assertion of the need for religion and social justice—all these are presented by Bahá'u'lláh as systematic expressions of the same underlying principle of the removal of the sword."[28]

The doctrine of oneness also implies a new form of politics. Ulrich Gollmer summarizes a primary Bahá'í concern that "politics should not be conducted on the basis of a categorization into 'friends' and 'foes.'"[29] As further elaborated by Arash Abizadeh, what is at stake in the Bahá'í critique is the consequence of "thinking of politics as a form of war or combat," an ideology with far-reaching consequences, including the "division of humanity into essentially warring camps."[30] In Bahá'í doctrine, this has led to the prohibition against the involvement of Bahá'ís in partisan politics.

Furthermore, the principle of oneness—which, as discussed earlier, is also an affirmation of diversity—does not allow for coercive programs of conversion, nor even the expectation that the world will, in the future Golden Age, be part of one confession. Bahá'u'lláh instructs His followers to "Consort with all religions with amity and concord."[31] While Bahá'ís do teach their Faith to others, and do expect that masses of humanity will adhere to it in the future, such an achievement could never be accomplished by anything other than the wholly voluntary choice of each individual human being. At the same time, through the doctrine of progressive revelation, Bahá'ís are committed to the idea that religion is one, that all of the major world religions have been expressions of God's eternal relationship with humanity, and that all of these religions are seen as responses to His continuous revelation.

Given these various ramifications of the principle of oneness, it is clear that the Bahá'í Faith not only rejects conventional forms of political involvement to effect change but also limits the introduction of a Bahá'í doctrinal agenda into the political sphere. Any such action in these directions within the political sphere would inevitably be a source of division and would thus contradict the principle of oneness. What the Bahá'í Faith does consciously engage in, however, is action at the level of social meanings. A social meaning is the "semiotic content attached to various actions, or inactions, or statuses, within a particular context."[32] Social meanings are thus constructed, shared, and dynamic. From a Bahá'í perspective, the construction of social meanings that increasingly reflect the principle of oneness is a form of action for social change toward a post-hegemonic world that does not, in the process, advocate for the hegemony of a particular and limited historical structure. Indeed, this is the very method seen in Shoghi Effendi's statement, cited above, about how certain events reflect the principle of oneness. In associating, for example, the opposition to the Geneva Protocol with the principle of oneness, Shoghi Effendi contested the conventional meanings associated with that particular historical event. In so doing, he was illustrating how human beings can "look on all things with the eye of oneness."[33] Indeed, whenever we associate a meaning of oneness or unity with an entity, event, activity, or happening, we are, in Bahá'í terms, indirectly reflecting the revelation of Bahá'u'lláh, and thus reflecting the hegemony of that revelation for this age in human affairs.

Returning to the Coxian principles of intersubjective meanings, it is clear from the Bahá'í perspective that the supra-intersubjectivity required for a post-hegemonic world can only be established by consciously targeting the creation of meanings that reflect the principle of oneness. As such, the challenge is not a search for common ground or the identification of what may lie between the constituent traditions of the world. Rather, it is about the "eye" through which the peoples who make up the constituent traditions of the world view their own traditions, and how those traditions relate with others. By gradually viewing one's own traditions through the lens of the oneness of humanity, the foundations within those traditions for patterns of peaceful and sustainable engagement with other traditions will be found. Such a process of change is, no doubt, rooted in the longue durée, but it is one that respects the autonomy of individuals and collectives, and recognizes the important contribution of all human beings at all levels of society to the creation of a peaceful world. Thus, a post-hegemonic world must be created by non-hegemonic means. This can take place through changes in social meanings that allow for the emergence of supra-intersubjective meanings.

A Hegemonic Bahá'í World Commonwealth in the New World Order?

Within popular Bahá'í discourse, one can find expressions of a view that the institutions of the Bahá'í administrative system—including the Universal House of Justice, the preeminent institution of that system—will, in the future, hold temporal power. For example, one finds statements to the effect that there will be: "a time when the authority of the Universal House of Justice will have been recognized by the nations of the world. At that time the legislature and executive constituting the essential components of the World Order of Bahá'u'lláh will harmoniously interact. The supreme authority of the House of Justice, divinely conferred upon it, will be the guarantor of the unity of the nations and peoples of the world."[34]

Others have suggested that the Bahá'í local assemblies will become the world's local governments and that the national assemblies will become the national governments. On the other hand, one finds arguments that Bahá'u'lláh intended clear forms of distinction and separation of political and religious institutions.[35] As has been discussed in detail elsewhere, drawing such firm conclusions is problematic, most notably to the degree that such views commit to a particular, fixed, and expected future relationship between religious institutions and political institutions.[36]

Shoghi Effendi speaks of the Bahá'í Faith potentially becoming an established religion, and the possibility of a "Bahá'í theocracy."[37] The notes in the Kitáb-i-Aqdas describe the relationship between the Bahá'í administrative order and the "new World Order" in the following terms:

The features of the *"new World Order"* are delineated in the Writings of Bahá'u'lláh and 'Abdu'l-Bahá and in the letters of Shoghi Effendi and the Universal House of Justice. The institutions of the present-day Bahá'í Administrative Order, which constitute the "structural basis" of Bahá'u'lláh's World Order, will mature and evolve into the Bahá'í World Commonwealth. In this regard, Shoghi Effendi affirms that the Administrative Order "will, as its component parts, its organic institutions, begin to function with efficiency and vigour, assert its claim and demonstrate its capacity to be regarded not only as the nucleus but the very pattern of the New World Order destined to embrace in the fullness of time the whole of mankind."[38]

From one perspective, this description highlights the distinction between the Bahá'í administrative order and the "new World Order." In stating that the internal order of the Bahá'í Faith will form the "nucleus" and "pattern" of the "new World Order," stress is being placed on the fact that the Bahá'í institutions are a conscious attempt to structure a global pattern of governance that reflects the principle of oneness. In other words, from one perspective, the Bahá'í order can be thought of as an experiment, begun in earnest in the nineteenth century, that aims to be of assistance to the global project of creating an all-encompassing system of world order.

Although the Bahá'í system is in its early stages of development, some of the principles of governance that Bahá'u'lláh implanted at the core of the Bahá'í administrative order are already clear. As a governing structure, the Bahá'í administrative order clearly favors the principle of federalism, with multiple levels of government having authority over different regions and populations. Related to federalism, but more implicit in the Bahá'í writings, is the principle of subsidiarity. The Bahá'í administrative order was built, after all, from the lowest authorities upward. Local governing bodies began to be formed in the

Bahá'í community as part of a conscious and deliberate plan to establish national and international institutions gradually. This pattern of development reflects an orientation in the Bahá'í writings emphasizing the handling of as many matters as possible at the local and regional level. Indeed, in recent years, one sees this focus on the local level increasing, with the creation of new regional administrative bodies exercising responsibilities effectively devolved from the national institutions.

The links between the Bahá'í concept of unity—with its full recognition of the value of diversity—and federalism and subsidiarity are quite obvious. It is through decentralization and an emphasis on the local level that distinctiveness can be maintained within a global order and the diverse needs of specific peoples and communities addressed. The principles of unity are similarly present in the modes of operation and decision-making within the Bahá'í administrative system. As noted earlier, the Bahá'í writings contain significant criticisms of models of politics as a war of opposing forces, a predominant criticism being the excessive partisanship in contemporary multiparty democracies. Consistent with this teaching, the Bahá'í administrative order explicitly bans partisanship in its electoral process and functioning. At the same time, it utilizes a process of decision-making, called consultation, that is oriented toward maintaining and building unity among those charged with making decisions. For example, consultation encourages the unfettered expression of all points of view but commits participants to an ethic of detachment, so that differences of opinion do not become a source of division among the participants. At the same time, consultation asks participants to be oriented toward maintaining unity of the decision-making group at the end of the day, even if a decision is not based on consensus and the discussion may have been marked by serious differences of opinion.

Undergirding the Bahá'í administrative order is a highly contextual mode of implementation and application. This expresses itself in a number of ways. First, there is no expectation that the structures and institutions within the system will always be parallel with one another. For example, in response to distinctive community needs, there are some differences in the structures of the administrative orders in different communities. One example is that regional institutions only exist in some countries.[39] More significantly, the application of Bahá'í law by local and national Bahá'í institutions is characterized by variations based on population and context.[40]

Viewing these few principles of the Bahá'í administrative order as a "nucleus" or "pattern" of the "new World Order," one sees some clear aspects of Bahá'u'lláh's design for governance in the Most Great Peace. Bahá'u'lláh envisions a global federal system in which a supranational state is formed by the nations of the world. The modes of government within the nations of the world and the relationship between national governments and the supranational government will be contextually driven, and will vary from nation to nation. Similarly, while the Most Great Peace is associated with the progressive spiritualization of human affairs and individual and collective life, the relationship between religion and politics will be diverse and dynamic. For example, indigenous traditions and historical patterns of religious expression (including Bahá'í) may develop an intimate interrelationship with civil institutions, thus giving meaning to Shoghi Effendi's term *Bahá'í theocracy*. At the same time, other nations will develop new patterns of interaction between religion and politics that, in some respects, may maintain or evolve new traditions of distinctions between the religious and the temporal. Furthermore, there is no reason to expect that the relationship between an international religious institution—such as the Universal House of Justice—and the supranational and national institutions of government would not also be contextual and driven by local and national differences. In other words, the Universal House of Justice would interact with supranational and national governments in a variety of ways, fulfilling a range of roles consistent with the principle of unity.

Conclusion

The principle of the hegemony of revelation, and the privileging of oneness by the Bahá'í revelation, forecloses any claim that the *intention* of Bahá'u'lláh's "new World Order" is for Bahá'í political institutions, and the Bahá'í community, to claim, and acquire, temporal power. The "new World Order" is an articulation of some of the aspects of a system of ordering human affairs that, in Bahá'u'lláh's vision, reflects the fundamental principle of the oneness of humanity. Like revelation itself, the emergence of such a system is relative and dynamic. It is partially contingent upon human choices, responses, and actions. In other words, the intent in laying out a vision of a "new World Order" is not to claim future temporal power, but to lay out a general architecture for the structuring and exercise of power that strives to reflect the principle of oneness. It is not a claim to power, but a claim *about* power, including its proper uses, manifestations, and limitations, in a truly global society.

5 / Church and State in the Bahá'í Faith: An Epistemic Approach

[FIRST PUBLISHED IN *JOURNAL OF LAW AND RELIGION*, VOL. XXIV, NUMBER 1, 2008–2009.]

When Mírzá Ḥusayn 'Alí (1817–92)—the founder of the Bahá'í Faith Who was known as Bahá'u'lláh (the "Glory of God")—died, there was a clear and unambiguous answer about who had the authority to lead His small but growing religious community. In His Book of the Covenant, Bahá'u'lláh identified His eldest son, 'Abbás Effendi, who later took the name 'Abdu'l-Bahá ("Servant of Bahá") (1844–1921) as His successor and head of the community, as well as the authoritative interpreter of His writings.[1] When 'Abdu'l-Bahá assumed the reins of community leadership upon Bahá'u'lláh's death, His claim to authority went largely unchallenged, and He remained in that role until His own death.[2]

While this seeming affirmation of a principle of primogeniture would appear to establish a clear pattern for the future organization and structure of the Bahá'í community, it was only one part of the leadership of the community envisioned by Bahá'u'lláh. Equally unambiguous was Bahá'u'lláh's vision of houses of justice—elected bodies that would serve governance functions—existing throughout the world. In the Kitáb-i-Aqdas, Bahá'u'lláh states that "[t]he Lord hath ordained that in every city a House of Justice be established," whose members are

79

to "take counsel together and to have regard for the interests of the servants of God. . . ."[3] In that same book, Bahá'u'lláh contemplated an international house of justice, in addition to the local houses of justice.[4]

Leadership and governance of the community, despite very minor schisms, have recently reached the point where the principle of elected institutions leading the community has been fully established, and the authority vested in single individuals who descend from Bahá'u'lláh has come to an end.[5] 'Abdu'l-Bahá's Will and Testament clearly and unequivocally appointed His grandson Shoghi Effendi (1897–957), then a student at Oxford, to be the "Guardian" of the Bahá'í Faith and the interpreter of the sacred writings, and provided that the Guardianship could pass down through the male descendants of Shoghi Effendi.[6] But, at the same time, 'Abdu'l-Bahá, Who during His life had begun the process of institution building, made clear that the evolution of the community would be toward the election of houses of justice locally, nationally, and internationally. Shoghi Effendi made the construction of this "Administrative Order" a cornerstone of his thirty-six years as head of the Bahá'í Faith.[7] When Shoghi Effendi died childless in 1957, *de facto* the door was closed on the era of individual leadership in the Bahá'í Faith. The community carried out Shoghi Effendi's plan to elect the first Universal House of Justice[8] in 1963, and with that event, the transfer from individual charismatic authority to a model of elected institutional authority was complete.

While this transition from individual to institutional authority removed many questions that could have bedeviled the community— including potential disputes among individual claimants—with the emergence of institutional authority, there arose a new set of challenges and questions. Bahá'u'lláh, 'Abdu'l-Bahá, and Shoghi Effendi never made any claim of political power in the societies in which they lived. But just because individual Bahá'í leaders did not claim political authority from the religion's founding in 1863 until Shoghi Effendi's death in 1957 does not mean that Bahá'u'lláh did not envision some public role for the institutions that would assume the leadership of His religious community. Indeed, many indicators within Bahá'í primary literature[9] anticipate a role for Bahá'í institutions in civil governance. For example, the terms "Bahá'í state" and "Bahá'í theocracy"[10] appear in authoritative Bahá'í writings, and the Universal House of Justice has spoken of a future that will see the union of spiritual and civil authority.[11] In these statements, one finds a reflection of Bahá'u'lláh's statement that "all matters of State should be referred to the House of Justice."[12] At the same time, however, the primary literature is also laden with statements that imply some form of separation or distinction between civil and religious institutions, to reflect Bahá'u'lláh's teaching that "[t]he one true God . . . hath bestowed the government of the earth upon kings. . . . That which He hath reserved for Himself are the cities of men's hearts . . . ."[13]

Discussion of the public role, if any, of Bahá'í institutions is in its infancy. This discussion is growing, however, and it is a significant one. The evolution of discussion of issues around "church and state"[14] in the Bahá'í Faith will contribute to the shape of Bahá'í communities and the nature of their interaction with the governments and populations of the countries in which they reside. At the same time, in an era when religious leaders clearly claim more authority in the political sphere around the world, and with the attendant potential dangers, there is value in assessing all growing religious systems and their views on the place of religion in public life.

The goal of this article is to explore some of the challenges in discussing the relationship between religious and civil institutions in the Bahá'í Faith as outlined in primary and secondary literature, and to examine some directions in which such a discussion might develop. After an overview of the conclusions that have been reached in secondary literature on this relationship in the Bahá'í Faith, the article examines some themes found in the primary literature to offer new approaches and understandings.

The Current Secondary Literature on Church and State
in the Bahá'í Faith

A traditional view expressed in secondary literature on the Bahá'í Faith—much of it apologetic in nature—has been to assert that Bahá'u'lláh intended the complete integration of Bahá'í institutions with civil government. This tradition has been expressed in various forms throughout Bahá'í history and continues to be expressed today. A typical statement of this view is that "Bahá'í spiritual assemblies will be the local government and the national spiritual assemblies the national government."[15] Stated another way, "every community, village, town, city, and nation will be under the control of one of these [Houses of Justice]."[16] Such conclusions are often embedded within a consciously evolutionary framework—but with the clear identification of a complete integration of religious and civil institutions as the intended endpoint.

While the Guardian identified various stages in the evolution of the Faith (see text at note 94), the following non-authoritative statement was reported by a pilgrim regarding a description by Shoghi Effendi of the following stages in the evolution of the Bahá'í Faith:

Obscurity: The first stage is that of obscurity, the stage where, as in South Africa in 1955, the Bahá'í Faith is not known. People pay no attention to it or its followers.

Persecution: This is the stage where the authorities, religious or civil, sense danger to their own institutions. They oppose the Bahá'í Faith and do all they can to harm and obliterate it. It was like this in Persia.

Emancipation: This is where the Bahá'í Faith is known, and the opposition has ceased. The people and authorities tolerate it but pay little attention to it. This was the situation in Egypt in 1955.

Recognition: As in the United States today [1955], the Bahá'í Faith is considered as one of the religions of the country, and it is known to the people and the authorities. Assembly incorporations are granted, the right to perform marriages is recognized, and its institutions are permitted to function freely as an independent religion.

Establishment (or State Religion): Like the Church of England in England, the Bahá'í Faith will be recognized and its institutions will function with the full approval of the majority of the people. People accept the teachings, realize their importance, and become followers. The Bahá'í Faith would then become a State religion, as the Christian Church in the time of Constantine was the State religion of Rome. The Bahá'í Faith has not been accepted in this way anywhere as yet.

The Bahá'í State: This will come when the Bahá'í spiritual assemblies will be the local government and the national spiritual assemblies the national government. The State will be governed by the laws, the principles, and the institutions of Bahá'u'lláh.

The Bahá'í Commonwealth: The commonwealth will follow at a time when a number of states combine to work together under the laws, the principles, and the institutions of Bahá'u'lláh.

The Bahá'í Civilization: The Bahá'í Civilization and the Golden Age of Bahá'u'lláh will be the culmination of this evolutionary process.[17]

This evolutionary perspective essentially asserts that although the power and authority of Bahá'í institutions need not be established immediately, there will come a time when Bahá'í institutions assume the full mantle of power. It must be noted, however, that this vision is not univocal. Within the theme of integration, the literature also contains references to the vision of the merging of religious and civil authority focused on, for example, the legislative or judicial sphere.[18]

In the last decade or so, a few writers have emphasized the counter-tradition that challenges this integrationist vision of a complete merging of religious and civil authority. This counter-tradition is also diverse, but the common thread is the assertion that Bahá'u'lláh intended institutional separation. In at least one contemporary work by Juan Ricardo Cole, this institutional separation is complete; and the Universal House of Justice is seen as an internal administrative authority only, with the power of setting punishments for the religious community.[19] Bahá'u'lláh's broader vision of how religious and civil institutions should interact, Cole suggests, can be illustrated through contemporary debates and categories within political philosophy. Specifically, Cole finds parallels between "communitarian" philosophies—he makes reference to Michael Sandel's notion of republicanism—and Bahá'u'lláh's intended vision, with the caveat that Bahá'u'lláh undergirded His vision with an internationalist orientation.[20]

A distinct but nonetheless separationist view is expressed by Sen McGlinn, who has developed his approach more fully than any other writer on the subject. McGlinn concludes that Bahá'u'lláh intended some separation: "Religious and state institutions are distinct organs in the body politic. Religious institutions should not be involved in civil administration or policy matters. The separation of church and state is a sign of human maturity and is irrevocable. . . . Religion should be established: should have a constitutional role and at least moral support, without implying the exclusive establishment of any one confession."[21]

McGlinn reaches these conclusions, starting from his thesis, that the state exists and is validated in Bahá'í theology to a degree that is not seen in any other major religion, including models of Christian dualism.

McGlinn contends that the Bahá'í eschatological model of the ideal society envisions a coexistence of the state and the Messiah. McGlinn further argues that the specific model of church-state relations endorsed by Bahá'u'lláh is somewhat akin to that of modern-day England. McGlinn understands this model in the following terms: "The Church of England is within the state, broadly defined, but is not in government. It is in a position to be consulted and to criticize but not to rule or coerce belief."[22] Such a model manages Bahá'u'lláh's commitments to pluralism and freedom from coercion, the need for religion to undergird society and social life, and the need for government to seek out the expert opinion of religious leaders. Indeed, McGlinn goes on to clarify that "[t]his interdependent relationship implies that the state should support religion in general, but it will be noted that Bahá'u'lláh does not suggest that it support any particular confession, including his own."[23]

Bahá'í apologetics has also been undergoing contemporary development, and as such, a more nuanced and cautious approach to the traditional commitment to the ideal of merging of civil and religious authority has been occurring. For example, in 1995, three German Bahá'í scholars—Ulrich Gollmer, Udo Schaefer, and Nicola Towfigh—published *Desinformation als Methode* (lit. trans. Disinformation as Method),[24] an extensive defense in response to Francesco Ficicchia's attack on the Bahá'í Faith, *Der Bahá'ismus: Religion der Zukunft? Geschichte, Lehre und Organisation in kritischer Anfrage (Bahá'ism: Religion of the Future? A Critical Inquiry into its History, Teachings and Organization).*[25]

One of Ficicchia's core allegations against the Bahá'í Faith was that it advocates political Mahdism—that Bahá'ís seek "the creation of a theocratically unified world state."[26] Ficicchia undoubtedly raised this allegation in this manner to suggest that the Bahá'í community was bent on seizing power and coercing adherence to particular norms and values—an especially incendiary accusation in post-World War II Germany. Gollmer cites numerous flaws in Ficicchia's analysis and demonstrates Ficicchia's misunderstanding of sources and evidence, as well as of basic foundations of Bahá'í doctrine. Ficicchia's assertion, framed as a piece of fear-mongering, is revealed as inaccurate and wrong.

At the same time, however, at the core of Ficicchia's assertion is an inquiry into theocratic impulses in the Bahá'í Faith, and on this point the author's response is somewhat vague. Gollmer correctly distinguishes between claims to political power and eschatological claims concerning the Kingdom of God on earth and illustrates that Ficicchia has collapsed eschatological claims into political power ones.[27] Gollmer does note, echoing the writing of Shoghi Effendi, that Bahá'ís expect that in the "Golden Age" of the Bahá'í Faith, the "internal affairs of the community and the process of world history will fuse. Religion and politics will be reconciled,"[28] but Gollmer offers little beyond this except to say that "every glimpse of the future that God grants to mankind is an expression of his mercy, consolation and guidance."[29] The authors largely avoid the subject of theocracy per se, with Schaefer discussing it in a footnote, but only in reference to the administration of the community, not in relation to society at large.[30]

As the above examples illustrate, between them, the integrationist and separationist traditions in the secondary literature provide arguments for almost every conceivable construction of the relationship between Bahá'í institutions and civil institutions. There is clearly dissensus on this subject in the secondary literature, in terms of both method and conclusion. There is, however, one common characteristic in the secondary literature: it is predominantly essentialist in character. To date, the literature on the subject has primarily attempted to provide answers to the following question: What is the intended essential relationship between Bahá'í institutions and civil institutions? The answers provided in the secondary literature have tended to conclude that there is *a* Bahá'í model of church-state relations that can be uncovered by searching for *the* intention of Bahá'u'lláh. That is, the literature assumes that there is a single, particular form of government which is to predominate,[31] and that this particular form—which represents a definite political structure to Bahá'u'lláh's eschaton of the future—can be found within the

Bahá'í writings. These authors presume that institutional arrangements of the anticipated Kingdom of God on Earth can thus be identified and articulated.

To say that discourse concerning Bahá'í concepts of church and state has been primarily institution-focused and essentialist in nature—in the sense of seeking to identify the intended and proper institutional arrangement—does not distinguish Bahá'í discourse. A preoccupation with identifying institutional patterns and dynamics has been one of the central foci of discussion about the relationship between religious and political institutions throughout the history of Christianity, most notably since the Papal Revolution of the eleventh century.[32] Further, the subordination of church and state discourse to constitutional paradigms, such as in the United States, has highlighted a focus on institutional-jurisdictional demarcation. The question to be addressed, however, is whether a focus on identifying the intended pattern of relationship between religious and political institutions in the Bahá'í Faith is a helpful approach to studying Bahá'í understandings of such a relationship.

Questioning Essentialisms: An Epistemic Approach to the Question of Church and State

As noted above, it is possible to find statements in the primary litera-ture being used to support almost every conceivable construction of the institutional relationship between church and state in the Bahá'í Faith, and accordingly, writers have presented wildly divergent conclusions. But the issue that this divergence poses is whether within the primary literature, one can find any greater indicia of a clear position than what currently appears in the secondary literature. As will be argued below, there *is* a coherent understanding to be found within the primary lit-erature. This understanding, however, does not coincide with any of the positions that appear in the current secondary literature. Rather, this position denies that Bahá'u'lláh intended to advocate for any single particular model of relationship between Bahá'í institutions and civil institutions, and that, consistent with his notions of social change and the principle of unity in diversity, He envisioned a future with a multiplicity of models of institutional relationships between church and state.

As opposed to an essentialist approach, this approach might be termed epistemic. It emphasizes Bahá'u'lláh's privileging of the formation of common understandings and shared meanings, which influence and shape the appearance of particular patterns of institutional relationships. In such an epistemic vision, an open, diverse, and contingent understanding of institutional forms is evident. In practice, this vision would potentially justify a wide range of institutional arrangements in distinct contexts and at various stages of development—arrangements, which, in contemporary categories, might cover a wide range of separationist and integrationist possibilities. The themes below help identify the foundations, and aspects, of this epistemic vision.

Temporal Legitimacy and Divine Sovereignty

The starting point for illustrating the epistemic approach is to recognize that in Bahá'u'lláh's teachings, earthly sovereignty is presented as a proper expression of divine sovereignty, while at the same time, Bahá'u'lláh does affirm the legitimacy of human governance. Bahá'u'lláh writes that "[o]ur mission is to seize and possess the hearts of men,"[33] but at the same time, "Ye are but vassals, O kings of the earth!"[34] The two elements of this apparent tension—temporal legitimacy and divine sovereignty—are often repeated and reinforced throughout His writings. "The one true God, exalted be His glory, hath bestowed the government of the earth upon the kings," He writes, and "[t]hat which He hath reserved for Himself are the cities of men's hearts . . . ."[35] Also, there are statements of divine sovereignty that appear to contradict the previous statement: "[T]he precepts laid down by God constitute the highest means for the maintenance of order in the world and the security of its peoples."[36]

At first glance, these writings appear to affirm the principles that the Divine and divine Manifestations have complete sovereignty, though that complete sovereignty need not be expressed through a complete domination of the polity through a personage or institution imbued with divine sovereignty. Some authors, however, in writing about the question of church and state have asserted that Bahá'u'lláh's vision of divine sovereignty does not touch the realm of civil governance—and that earthly sovereignty is distinct and apart from the spiritual sovereignty of God and the Manifestations of God.[37] For example, McGlinn's conclusions with respect to Bahá'u'lláh's Kitáb-i-Íqán (The Book of Certitude) might be summarized as follows:

1. The doctrine of two sovereignties in the book is Bahá'u'lláh's engine for shifting the Bábí community from being a sect of Shi'i Islam to a new religion, which Bahá'u'lláh was on the cusp of announcing.

2. In order to effect this shift, Bahá'u'lláh had to establish the sovereignty of the Báb as the Qá'im "and then to provide a justification for the separate sovereignty of the state after the eschaton."[38]

3. "The distinction between earthly and spiritual sovereignty is proper to God's self."[39]

A review of McGlinn's conclusions is useful to clarify aspects of the Bahá'í notion of divine sovereignty and its implications for human governance.

The Kitáb-i-Íqán was written in 1861 in response to questions posed by Hájí Mírzá Siyyid Muhammad, a maternal uncle of the Báb.[40] In 1844, Siyyid 'Alí-Muhammad (1819–1850), the Báb, began making religious claims that would ultimately lead to His execution by the Iranian state.[41] The Báb simultaneously claimed to be the fulfillment of

Islamic prophecies, including the promised Qá'im; the bearer of a new revelation from God; and the founder of an independent religion. He also claimed to be a precursor to a future revelation.[42] The Bábí religion grew rapidly—and was heavily persecuted. It was in Bahá'u'lláh's capacity as a leader of the Bábí movement after the Báb's execution that the Báb's uncle sought answers to his questions.

Central to these questions was confusion concerning the claims of the Báb and their relationship to the claims of the Prophet Muhammad. A major part of the Kitáb-i-Íqán is thus taken up with theological themes, including the nature of sovereignty, the station of Manifestations of God, and explanations of how human beings can attain knowledge of the Manifestation of God.

McGlinn, opening his analysis with a statement about Bahá'u'lláh's hermeneutics, argues that in the Kitáb-i-Íqán, Bahá'u'lláh was offering instruction about how signs of the Qá'im should be read. This is accurate, as the first half of the Kitáb-i-Íqán is an explication of the following statement about interpretation: "No man shall attain the shores of the ocean of true understanding except he be detached from all that is in heaven and on earth. Sanctify your souls, O ye peoples of the world, that haply ye may attain that station which God hath destined for you and enter thus the tabernacle which, according to the dispensations of Providence, hath been raised in the firmament of the Bayán."[43]

The second half of the book applies Bahá'u'lláh's discussion of interpretation to the specific question of the sovereignty of the Qá'im and the method of understanding his signs. Bahá'u'lláh introduces the second half of the book as an interpretation of the following verse: "Verily He Who is the Daystar of Truth and Revealer of the Supreme Being holdeth, for all time, undisputed sovereignty over all that is in heaven and on earth, though no man be found on earth to obey Him. He verily is independent of all earthly dominion, though He be utterly destitute. Thus We reveal unto thee the mysteries of the Cause of God, and bestow upon thee the gems of divine wisdom, that haply thou mayest soar on the wings of renunciation to those heights that are veiled from the eyes of men."[44]

McGlinn further suggests that Bahá'u'lláh's purpose is to highlight that the question of the sovereignty of the Qá'im (in this context, the Báb) cannot be separated from the question of the sovereignty of the Prophets generally.[45] This is a limited rendering of Bahá'u'lláh's purpose, but it does resonate with the text and the general opinion of commentators. In context, the Kitáb-i-Íqán must be read as an apologetic defense of the Báb, both in response to the doubts of the Báb's maternal uncle as well as to the general slander that had been leveled at the Báb and His followers both during His lifetime and after His execution. Bahá'u'lláh is thus interested in standards and methods of interpretation of revelation and the signs of the future they contain. His method of analysis on this point is to absolutely distinguish the category of Manifestation of God from the category of human being, whether learned or not. Only Manifestations of God can uncover the hidden and real meanings of the words of God, and, as such, the basis for all inquiries into truth must be conducted through the Manifestation or His revelation.[46] What all human beings do possess is the capacity, as stated in the opening paragraph of the Kitáb-i-Aqdas, to recognize and obey God.[47]

As Nader Saiedi has explained, this distinction between the Manifestation of God and humans extends dynamically throughout history through Bahá'u'lláh's reading of the principle of the unity of God. While the unity of God has long stood for the rejection of idol worship, Bahá'u'lláh extends it to require "recognizing the Will of God beyond particular instances of that Will."[48] In other words, this is an expression of the Bahá'í concept of progressive revelation—or the idea that divine revelation is both progressive and relative. Revelation, in Bahá'í thought, is a unitary but historically and contextually bound phenomenon: God has intervened in human history periodically and continually through Manifestations of God who bring a message in the form of revelation. Each of these instances of revelation has absolute legitimacy and authority as the word of God.[49] Revelations differ in the mode of expression, emphasis, structure, and details, depending upon the period of history and context into which the revelation is born. Revelation is thus in a reflexive relationship with history. Just as revelation demands and motivates particular human actions and movements, the course of human history comes to require and necessitate new revelations. The particular expression of the will of God in the revelation of the Báb, while specific, is also an expression of the same will that produced the Qur'án. To reject the Báb, by citing the words of the Qur'án or any other scripture, is thus invalid and a form of idol worship.

Within the interpretation of these references, Bahá'u'lláh is laying the basis for the claim of the complete sovereignty of the Manifestations of God, and indeed of Himself. The Christian rejection of Muhammad and the Muslim rejection of the Báb are rooted in the clinging to literal traditions and expectations of prophecy that are the accretions of time and human learning, as well as rooted in the failure to accept that the only measurable standard of the Messiah or the Promised One is the person of the Manifestation Himself and the revelation He brings.[50]

While McGlinn's analysis appears consistent with these general points concerning divine sovereignty, on the issue of earthly sovereignty, his argument becomes unclear and in some respects questionable. It is worth quoting McGlinn's paragraphs in full:

In part two of the Kitáb-i-Íqán, Bahá'u'lláh explains the nature of the sovereignty of the Qá'im:

. . . by sovereignty is meant the all-encompassing, all-pervading power which is inherently exercised by the Qá'im whether or not He appear to the world clothed in the majesty of earthly dominion. . . . That sovereign is the spiritual ascendancy . . . which in due time revealeth itself to the world . . . .

He gives the example of Muhammad's lack of worldly power during the time he was in Mecca, and contrasts it with the spiritual authority that was accorded to Muhammad in Bahá'u'lláh's own time. The sovereignty of the prophets resides in the power to attract devotion and to change hearts, to reform morals, to call forth sacrifices, and to create a new form of human community. While clearly differentiated from worldly dominion, and superior inasmuch as it is long-lasting, Bahá'u'lláh does not say that it overrules or displaces temporal government:

> Were sovereignty to mean earthly sovereignty and worldly dominion, were it to imply the subjection and external allegiance of all the peoples and kindreds of the earth—whereby His loved ones should be exalted and be made to live in peace, and His enemies be abased and tormented—such [a] form of sovereignty would not be true of God Himself, the Source of all dominion, Whose majesty and power all things testify. . . .

Bahá'u'lláh is saying that the ways of God do not change: if God does not force belief or obedience on humanity, then the Qá'im cannot. But he is also saying that the distinction between earthly and spiritual sovereignty is proper to God's self: that the Kingdom of God created by the Qá'im must be "true of God Himself," it must reflect the nature of dominion, majesty, and power in the Kingdom in Heaven. We will return to this point in "A Speculative Theology."[51]

This argument is not well supported. McGlinn implies that the first quotation he cites suggests that the Qá'im is not interested in earthly sovereignty. There is an argument that the quotation implies the opposite. Allowing for the sovereignty of the Qá'im "whether or not He appear to the world clothed in the majesty of earthly dominion" merely suggests that earthly sovereignty is a possible but not necessary criterion for His appearance. The fact that earthly sovereignty is a viable expression of the spiritual sovereignty of the Qá'im is further supported in the next sentence of the excerpt from the Kitáb-i-Íqán, which McGlinn does not quote: "Furthermore, by sovereignty is meant the all-encompassing, all-pervading power which is inherently exercised by the Qá'im whether or not He appear to the world clothed in the majesty of earthly dominion. *This is solely dependent upon the will and pleasure of the Qá'im Himself.*"[52]

This acceptance that the Qá'im might properly exercise earthly sovereignty fits with the general theory of sovereignty that Bahá'u'lláh develops in the Kitáb-i-Íqán. Bahá'u'lláh's central point is that the sovereignty of the Manifestation of God (including the Qá'im) is absolute and self-defining. Manifestations have "all-compelling power" and are "invested with invincible sovereignty."[53] Further, "[t]his sovereignty . . . is not the sovereignty which the minds of men have falsely imagined."[54] This sovereignty can only be defined by God and the Manifestations, because it is possessed by Manifestations in their character of embodying the attributes of God.

Bahá'u'lláh writes in reference to the Manifestations that "each and every one of them [has] been endowed with all the attributes of God, such as sovereignty, dominion, and the like, even though to outward seeming they be shorn of all earthly majesty."[55] Saiedi summarizes the relationship between the sovereignty of God and the sovereignty of the Manifestations in the following terms:

> The unconditional sovereignty of God implies that divine revelation cannot be bound by the limited categories and interpretations of the human mind. So all ordinary presuppositions about the meanings of the words of God and the holy traditions must be discarded, and reliance on such arbitrary human constructions

and standards amounts to "chaining up the hand of God" and, in fact, denying divine sovereignty. . . .

Bahá'u'lláh also affirms the sovereignty of the Prophets through the fundamental concept of manifestation theology. The Prophets are all Manifestations of the attributes of God. Their very existence is the supreme manifestation of the divine attribute of sovereignty. Therefore, the being of the Prophet is itself absolute sovereign over all things.[56]

Furthermore, Saiedi writes, "At the level of creation, the world has come into existence through the Word of God, which is the essence of the Manifestations of God. The existence of all things depends on them since it is through them that all things have been created. This is absolute, unconditional, and essential dominion and sovereignty. This dominion is never alienated from the Manifestations of God because the entire creation would cease to exist if divine grace and effulgence were to stop for one moment. . . ."[57]

In this vision of all-encompassing sovereignty, whether or not the Qá'im holds earthly sovereignty is beside the point. While human beings may expect the Qá'im to exert earthly sovereignty in his lifetime, it is completely up to the Qá'im whether or not he will. As Gollmer comments, ". . . the fact that the Qá'ím—and most previous manifestations—are, at least initially, not in possession of any earthly power, is regarded as a test for mankind."[58] Furthermore, he writes, "unrestricted power is the prerogative of God and his manifestations alone: 'He doeth what He pleaseth.' It is up to the manifestations themselves how they employ the secular and spiritual powers bestowed upon them by God, and how they transfer these powers to the respective institutions appointed to succeed them."[59]

Earthly sovereignty is within the sovereignty of the Qá'im, as is the choice whether or not to exert it—the operative principle being the absolute sovereignty of God and the Manifestations. For example, in relation to law, Bahá'u'lláh writes, "Were He to decree as lawful the thing which from time immemorial had been forbidden, and forbid that which had, at all times, been regarded as lawful, to none is given the right to question His authority. Whoso will hesitate, though it be for less than a moment, should be regarded as a transgressor."[60]

Bahá'u'lláh makes this clear in His discussion of the treatment of Muhammad. After recounting how Muhammad was debased in His lifetime, Bahá'u'lláh celebrates how many of the governments of the world have become identified with Muhammad and Islam. Bahá'u'lláh notes that "[e]ven those Kings of the earth who have refused to embrace His Faith and to put off the garment of unbelief, nonetheless confess and acknowledge the greatness and overpowering majesty of that Day-star of loving kindness."[61]

He then goes on to explicitly state that the Qá'im and Manifestations do have earthly sovereignty:

Such is His earthly sovereignty, the evidences of which thou dost on every side behold. This sovereignty must needs be revealed and established either in the lifetime of every Manifestation of God or after His ascension unto His true habitation in the realms above. What thou dost witness today is but a confirmation of this truth. That spiritual ascendancy, however, which is primarily intended, resideth within, and revolveth around Them from eternity even unto eternity. It can never for a moment be divorced from Them. Its dominion hath encompassed all that is in heaven and on earth.[62]

McGlinn's argument that a distinction between spiritual and earthly sovereignty is proper to God's self and that an implication of this is that Manifestations do not properly exert an earthly sovereignty is weak. It is clear in Bahá'í thought that the sovereignty of the Manifestations is all-encompassing, although earthly sovereignty is often not exercised by the Manifestation Himself in His lifetime, but will come to be expressed later. In the second quotation cited by McGlinn, Bahá'u'lláh is refuting the traditional interpretations of the coming of the Qá'im that demand His earthly sovereignty to be expressed through His person. At the same time, Bahá'u'lláh is defining a type of earthly sovereignty that He deems inappropriate—one characterized by coercion and force. Further, Bahá'u'lláh is confirming that earthly sovereignty is not the measure or standard for establishing the sovereignty of a Manifestation; nor are earthly sovereignty and spiritual sovereignty wholly distinct. Thus, earthly sovereignty is a valid expression of the spiritual sovereignty of Manifestations, but its absence at a particular time is not proof of an invalid claim to being a Manifestation (or the Qá'im, in the specific case of the Báb).

Interaction of Religion and Politics

Bahá'u'lláh's affirmation of God's earthly sovereignty, as expressed through His Manifestations, is reflected in the general proposition expressed in the writings of the Bahá'í Faith that religion and politics can and should inform and interact with one another.

The Bahá'í teachings envision religion as essential to all aspects of human life, including public life. 'Abdu'l-Bahá writes that

[i]t is certain that man's highest distinction is to be lowly before and obedient to his God; that his greatest glory, his most exalted rank and honor, depend on his close observance of the Divine commands and prohibitions. Religion is the light of the world, and the progress, achievement, and happiness of man result from obedience to the laws set down in the holy Books. Briefly, it is demonstrable that in this life, both outwardly and inwardly the mightiest of structures, the most solidly established, the most enduring, standing guard over the world, assuring both the spiritual and the material perfections of mankind, and protecting the happiness and the civilization of society—is religion.[63]

Furthermore, 'Abdu'l-Bahá writes, "It is certain that the greatest of instrumentalities for achieving the advancement and the glory of man, the supreme agency for the enlightenment and the redemption of the world, is love and fellowship and unity among all the members of the human race. Nothing can be effected in the world, not even conceivably, without unity and agreement, and the perfect means for engendering fellowship and union is true religion."[64] This emphasis on the essentiality of religion is echoed in 'Abdu'l-Bahá's statement that the Bahá'í Faith "embraceth all spiritual and temporal matters."[65]

This affirmation of the fundamental role of religion does not answer the question of the proper relationship between religious and civil institutions—and whether institutional integration is required by the Bahá'í writings. There are other ways besides institutional integration in which religion and politics may interact. For example, the integration may be cultural and social—meaning that religion is in the public sphere, an active force within public discourse, but religious and civil political institutions remain distinct from one another. Furthermore, there are many possible forms and structures where religious and political institutions have varying degrees of formal (and informal) relationships with one another, but remain legally and politically distinct entities. Through a review of some Bahá'í primary literature, it is argued that the Bahá'í teachings do not definitively insist on any particular model of institutional interaction as essential and correct.

The starting point for analysis of the possible public role of Bahá'í institutions is to review the nature, structure, and role of the Universal House of Justice. It is important at the outset to review and consider the following statement of Bahá'u'lláh concerning the Universal House of Justice:

This passage, now written by the Pen of Glory, is accounted as part of the Most Holy Book: The men of God's House of Justice have been charged with the affairs of the people. They, in truth, are the Trustees of God among His servants and the daysprings of authority in His countries.

O people of God! That which traineth the world is Justice, for it is upheld by two pillars, reward and punishment. These two pillars are the sources of life to the world. Inasmuch as for each day there is a new problem and for every problem an expedient solution, such affairs should be referred to the House of Justice that the members thereof may act according to the needs and requirements of the time. They that, for the sake of God, arise to serve His Cause, are the recipients of divine inspiration from the unseen Kingdom. It is incumbent upon all to be obedient unto them. All matters of State should be referred to the House of Justice, but acts of worship must be observed according to that which God hath revealed in His Book.[66]

The primary focus of debate in this passage is the statement that "all matters of State should be referred to the House of Justice."[67] This translation remains the standard one used within the Bahá'í community and is often used to support the apologetic assertion that the Universal House of Justice is intended to be the future governing institution for the entire world. In contrast to the predominant approach, Cole has argued that it has been mistranslated—particularly, the phrase *umúr-i-siyásiyyih*.[68] Cole argues that this phrase should be translated as referring to leadership and setting punishments, as opposed to the political role implied in the use of the term *state*.[69]

Cole's interpretation, however, does not account for the reality that over the course of hundreds of years, *siyása* became the term for politics in all Middle Eastern languages. As early as the eleventh and twelfth centuries, one finds derivations of *siyása* with significant political connotations.[70]

The question remains, however, what are the implications of this statement? The statement could imply a vision of the Universal House of Justice as the sole religious and civil authority. But it can also be read in other ways, as saying, for example, that all political (state) matters impacting the community should be addressed by the Universal House of Justice. A review of some of the key writings concerning the Universal House of Justice demonstrates that the institution is certainly discussed and structured similar to a contemporary political legislative institution. At the same time, however, there are not explicit statements about the Universal House of Justice and civil institutions that necessitate a fully integrationist conclusion.

In writing that "acts of worship" must be obeyed according to the teachings of scripture, Bahá'u'lláh removes them from the purview of the House of Justice, and as such reforms the classical Islamic scheme. The realm of worship (*'ibádat*) is historically drawn within Islamic law as distinct from the realms of societal relations (*mu'ámalát*) and politics (*siyása*).[71] In the classical Sunni Islamic theory, the methods and rules developed by the *ulama* control the realms of *'ibádat* and *mu'ámalát*, thereby lending significant public power to the clerics. Over time the *ulama* also developed theoretical justifications for roles in the realm of *siyása*, though in practice, the ruler exercised some legal (legislative) power in the realm of *siyása*.

Bahá'u'lláh's scheme maintains a distinction between *'ibádat*, *mu'ámalát*, and *siyása* but reconfigures the power arrangements. There is only one legal authority, the Universal House of Justice, and it is restricted from operating in the realm of *'ibádat*.[72] The Universal House of Justice is also a form of legal actor that operates outside of the parameters of the classical Islamic legal theory. In particular, the Universal House of Justice has an explicit grant of legislative powers.[73] As well, there is no public or legal role for a clerical class in this scheme, and no authority over the sacramental aspects of religious life.[74]

It is also important to emphasise other ways that the Universal House of Justice does not represent an institutionalized and rationalized clerical authority mirroring the *ulama* of Islam. In the classical Islamic legal theory, no authority was granted to any institution or class of individuals to pass generally binding legislation. In pursuit of the need to act according to divine sanction in all aspects of life, the mechanism for identifying the divine law applicable in a particular situation was to be done through *ijtihád*.[75] A new engagement with the sources (*usúl*) of law through *ijtihád* was to occur every time a legal question arose. Within the strivings of conscience entailed in *ijtihád*, it was believed, the most pristine and sanctified legal rule applicable to a situation could be discovered.[76] Frank Vogel refers to law-making through *ijtihád* as a "microcosmic" and "inner-directed" paradigm of "instance-law."[77]

Within such a legal methodology, an act of legislation is inferior to and at odds with the method of *ijtihád* itself. To this degree, however, the ideal theory is also anarchic and impractical—with the expected historical consequence of a great diversity of laws (typically organized into "schools"); the emergence of schemes for general law-making; and the balancing of power between the learned (*ulama*) and the rulers (Caliph, Sultan, King).[78] This balance was always a compromise, however, viewed to some degree as a deviation from the ideal method of *ijtihád*.

In contrast to this Islamic scheme, it is crucial to recognize the Universal House of Justice as a democratic institution that passes legislation through a non-intentionalist paradigm. Quite explicitly, the Universal House of Justice is instructed to pass legislation based on the exigencies of the time, not on the principles within the holy scripture where specific laws for all circumstances for all time can be found. 'Abdu'l-Bahá explains the rationale of the Universal House of Justice in a comparison and distinction with the traditional legal role of the *ulama:*

> Those matters of major importance which constitute the foundation of the Law of God are explicitly recorded in the Text, but subsidiary laws are left to the House of Justice. The wisdom of this is that the times never remain the same, for change is a

necessary quality and an essential attribute of this world, and of time and place. Therefore the House of Justice will take action accordingly. . . .

Briefly, this is the wisdom of referring the laws of society to the House of Justice. In the religion of Islám, similarly, not every ordinance was explicitly revealed; nay not a tenth part of a tenth part was included in the Text; although all matters of major importance were specifically referred to, there were undoubtedly thousands of laws which were unspecified. These were devised by the divines of a later age according to the laws of Islamic jurisprudence, and individual divines made conflicting deductions from the original revealed ordinances. All these were enforced. Today this process of deduction is the right of the body of the House of Justice, and the deductions and conclusions of individual learned men have no authority, unless they are endorsed by the House of Justice.[79]

'Abdu'l-Bahá further states that "[u]nto [the Universal House of Justice] all things must be referred. It enacteth all ordinances and regulations that are not to be found in the explicit Holy Text";[80] that "unto the Most Holy Book every one must turn and all that is not expressly recorded therein must be referred to the Universal House of Justice";[81] and "whatsoever they decide has the same effect as the Text itself. And inasmuch as this House of Justice hath power to enact laws that are not expressly recorded in the Book and bear upon daily transactions, so also it hath power to repeal the same."[82]

It seems clear that the legal power (*tashrí*) granted to the Universal House of Justice is a legislative one where an institution has the power to enact new laws. Only such a reading can adequately account for a power such as repeal.

This construction of the Universal House of Justice certainly appears to be analogous to a political legislative institution. 'Abdu'l-Bahá notes this when He writes: "This House of Justice enacteth the laws and the government enforceth them. The legislative body must reinforce the executive, the executive must aid and assist the legislative body so that through the close union and harmony of these two forces, the foundation of fairness and justice may become firm and strong, that all the regions of the world may become even as Paradise itself."[83]

Implied in this text is a connection between the legislative role of the Universal House of Justice and actions by world governments generally.

The scope of its legislative authority is defined by 'Abdu'l-Bahá in the following expansive terms:

It is incumbent upon these members (of the Universal House of Justice) to gather in a certain place and deliberate upon all problems which have caused difference, questions that are obscure and matters that are not expressly recorded in the Book. Whatsoever they decide has the same effect as the Text itself. And inasmuch as this House of Justice hath power to enact laws that are not expressly recorded in the Book and bear upon daily transactions, so also it hath power to repeal the same. Thus for example, the House of Justice enacteth today a certain law and enforceth it, and a hundred years hence, circumstances having profoundly changed and the conditions having altered, another House of Justice will then have power, according to the exigencies of the time, to alter that law. This it can do because that law formeth no part of the Divine Explicit Text. The House of Justice is both the initiator and the abrogator of its own laws.[84]

Finally, it is important to note that the Universal House of Justice is described by 'Abdu'l-Bahá and Shoghi Effendi as possessing "conferred infallibility" (al-'isma al-sifátíya).[85] The implication of this claim is that the Universal House of Justice is believed to be free from error or not liable to errors in judgment. This infallibility rests on the institution and not on its members, and, as such, there are no implications of sinlessness or immaculateness attached to this claim.[86] There exists some discussion in the secondary literature about whether this claim of infallibility applies to all decisions and actions of the Universal House of Justice, but it is generally accepted that it attaches to their legislative enactments.[87] While this does not address the question of the relationship between church and state per se, the belief in infallibility clarifies the theocratic nature of the Bahá'í model of administration in the sense that it implicates the Divine in Bahá'í law-making.

What can we conclude from these writings about the structure and nature of the Universal House of Justice? Collectively, these various aspects of the Universal House of Justice appear to affirm its character as a legislative institution, distinct from the traditions of the *ulama* and reflecting notions of political power indicative of the realm of *siyása* that imply a role beyond solely administering the life of the religious community. This does not, however, tell us the substance of what the relationship between church and state—or more specifically, the relationship between the Universal House of Justice and civil governments—will look like in Bahá'í terms. It already appears that there is enough evidence to question firm separationist positions. However, this does not lead necessarily to the fully integrationist conclusion.[88]

While not providing specificity on actual institutional arrangements or foreclosing all arguments for some forms of institutional separation, the following statements, written on behalf of Shoghi Effendi, or explicitly confirmed as conforming to his views, and considered as authoritative by the Bahá'í community, further make clear that a public role is anticipated for Bahá'í institutions:

In the light of these words, it seems fully evident that the way to approach this instruction is in realizing the Faith of Bahá'u'lláh as an ever-growing organism destined to become something new and greater than any of the revealed religions of the past. Whereas former Faiths inspired hearts and illumined souls, they eventuated in formal religions with an ecclesiastical organization, creeds, rituals and churches, while the Faith of Bahá'u'lláh, likewise renewing man's spiritual life, will gradually produce the institutions of an ordered society, fulfilling not merely the function of the churches of the past but also the function of the civil state. By this manifestation of the Divine Will in a higher degree than in former ages, humanity will emerge from that immature civilization in which [C]hurch and [S]tate are separate and competitive institutions, and partake of a true civilization in which spiritual and social principles are at last reconciled as two aspects of one and the same Truth.[89]

Regarding the question raised in your letter, Shoghi Effendi believes that for the present the Movement, whether in the East or the West, should be dissociated entirely from politics. This was the explicit injunction of 'Abdu'l-Bahá. . . . Eventually, however, as you have rightly conceived it, the Movement will, as soon as it is fully developed and recognized, embrace both religious and political issues. In fact Bahá'u'lláh clearly states that affairs of state as well as religious questions are to be referred to the House of Justice into which the Assemblies of the Bahá'ís will eventually evolve.[90]

The Bahá'ís will be called upon to assume the reins of government when they will come to constitute the majority of the population in a given country, and even then their participation in political affairs is bound to be limited in scope unless they obtain a similar majority in some other countries as well.[91]

The Bahá'ís must remain non-partisan in all political affairs. In the distant future, however, when the majority of a country have become Bahá'ís then it will lead to the establishment of a Bahá'í State.[92]

Shoghi Effendi himself wrote the following:

Not only will the present day Spiritual Assemblies be styled differ-
ently in future, but they will be enabled also to add to their present
functions those powers, duties, and prerogatives necessitated by
the recognition of the Faith of Bahá'u'lláh, not merely as one of
the recognized religious systems of the world, but as the State Religion of an independent and Sovereign Power. And as the Bahá'í
Faith permeates the masses of the peoples of East and West, and
its truth is embraced by the majority of the peoples of a number of
the Sovereign States of the world, will the Universal House of Justice attain the plenitude of its power, and exercise, as the supreme
organ of the Bahá'í Commonwealth, all the rights, the duties, and
responsibilities incumbent upon the world's future super-state.[93]

This present Crusade, on the threshold of which we now stand,
will, moreover, by virtue of the dynamic forces it will release and its
wide repercussions over the entire surface of the globe, contribute
effectually to the acceleration of yet another process of tremendous significance which will carry the steadily evolving Faith of
Bahá'u'lláh through its present stages of obscurity, of repression,
of emancipation and of recognition—stages one or another of
which Bahá'í national communities in various parts of the world
now find themselves in—to the stage of establishment, the stage
at which the Faith of Bahá'u'lláh will be recognized by the civil
authorities as the state religion, similar to that which Christianity
entered in the years following the death of the Emperor Constantine, a stage which must later be followed by the emergence of the
Bahá'í state itself, functioning, in all religious and civil matters,
in strict accordance with the laws and ordinances of the Kitáb-i-
Aqdas, the Most Holy, the Mother Book of the Bahá'í Revelation,
a stage which, in the fullness of time, will culminate in the establishment of the World Bahá'í Commonwealth, functioning in the
plenitude of its powers, and which will signalize the long awaited
advent of the Christ promised Kingdom of God on earth—the

Kingdom of Bahá'u'lláh mirroring however faintly upon this humble handful of dust the glories of the Abhá Kingdom.[94]

The Universal House of Justice has described Shoghi Effendi's explanation of the "future Bahá'í World Commonwealth" as one "that will unite spiritual and civil authority" and rejects the assertion that the "modern political concept of 'separation of church and state' is somehow one that Bahá'u'lláh intended as a basic principle of the World Order He has founded."[95]

Given the above explications, one is hard-pressed to see how some scholars could have definitively concluded that the essential Bahá'í view is of a form of institutional separation—whether complete separation as in the case of Cole, or even the English model advocated by McGlinn. Only through failure to fully incorporate certain authoritative primary sources can such a conclusion be reached. McGlinn demonstrates such an omission in his 1999 article when he writes inaccurately that "Shoghi Effendi's own writings contain little that illuminates the church-state question" and that beyond stating definitely that the Bahá'ís must never "allow the machinery of their administration to supersede the government of their respective countries," and vigorously emphasizing the duty of obedience of government, he says nothing on the church-state issue.[96]

Furthermore, McGlinn not only dismisses the possibility of an integrationist endpoint argued for in much of the secondary literature on the subject but also insists that the notion the Bahá'í teachings on the subject might affirm a developmental or evolutionary approach is wrong.[97] Labeling such approaches "dispensationalist," McGlinn, as discussed earlier, argues that a particular separationist form of church-state relations is identified as intended, and as such that an evolutionary approach would require acceptance of change of fundamental teachings of the Bahá'í Faith over time.[98] In order to dismiss the dispensationalist approach, McGlinn classifies authoritative statements from the primary literature as being about "historical process" and not statements reflecting a fundamental teaching of the religion. For example, McGlinn dismisses the statements of Shoghi Effendi—such as those quoted above speaking of stages of "establishment" and formation of a "Bahá'í state"—as a reference to "historical change" and not support for a dispensationalist view.[99]

In such an approach, McGlinn appears guilty of a similar error he suggests is made by advocates of dispensationalism. McGlinn explains away apparently integrationist statements as only about "historical change" to help validate his separationist starting point.[100] This is similar to what he accuses the dispensationalists of—categorizing certain primary literature as referring to "stages" to explain away apparently separationist statements and affirm an integrationist endpoint. As will be further explored later, in an epistemic approach, the necessity and logic of change—which reflects fundamental principles of the Bahá'í Faith—is emphasized over the goal of identifying a particular and essential institutional endpoint, whether it be integrationist or separationist.

But still one must be cautious in concluding from these statements a firm commitment in the primary literature to any essential and specific model of church-state relations. Questions of the establishment of religion are not entirely analogous to the issue of the relationship between religious and civil institutions, and certainly not to the question of theocracy. Moreover, there are many models for what "establishment" and formation of a "Bahá'í state" might mean. Furthermore, as illustrated earlier, there are also statements in the primary literature that can be understood to suggest a more separationist view.[101] Statements of Shoghi Effendi seem to suggest a future with distinct national civil institutions.[102] It must also be noted that there is undeniably a firm commitment to democracy, human rights, and protection of minorities in the primary literature. Little has been offered in secondary literature to justify how an integrationist vision can be reconciled with these principles.

Given all of the above, it appears that there is no definitive evidence in the primary literature that insists on firm conclusions about an essential institutional model of church-state relations. In this respect, the majority of the secondary literature—whether it advocates for an integrationist or a separationist approach—is guilty of the same error. Nowhere do Bahá'í writings spell out in detail how Bahá'í and civil institutions are expected to interact structurally or describe the jurisdictional lines, if any, that will be drawn between them. The evidence for the complete disappearance of secular civil institutions is inconclusive, as is the evidence for McGlinn's proposed English model. While religion is unequivocally anticipated as having a role in public life, and there are clear statements envisioning a legitimate role for Bahá'í institutions in public affairs, even the uniting of spiritual and civil authority in the distant world commonwealth, a specific and definitive institutional role is not prescribed in any absolute sense. As will be argued in the next section, the reason for this absence of specificity is that core Bahá'í teachings of social maturation and unity necessitate an open and contingent approach to such social forms of the future.

Maturation and Unity

Much secondary literature, as noted earlier, has not been content to leave uncertainty to this future institutional role. By going further, however, such literature lapses into essentialist positions, which are irreconcilable with core teachings of Bahá'u'lláh and 'Abdu'l-Bahá, such as those on social maturation and unity.

The Bahá'í writings repeatedly employ developmental metaphors to describe the collective life of humanity. The lens for analyzing the current conditions of political and social life is through the category of social maturation. For example, in a typical statement of this idea by the Universal House of Justice, the Bahá'í Faith views "[t]he human race, as a distinct, organic unit, [which] has passed through evolutionary stages analogous to the stages of infancy and childhood in the lives of its individual members, and is now in the culminating period of its turbulent adolescence approaching its long-awaited coming of age."[103]

This vision of social maturation rests upon the idea of unity, which

is the axis of Bahá'í ontology. In the Bahá'í paradigm, unity is an ontological principle, the defining characteristic of the nature of reality. As
one scholar summarizes:

> According to the Bahá'í view, the nature of reality is ultimately a
> unity, in contrast to a view that would postulate a multiplicity of
> differing or incommensurate realities. The nature of truth, accord-
> ing to the Bahá'í writings, is thus fundamentally unitary and not
> pluralistic. In a talk delivered in New York City in December of
> 1912, 'Abdu'l-Bahá states that "oneness is truth and truth is one-
> ness which does not admit of plurality." At a talk in Paris early
> that year, 'Abdu'l-Bahá admits that "Truth has many aspects, but
> it remains always and forever one."[104]

This ontology argues that humanity's collective life on this planet
is in the process of evolving to reflect more fully the reality of unity
in diversity so as to maximize its potential for social order and organization. The social life of humanity has become more complex and
integrated, and thus humanity must develop its ability to organize
in patterns of unity in diversity. Society, however, is not static. It is a
human construct. It is the product of human imagination, devotion,
and will. This means that human society can and should change, but
it does not mean that the form society should take is completely open
and anarchic. Social forms, including legal and political institutions,
will endure and are most suited to meet the needs of human beings
when they are constructed and operate according to the principle of
unity. In fact, the Bahá'í writings argue that a general pattern in the
history of the organization of human society illustrates an awareness of
the need to construct enlarging patterns of unity: "Unification of the
whole of mankind is the hall-mark of the stage which human society
is now approaching. Unity of family, of tribe, of city-state, and nation
have been successively attempted and fully established. World unity is
the goal towards which a harassed humanity is striving."[105]

It is important to stress how essential the concept of diversity is to the Bahá'í notion of unity. The Bahá'í writings identify true unity as encompassing diversity. For example, 'Abdu'l-Bahá uses the following analogy to describe the relationship between unity and diversity:

As difference in degree of capacity exists among human souls, as difference in capability is found, therefore, individualities will differ one from another. But in reality this is a reason for unity and not for discord and enmity. If the flowers of a garden were all of one color, the effect would be monotonous to the eye; but if the colors are variegated, it is most pleasing and wonderful. The difference in adornment of color and capacity of reflection among the flowers gives the garden its beauty and charm. Therefore, although we are of different individualities, . . . let us strive like flowers of the same divine garden to live together in harmony. Even though each soul has its own individual perfume and color, all are reflecting the same light, all contributing fragrance to the same breeze which blows through the garden, all continuing to grow in complete harmony and accord.[106]

Inherent within and inseparable from this vision of unity are the well-known Bahá'í commitments to gender and racial equality and social justice that are essential for the creation of true unity in diversity.

According to such a view of reality, the mission and challenge of social forms is not to find patterns of harmony amongst differences—in other words, not merely to find patterns of harmonious coexistence—but, in recognizing the reality of unity, to increasingly discover patterns of integration that express the fundamental unity of diverse entities in ever more complex and fundamental ways. Indeed, the establishment of the Kingdom of God on Earth is a process of increasingly articulating underlying realities, such as unity, and embodying these realities in the patterns of social and personal life we create: "The kingdom of peace, salvation, uprightness, and reconciliation is founded in the invisible world, and it will by degrees become manifest and apparent through the power of the Word of God! As a result of consecrated human endeavour over decades, and indeed centuries, this spiritual reality is gradually expressed in physical form."[107]

It is instructive in this respect that the Bahá'í writings place the initial locus of meaningful action towards creation of patterns of unity within the realm of individual human consciousness. It is through becoming aware of the fundamental unity of reality and seeing the world through the eye of unity that social unity can be accomplished. Bahá'u'lláh writes that one should "looketh on all things with the eye of oneness, and seeth the brilliant rays of the divine sun shining from the dawning-point of Essence alike on all created things, and the lights of singleness reflected over all creation."[108] Through "singleness," the diversity implicit in unity can and should be recognized.

One failure of both the integrationist and separationist approaches lies in not recognizing that the Bahá'í notions of maturation and unity build contingency into the vision of the Kingdom of God on Earth, and part of that contingency is the theoretical possibility that a wide range of divergent institutional forms may be valid expressions of Bahá'í teachings. Progressive revelation and emphasis on change and gradualism highlight the importance of human response and choice in how the ultimate pattern of the Kingdom of God emerges and takes shape.[109] A relative and progressive vision of God's interaction with humanity makes committing to the final form of the Kingdom of God a futile and irrational act. The final form(s) will be a contingent and historical reality, as even revelation is subject to historical reason.[110]

This vision is particularly highlighted when one examines the approaches to political and social change advocated by Bahá'u'lláh and 'Abdu'l-Bahá. One finds in the Bahá'í writings a hierarchy of modes of political and social change. Action at the level of social meanings is most privileged, followed by changes at the level of behavioral norms, and finally political forms (such as laws and institutions). Simply stated, Bahá'u'lláh and 'Abdu'l-Bahá's method of change emphasizes the need to act at the level of meanings before seeking to make broad or comprehensive changes at the level of norms and forms. Indeed, such a diffuse approach to social change is dictated by the Bahá'í definition of unity. The Bahá'í notion of unity, with its embedded notion of diversity, does not allow for coercion as a means to change. This idea is expressed by the first principle—the removal of the sword—enunciated by Bahá'u'lláh when He declared Himself to be a Manifestation of God in 1863. Saiedi describes the implications of this principle in the following terms: "The prohibition of killing, violence, and religious coercion; the promotion of love, unity, and fellowship among peoples; the call for peace among the nations; the condemnation of militarism and of the proliferation of arms; the assertion of the necessity for education and productive employment; the condemnation of sedition; the assertion of the need for religion and social justice—all these are presented by Bahá'u'lláh as systematic expressions of the same underlying principle of the removal of the sword."[111]

The elevation of change at the level of meanings over norms and forms is reflected directly in, among other things, Bahá'í law. As has been described elsewhere,[112] there has been a distinct trend toward moving Bahá'í law to the background since the time of Bahá'u'lláh. This backgrounding is expressed in the suspension of the application of many laws until the existence of a particular matrix of social meanings in which that law may be received without being a source of conflict. As Bahá'u'lláh states:

Indeed, the laws of God are like unto the ocean and the children of men as fish, did they but know it. However, in observing them one must exercise tact and wisdom. . . . Since most people are feeble and far-removed from the purpose of God, therefore one must observe tact and prudence under all conditions, so that nothing might happen that could cause disturbance and dissension or raise clamour among the heedless. Verily, His bounty hath surpassed the whole universe and His bestowals encompassed all that dwell on earth. One must guide mankind to the ocean of true understanding in a spirit of love and tolerance. The Kitáb-i-Aqdas itself beareth eloquent testimony to the loving providence of God.[113]

In this scheme that continues today, the application of Bahá'í law is contingent on particular meanings being extant so that the application of laws (which are by nature coercive) will reinforce meanings conducive to unity.

This privileging of social meanings is also captured in the Bahá'í principle of non-participation in politics.[114] Bahá'u'lláh taught His believers to avoid partisan politics, a principle that could be interpreted as suggesting quietism and passivism. But such a rendering is inaccurate, for the issue is not politics itself, but whether engagement in contemporary political processes is an approach to social and political change reflective of the principle of unity. For Bahá'u'lláh, there was no value in Bahá'ís assuming positions of political power within current political systems.[115] It can be argued that one reason for this is that the methods used to secure such power and the institutions in place for the exercise of power are not reflections of an ontology of unity, and attempting to enforce a religious program, including through contemporary political methods and institutions, is antithetical to unity.[116] It is thus not surprising to find in the Bahá'í writings statements that clearly distinguish the Bahá'í Administrative Order from existing political institutions. As Shoghi Effendi states:

It would be utterly misleading to attempt a comparison between this unique, this divinely-conceived Order and any of the diverse systems which the minds of men . . . have contrived. . . . Such an attempt would in itself betray a lack of complete appreciation of the excellence of the handiwork of its great Author. . . . The divers and ever-shifting systems of human polity, whether past or present, whether originating in the East or in the West, offer no adequate criterion wherewith to estimate the potency of its hidden virtues or to appraise the solidity of its foundations.[117]

It is also for these reasons that Bahá'u'lláh informs the kings and rulers of the world that He is only concerned with the hearts of people, for it is through influence at the level of human knowledge and awareness—and, by consequence, social meanings—that unity can truly begin to be reflected in social forms.

A good example of the Bahá'í method of focusing on change at the level of social meanings is seen in 'Abdu'l-Bahá's 1875 treatise *Risáliy-i-Madaniyyih* (*Secret of Divine Civilization*). The *Risáliy-i-Madaniyyih* was written at the explicit instruction of Bahá'u'lláh, Who asked for an exploration of "the means and the cause of development and underdevelopment of the world in order to reduce the prejudices of the dogmatic conservatives."[118] As such, *Risáliy-i-Madaniyyih* is a commentary on Iranian political and social reform, written at a time when reform sentiment was running high in the face of increasing contact with, and threats by, the West. The repercussions of that contact were increasingly strident voices asserting the incompatibility of Islam with aspects of progress seen in the West (the so-called dogmatic conservatives).

'Abdu'l-Bahá's approach to reform argues for a change in the social meanings associated with politics within Iran and Twelver Shi'ism. 'Abdu'l-Bahá's opening address in *Secret of Divine Civilization* is to the traditional political actors who pursue political change—the Shah and the *ulama*. He begins by commending Nasiri'd-Din Shah (1831–96) for the efforts of his ministers in pursuing reform, but He then notes that reform has not gone far enough: Iran's apex of glory is found in the past, while presently Europe and America appear at the apex of material and technological development.[119] He next criticizes the *ulama* for their agitations against reform and condemns them for stalling progress.[120] After these brief statements to the main actors, 'Abdu'l-Bahá argues that the meaning of leadership and the role and character of government must change.[121] He attempts to free political narrative from the stagnating impact of the occultation of the twelfth Imam, which contributed to Twelver Shi'ism doctrine preaching the illegitimacy of government pending the end of the occultation.[122]

'Abdu'l-Bahá attempts to rehabilitate political dialogue about the nature of leadership itself. His discussion of the Shah and the *ulamá*'s leadership is not couched in theological niceties or eschatological condemnations. It is not colored by the past or the attitudes toward leadership that dominated. In some respects, its form echoes the "Mirrors of Princes" tradition, which often would outline how rulers need to rule with justice, and the role of religion and the *ulama* in relation to the ruler's power.[123] But 'Abdu'l-Bahá's focus is different in a number of respects. He does not adopt the typical position of the "Mirrors of Princes" tradition that accepts autocratic rule. Moreover, He does not focus solely on the role of the ruler in propagating justice, but rather includes the meanings that the masses of the people associate with leadership.[124] He engages in a detailed discussion of the need for rulers to associate themselves in the minds of the masses with freedom from political corruption, honesty, high levels of skill and education, personal integrity, and their practical performance as a leader.[125] 'Abdu'l-Bahá demonstrates the uniqueness of His approach when He begins applying His criteria of leadership to possible democratic reforms that may be pursued. Consider the following:

> While the setting up of parliaments, the organizing of assemblies of consultation, constitutes the very foundation and bedrock of government, there are several essential requirements these institutions must fulfill. First, the elected members must be righteous, God-fearing, high-minded, incorruptible. Second, they must be fully cognizant, in every particular, of the laws of God, informed as to the highest principles of law, versed in the rules which govern the management of internal affairs and the conduct of foreign

relations, skilled in the useful arts of civilization, and content with their lawful emoluments.[126]

Beyond the virtues of a righteous leader, 'Abdu'l-Bahá is arguing that Iranians must begin to achieve a mindset that focuses on the skills, utilities, and character of the people who lead them and of good governance. 'Abdu'l-Bahá illustrates His point with a strikingly cogent and contemporary example of the dilemmas for governments where virtue and skill are not combined: "If . . . the members of these consultative assemblies are inferior, ignorant, uninformed of the laws of government and administration, unwise, of low aim, indifferent, idle, self-seeking, no benefit will accrue from the organizing of such bodies."[127]

In some respects, this discussion of leadership sounds quite modern. However, 'Abdu'l-Bahá combines His pragmatic focus with a focus on the spiritualization of leadership that is dissociated from the religiosity of the past. He does link injustice with a "lack of religious faith," but, more significantly, He says it is due to "the fact that [the leaders] are uneducated."[128] He sees the necessity of an education in "self-respect, in high resolves and noble purposes, in integrity and moral quality, in immaculacy of mind"[129] for leaders who must be characterized by "excellent character, . . . high resolve, . . . breadth of learning, . . . and [the] ability to solve difficult problems."[130] This focus on character, integrity, nobility, and the education of leaders and their subjects is rooted in a view that the development of human capacities—intellectual, emotional, and spiritual—is the key to good governance and civil order. Religion proper only comes into this equation as relevant when it contributes to accomplishing this objective.[131]

While the specifics of 'Abdu'l-Bahá's definitions of leadership are interesting, His method is more crucial. His efforts focus on changing the collective associations that are applied to a social phenomenon. Shifting meanings is the prerequisite in His vision for meaningful political reform. This focus provides an important context for understanding how Bahá'í institutions may come to play a public role. 'Abdu'l-Bahá's mode of action is not to agitate for broad structural change, revolution, or even changes in leaders without an *a priori* change in meanings. In today's terminology, aspects of this approach to politics might be considered postmodern.[132] It focuses on the mindsets and frames of reference individuals bring to politics. It recognizes that structural changes often reinforce pre-existing patterns—often oppressive and negative ones—because the contexts in which those structures exist have not been altered. It also points to the relationship between identification and politics, holding that individual identity, self-actualization, and awareness are necessary for successful democratic participation. In His commenting on the constitutional revolution that began in 1905, 'Abdu'l-Bahá continually reinforced the idea that for reform to succeed "the Government and the People should mix together like honey and milk,"[133] and that if this did not occur, "the field [would] be open for the maneuvers of others."[134] A suggestion is that absent this identification of the general population with politics and their awareness of the political dimensions of their personal lives, politics is easily co-opted by the few and corrupted.

Other primary literature develops the theme that participation in contemporary political processes may potentially co-opt Bahá'í political ideas and practices and transform them into ones foreign to the core principles of the Bahá'í teachings.[135] Bahá'í formal prescriptions may mirror those that others are advocating, but the context—the meanings and norms—that 'Abdu'l-Bahá sees as fundamental to successful formal change and consistent with Bahá'u'lláh's teachings will not be present if the formal change occurs without the hard work needed for transformation at the levels of norms and meanings.

The hierarchical relationship among meanings, norms, and forms as modes of political action is a template against which the historical and contemporary Bahá'í community can be analyzed. A brief overview of the evolution of the structure and internal organization of the Bahá'í community illustrates this.

The first one hundred fifty years of Bahá'í history have been characterized by institutionalization and the development of an administrative system. The evolution of this system has had three distinct phases. The first phase, which occurred under the leadership of 'Abdu'l-Bahá, was characterized by a turn to the West, and in particular to the fostering and development of Bahá'í communities in North America. After 'Abdu'l-Bahá was freed from prison in 1908, He prepared for and undertook a 1911–12 journey throughout Europe, Canada, and the United States. During this journey, 'Abdu'l-Bahá propagated the Bahá'í Faith; encouraged the nascent Bahá'í communities to more audacious forms of action; spoke with countless social, political, and academic leaders; and spoke out on the "hot" issues of the day, such as the impending World War, race, suffrage movements, and unions. His journey also laid the groundwork for North American Bahá'í communities to bear the responsibility of building up Bahá'í communities and administrative organs around the globe.[136]

In the second phase of administration building, Shoghi Effendi guided the Bahá'í community to the fulfillment of 'Abdu'l-Bahá's plan. The original basic structure of the administrative order was to have elected bodies of nine individuals at municipal, national, and international levels. Additionally, appointed advisory positions were created. The process Shoghi Effendi employed for the construction of this system was to focus on local grassroots development that, when the community had reached a suitable size and degree of administrative sophistication, could elect a national institution. It was on the foundation of these national institutions that the international body, and supreme authority, the Universal House of Justice, would be elected.[137]

Shoghi Effendi died in 1957 before the election of the first Universal House of Justice, but under his guidance the institutionalization of the Bahá'í community had dramatically changed. The third phase in development began in 1963 when the Universal House of Justice was elected and the skeletal architecture of the administrative order was in essence completed.

Why does a community with a focus on cultivating a spiritual way of life and developing a mode of community life that reflected such spirituality, turn towards institutionalization in such a systematic way?[138] The process of institutionalization further clarifies the nature of politics and political action in the Bahá'í Faith. This experiment with the forms of politics, constructed completely apart from and without any direct engagement with external political processes and institutions, positions the Bahá'í Faith to have a global character to its administrative order. But this system of government is, for want of a better term, an experimental zone in which the Bahá'í community is attempting to erect institutions rooted in the meanings and reflecting the norms that the Bahá'í Faith argues should govern political life.

Neither McGlinn's English model nor Cole's separationist model, or even the tradition of integrationist theocracy, fit with this epistemic vision of political change. There is an inherent gradualism in the Bahá'í approach of being open to a vision of maturation, wherein a number of different forms of governance—and patterns of relationships between civil and religious institutions—may be affirmed. Social meanings may develop in such a way that choices to move in a direction toward a Bahá'í theocracy, as articulated in integrationist perspectives, dominate in certain places. However, such a "theocracy," were it ever to emerge, would have to remain consistent with the overarching principle of unity in diversity—including the essential implications for human rights and equality—and the predominance of the democratic principle within the Bahá'í Administrative Order. By consequence, this suggests great care and caution must be used in ascribing contemporary definitions and categories to the term "Bahá'í theocracy" or "Bahá'í state."[139] At the same time, social meanings may emerge elsewhere to give another form to institutional integration; while in yet other contexts, institutional arrangements that appear as separationist in contemporary terms may be deemed as reflecting the most legitimate and appropriate interaction between the religious and political.

Such an open approach to forms of church and state in the Bahá'í Faith reflects the self-identity of the Universal House of Justice, which has expressed its commitment to an open and contingent vision of its own role in political affairs. In response to questions concerning the appearance of a Bahá'í theocracy, the Universal House of Justice stresses themes of gradualism, openness, and contingency. It states that a "fundamental principle which enables us to understand the pattern towards which Bahá'u'lláh wishes human society to evolve is the principle of organic growth which requires that detailed developments, and the understanding of detailed developments, become available only with the passage of time."[140] Employing a simple analogy, "if a farmer plants a tree, he cannot state at that moment what its exact height will be, the number of its branches or the exact time of its blossoming. [H]e can, however, give a general impression of its size and pattern of growth and can state with confidence which fruit it will bear. The same is true of the evolution of the World Order of Bahá'u'lláh."[141]

Similarly, the Universal House of Justice states that "the Administrative Order is certainly the nucleus and pattern of the World Order of Bahá'u'lláh, but it is in embryonic form, and must undergo major evolutionary developments in the course of time."[142] It also echoes the vision of political action of 'Abdu'l-Bahá by stating that "clearly the establishment of the Kingdom of God on earth is a 'political' enterprise," but "the Bahá'ís are following a completely different path from that usually followed by those who wish to reform society."[143] They "concentrate on revitalizing the hearts, minds, and behaviour of people and on presenting a working model as evidence of the reality and practicality of the way of life they propound."[144] Finally, the Universal House of Justice stresses the contingency of any shift toward a Bahá'í state or Bahá'í theocracy by stating that there are certain principles that may be identified as key to Bahá'u'lláh's vision of the unfoldment of the Kingdom of God on earth.[145] These principles stress that a movement toward a Bahá'í state is wholly in the hands of the state that wishes to pursue such a course.[146] The decision by a state and its citizens to adopt the Bahá'í Faith as the "State Religion, let alone to the point at which a State would accept the Law of God as its own law and the National House of Justice as its legislature, must be a supremely voluntary and democratic process."[147]

As a general principle, such a transition would have to occur "by constitutional means"[148]—while Bahá'ís would still observe principles of abstention from certain forms of political action—and this transition would have to be consistent with the core Bahá'í commitments to democracy and human rights.

It is curious that statements such as these have not been subject to more scholarly analysis or incorporated to a greater degree into the debate about church-state relations in the Bahá'í Faith. The self-perception and identity of the institution that is at the core of the church-state question are necessary corollaries to a close textual analysis of the statements of Bahá'u'lláh. Perhaps, as discourse on this subject develops, scholars will place further emphasis on analyzing and understanding the institution of the Universal House of Justice and the range of its possible future political role and relationship with civil governments.

An Open Vision of Church and State

An epistemic vision of church and state is ultimately an open vision. Bahá'u'lláh's teachings represent an eschatological vision that consciously accepts the human dimension in how religions evolve in reality. With unity in diversity as the guiding principle, a firm commitment to a specific pattern and structure of church and state is inconceivable, even as Bahá'ís anticipate an increasing role for religion in public life. There is no linear form or expression to social maturation—there are only general directions of development. And, within limits, the end points are relative. In cultures with long traditions of theocratic structures, one might expect a transition to forms of theocracy to occur. In societies with a long tradition of separationist structures, the transition to increasing interaction between religion and politics will likely be very different, and the institutional forms might appear quite distinct from those in another context. The relationships between national Bahá'í institutions and civil governments in one setting will be very different than in another. By extension, the relationship of the Universal House of Justice to the state apparatus of one country may be quite different from another. Reflecting the non-coercive nature of unity, those relationships, should they ever emerge, would be constitutional and voluntary in nature. By failing to recognize the innate openness in Bahá'u'lláh's vision, both separationists and integrationists have made the same essentialist error; and by so doing, they have failed to explore a distinct religious vision of how church and state may interact. Indeed, what one sees in scholarship so far is a tendency to frame the debate through the often used polarizing lenses of theocracy and democracy—a debate seemingly indistinguishable from the poles that dominate general debates about religion and politics. The emphasis found in the Bahá'í writings on action at the epistemic level and the core principle of unity in diversity may well inform better approaches to this important subject.

6 / Internationalism and Divine Law: A Bahá'í Perspective

[FIRST PUBLISHED IN *JOURNAL OF LAW AND RELIGION*, VOL. XIX, NO. 2, 2003–2004.]

Abstract

This article introduces the internationalism motif in Bahá'í political and legal thought and Bahá'í arguments concerning the place of divine legal claims in contemporary debates about models of world order. In contrast to theories such as the clash of civilizations thesis of world politics—which view divine legal and political claims as a likely source of conflict and violence—the relative and progressive concept of revelation in the Bahá'í Faith argues for religion as a potentially unifying and foundational force in the evolution of a universal civilization. Bahá'í perspectives on internationalism also illustrate a distinct concept of divine law articulated within the Persianate and Muslim traditions of nineteenth century political and legal thought.

Nineteenth-century Iran was a hotbed of reform sentiment. While the prescriptions for change that were offered varied greatly, the drive and expectation for both religious and political change were fervent. Among the more unique movements arguing for reform was the Bahá'í Faith. Founded by Mírzá Ḥusayn-'Alí (1817–1892)—known as Bahá'u'lláh ("Glory of God")—the Bahá'í Faith arose out of the upheavals precipitated by the Bábí religion. Bahá'u'lláh articulated a theology of oneness that was reflected in pacifist and progressive social practices. Central to His teachings was the idea that all the founders of the world's great religions—including Moses, Buddha, Christ, and Muhammad—were "Manifestations" of God, charged with revealing a message from God relevant to that period in humanity's collective history. As such, all religions are ultimately united; they come from the same source, share the same core precepts, and engage in the same process of articulating God's relationship with His creation. However, this unity is expressed in historical, contextual, and contingent terms, which result in different texts, patterns of worship, doctrines, laws, and modes of community life in the world's great religions.

Internationalism—implying the establishment of universal peace and global unity—was a core theme of Bahá'u'lláh's teachings. Humanity was reaching a time of maturation, when the unity of humanity would be fully realized and manifested. Many aspects of His religious system reflect this idea of maturation: His criticism of religious hierarchies and the prohibition of any Bahá'í clergy; His emphasis on interreligious dialogue and unity; and His call for the establishment of an international auxiliary language. Bahá'u'lláh argued that it was both possible and necessary that individual identities be affiliated with the entire globe. In a well-known statement—which Cambridge Orientalist E.G. Browne saw as lacking pragmatism and utopian—Bahá'u'lláh stated, "[i]t is not for him to pride himself who loveth his own country, but rather for him who loveth the whole world."[1]

This paper examines the relationship between Bahá'u'lláh's motif of internationalism and the legal teachings and practices within His religious system. After a brief introduction to Bahá'í law, two axes for analyzing tensions between internationalism and divine law are examined. First, the struggle of human beings to translate divine law into social forms is explored, with a focus on the Bahá'í fidelity to a relative and dynamic vision of how the divine will may gain positive legal form.

Second, the challenge to articulate positive ways in contexts of diversity is analyzed in light of the Bahá'í privileging of an ontology of unity.

In the contemporary world, there exist basic and obvious tensions between commitments to global order and international law, and religious commitments to a divine law. Is a claim to a divine law inevitably in conflict with the forces of globalization and visions of world order? From a Bahá'í perspective, internationalism and divine law do not have to be in conflict, but rather are expressions of shared dynamic and historical processes. It is within the Bahá'í vision of a progressive and socially responsive divine law—with similarly dynamic mechanisms for the reflection of God's will in legal institutions and practices—that the Bahá'í commitment to internationalism can be understood.

A Brief Introduction to Bahá'í Law

Before examining Bahá'í arguments concerning internationalism and divine law, it is necessary to briefly introduce some of the basic texts and principles of Bahá'í law. Udo Schaefer's recent article, *An Introduction to Bahá'í Law: Doctrinal, Foundations, Principles, and Structures*,[2] provides a comprehensive background to the rules and legal categories found in Bahá'í texts. This introduction focuses more on contextual and thematic issues.

Legal themes are addressed throughout Bahá'u'lláh's writings, as well as those of the authorized interpreters of His writings—His son 'Abdu'l-Bahá (1844–1921) and great-grandson Shoghi Effendi (1897–1957). Using Islamic categories, one finds in Bahá'u'lláh's writings laws of worship (*'ibádat*) as well as those that relate to societal relations (*mu'ámalát*) and politics (*siyása*).

Bahá'u'lláh's Kitáb-i-Aqdas (the "Most Holy Book") is the core legal text. Written in 1873 and comprised of 190 paragraphs, almost all of which are no longer than a few sentences, the Kitáb-i-Aqdas is by no means Bahá'u'lláh's longest work, nor in many respects is it His most complex. Indeed, to the student of law, the Kitáb-i-Aqdas is in some respects quite familiar. This familiarity is found in its straightforward enunciation of legal rules, supported by a set of principles of textual (or legislative or statutory) interpretation. While the rules stated are not many, numbering less than one hundred, their scope is broad—touching on a range of civil and criminal law issues. As the following examples illustrate, regardless of which category of law one is discussing, the mode of delivery—brief and clear—is the same:

It hath been ordained that obligatory prayer is to be performed by each of you individually. Save in the Prayer for the Dead, the practice of congregational prayer hath been annulled.[3]

We have divided inheritance into seven categories: to the children, We have allotted nine parts comprising five hundred and forty shares; to the wife, eight parts comprising four hundred and eighty shares; to the father, seven parts comprising four hundred and twenty shares; to the mother, six parts comprising three hundred and sixty shares; to the brothers, five parts or three hundred shares; to the sisters, four parts or two hundred and forty shares; and to the teachers, three parts or one hundred and eighty shares.[4]

Gambling and the use of opium have been forbidden unto you.[5]

Should anyone unintentionally take another's life, it is incumbent upon him to render to the family of the deceased an indemnity of one hundred mithqáls of gold.[6]

These statements of rules are also interspersed with principles to guide interpretation. The foundational principle is the interpretive authority of 'Abdu'l-Bahá and His position of successorship. This interpretive authority is typically labeled as a feature of the covenant established by

Bahá'u'lláh. Bahá'u'lláh reiterates the relationship between God's law and God's covenant at the beginning of the Kitáb-i-Aqdas:

They whom God hath endued with insight will readily recognize that the precepts laid down by God constitute the highest means for the maintenance of order in the world and the security of its peoples. He that turneth away from them is accounted among the abject and foolish. We, verily, have commanded you to refuse the dictates of your evil passions and corrupt desires, and not to transgress the bounds which the Pen of the Most High hath fixed, for these are the breath of life unto all created things. The seas of Divine wisdom and Divine utterance have risen under the breath of the breeze of the All-Merciful. Hasten to drink your fill, O men of understanding! They that have violated the Covenant of God by breaking His commandments, and have turned back on their heels, these have erred grievously in the sight of God, the All-Possessing, the Most High.[7]

The issue of the successorship of 'Abdu'l-Bahá and His interpretive authority is also made explicit.[8] The successorship and authority of Shoghi Effendi became explicit in 'Abdu'l-Bahá's own writings.[9]

In addition to the foundational principle of covenant, Bahá'u'lláh provides a number of other guides to reading the Kitáb-i-Aqdas. In some instances a clear injunction to look for the plain meaning of the text is made:

Whoso layeth claim to a Revelation direct from God, ere the expiration of a full thousand years, such a man is assuredly a lying impostor. We pray God that He may graciously assist him to retract and repudiate such claim. Should he repent, God will, no doubt, forgive him. If, however, he persisteth in his error, God will, assuredly, send down one who will deal mercilessly with him.

Terrible, indeed, is God in punishing! *Whosoever interpreteth this verse otherwise than its obvious meaning is deprived of the Spirit of God and of His mercy which encompasseth all created things. Fear God, and follow not your idle fancies.*[10]

More generally, invoking the premise that the Kitáb-i-Aqdas represents the revealed word of God, Bahá'u'lláh repeatedly makes the claim that if the book is to be understood the principles of interpretation must be self-referential, or discovered within the text itself: "Weigh not the Book of God with such standards and sciences as are current amongst you, for the Book itself is the unerring Balance established amongst men. In this most perfect Balance whatsoever the peoples and kindreds of the earth possess must be weighed, while the measure of its weight should be tested according to its own standard, did ye but know it."[11]

The Kitáb-i-Aqdas will also appear familiar to the student of religious law. While the statement of rules and commandments is a prominent aspect of the text, these rules are embedded within a discussion of themes of divine sovereignty, the duties owed to God by human beings, and exhortations to obedience. There exists a clear enunciation of the divine command underlying the laws of Bahá'u'lláh—"These are the ordinances of God that have been set down in the Books and Tablets by His Most Exalted Pen."[12] This call of the divine demands a human response, which Bahá'u'lláh makes explicit in the opening verse of the Kitáb-i-Aqdas:

The first duty prescribed by God for His servants is the recognition of Him Who is the Dayspring of His Revelation and the Fountain of His laws, Who representeth the Godhead in both the Kingdom of His Cause and the world of creation. Whoso achieveth this duty hath attained unto all good; and whoso is deprived thereof hath gone astray, though he be the author of every righteous deed. It behooveth everyone who reacheth this most sublime station, this summit of transcendent glory, to observe every ordinance of Him

Who is the Desire of the world. These twin duties are inseparable. Neither is acceptable without the other. Thus hath it been decreed by Him Who is the Source of Divine inspiration.[13]

As is common in a number of scriptures, one also finds evocations supportive of both legalistic and mystical orientations. Bahá'u'lláh writes that "the precepts laid down by God constitute the highest means for the maintenance of order in the world and the security of its peoples,"[14] and "[t]hese, verily, are the Laws of God; transgress them not at the prompting of your base and selfish desires. Observe ye the injunctions laid upon you by Him Who is the Dawning-place of Utterance."[15] However, Bahá'u'lláh also writes that one should "[o]bserve My commandments, for the love of My Beauty."[16] Further, the reader is cautioned to: "Think not that We have revealed unto you a mere code of laws. Nay, rather, We have unsealed the choice Wine with the fingers of might and power. To this beareth witness that which the Pen of Revelation hath revealed. Meditate upon this, O men of insight!"[17]

There are also extensive ethical teachings within the Kitáb-i-Aqdas that reflect the Bahá'í belief in the physical world as an arena for the acquisition of spiritual tools to facilitate the eternal journey of the human soul. Within the Kitáb-i-Aqdas, Bahá'u'lláh exhorts individuals to fulfill their duties to obey and recognize God, show love and fellowship to the entire human race, and avoid any acts that might cause sadness to the hearts and souls of others. He also discusses the implications for human action of principles of liberty and unity.

Yet, for all that is familiar in the construction and content of the Kitáb-i-Aqdas, it has many aspects that set it apart from traditions of both legal writing and scripture. It must always be remembered that the canon of Bahá'í scripture does not constitute a "Book" but rather an extensive collection of works. The Kitáb-i-Aqdas is the "mother book" of this body of scripture, implying that within it one finds an encapsulation of the entirety of Bahá'u'lláh's revelation.[18] A text primarily preoccupied with legal themes is an integration of theology, philosophy, social and political thought, and the dynamics of the individual's relationship with the divine. The Kitáb-i-Aqdas and its succinct statement of rules thus becomes a vehicle through which the totality of Bahá'u'lláh's religious teachings is integrated. In this construction of legal text as the epicenter of a large and complex body of religious literature, a holistic and comprehensive vision of religious law is expounded—one that is indivisible from other areas of knowledge and religious teaching.

For example, the foundations of Bahá'í theology stress the relative and progressive nature of God's revelation to humanity, which has resulted in the incorporation of significant intertextual reflection in Bahá'u'lláh's laws. The Kitáb-i-Aqdas does not only reveal the laws of the Bahá'í Faith, but it also explicitly reacts to the revealed laws of earlier religions—through abrogation, explanation, and reformation. While such intertextuality between scriptures is not unique, the nature of Bahá'í theology renders the interreligious dialogue underlying the laws of the Kitáb-i-Aqdas a significant representation of the Bahá'í viewpoint on the progressive nature of religion. As Bahá'í authorities stated at the time of the publication of the Kitáb-i-Aqdas:

Its provisions rest squarely on the foundation established by past religions, for, in the words of Bahá'u'lláh, "*This is the change-less Faith of God, eternal in the past, eternal in the future.*" In this Revelation the concepts of the past are brought to a new level of understanding, and the social laws, changed to suit the age now dawning, are designed to carry humanity forward into a world civilization the splendors of which can as yet be scarcely imagined.

In its affirmation of the validity of the great religions of the past, the Kitáb-i-Aqdas reiterates those eternal truths enunciated by all the Divine Messengers: the unity of God, love of one's neighbor, and the moral purpose of earthly life. At the same time it removes those elements of past religious codes that now constitute obstacles to the emerging unification of the world and the reconstruction of human society.[19]

In the introduction to the Kitáb-i-Aqdas, we continue to read more explicitly:

The Law of God for this Dispensation addresses the needs of the entire human family. There are laws in the Kitáb-i-Aqdas which are directed primarily to the members of a specific section of humanity and can be immediately understood by them but which, at first reading, may be obscure to people of a different culture. Such, for example, is the law prohibiting the confession of sins to a fellow human being which, though understandable by those of Christian background, may puzzle others. Many laws relate to those of past Dispensations, especially the two most recent ones, those of Muhammad and *the Báb* embodied in the Qur'án and the *Bayán*. Nevertheless, although certain ordinances of the Aqdas have such a focused reference, they also have universal implications. Through His Law, Bahá'u'lláh gradually unveils the significance of the new levels of knowledge and behavior to which the peoples of the world are being called. He embeds His precepts in a setting of spiritual commentary, keeping ever before the mind of the reader the principle that these laws, no matter the subject with which they deal, serve the manifold purposes of bringing tranquility to human society, raising the standard of human behavior, increasing the range of human understanding, and spiritualizing the life of each and all. Throughout, it is the relationship of the individual soul to God and the fulfillment of its spiritual destiny that is the ultimate aim of the laws of religion.[20]

The Bahá'í concept of unity that underlies the theology of progressive revelation and its impact on law is also made explicit in the Kitáb-i-Aqdas. For example, it is articulated as a social ethic: "We shed upon the whole of creation the splendors of Our most excellent Names and Our most exalted Attributes. This, verily, is a token of My loving providence, which hath encompassed all the worlds. Consort ye then with the followers of all religions, and proclaim ye the Cause of your Lord, the Most Compassionate; this is the very crown of deeds, if ye be of them who understand."[21]

Similarly, the all-encompassing nature of Bahá'u'lláh's discussion of law is evidenced in how the Kitáb-i-Aqdas becomes a vehicle for Bahá'u'lláh to address various kings and rulers including Kaiser William I, Emperor Francis Joseph, the "Rulers of America and the Presidents of the Republics therein," and Sultan 'Abdu'l-'Azíz. While stating "it is not Our wish to lay hands on your kingdoms,"[22] Bahá'u'lláh nonetheless is asserting Divine sovereignty through discussion on the nature of Divine power and temporal power. Bahá'u'lláh's law becomes the "Most Great Law,[23] Himself the "King of Kings."[24] Fidelity to Bahá'u'lláh is demanded as kings and rulers are to "arise to aid My Cause in My kingdom."[25] In these statements and others, the political dimensions of Bahá'u'lláh's teachings are being integrated with discussion concerning the nature of divine law and its place in ordering the temporal world.

A distinctive aspect of the Kitáb-i-Aqdas that also merits attention is its explicit discussion of succession and legislative power. The authority of 'Abdu'l-Bahá has already been noted, but also explicit is Bahá'u'lláh's structuring of legislative power and a system of order. He states a "'House of Justice'"[26] needs be established in "'every city.'"[27] In a subsequent letter that He states is "part of the Most Holy Book," He establishes the legislative authority of the House of Justice.[28] Distinct from many other religious traditions in which questions of succession and authority become a source of schism and dissent, Bahá'u'lláh engages questions of constitutional and public law directly and explicitly enough that significant schism has been avoided in Bahá'í history.

While the Kitáb-i-Aqdas establishes the foundations of Bahá'í law, it is not an explicit source of the internationalism motif, nor does it explicitly explore the relationship between Bahá'u'lláh's law and His vision of world order. Internationalism was more systematically developed in the authoritative interpretations of 'Abdu'l-Bahá and Shoghi Effendi. In particular, in His 1875 political treatise *The Secret of Divine*

Civilization,[29] 'Abdul-Bahá addressed the reform of Iranian society by linking reform to both a need to be guided by divine law and a need to organize and act at an international level. Similarly, Shoghi Effendi wrote extensively about Bahá'í ideas of "world order," most notably in the letter "Goal of a New World Order."[30] As will be discussed later in this paper, it is in the writings of 'Abdu'l-Bahá and Shoghi Effendi that the structure of legal institutions within the Bahá'í Faith, as well as the institutions of a future world order, are more systematically articulated.

Divine Law and Human Law-Making

When a claim has been made that God has spoken, and law forms part of this speech, the central challenge is identifying its relationship with what already exists legally—both from God and from human beings—and with future lawmaking. Claims of a divine law always connote a sense of being absolute and universally valid. This triumphal intuition is often deeply ingrained in the popular religion, whose followers perceive a sense of inevitability to the ascendancy of their divine law. But typically, in both theory and practice, there is a careful modulation of divine legal claims as they confront existing systems of human lawmaking.

In the Bahá'í Faith, there exists a somewhat unique relationship between divine law and human lawmaking. Eschewing any overly ambitious drive to order human societies according to divine precepts, the Bahá'í approach has emphasized themes of delay and social context. As will be argued, such an approach distingtuishes the Bahá'í Faith from certain predominant tendencies in Muslim legal history, even while scholars remain preoccupied with viewing Bahá'í law through the experience of Muslim history and societies.

It could be said that claims of divine law tend to remain primarily theological until certain contextual factors prompt development. Discussions of divine law are often initially focused on themes of absoluteness and universality, but when and if pushed to become practical, divine law claims tend to modulate their absolute character and struggle with the contextualized values inherent in human lawmaking.

In early Christianity, for example, the relationship between what Christians considered to be the new revelation, divine law, and human lawmaking played itself out at multiple levels, largely as a result of the fact that the new revelation was born into two legalistic cultures—Jewish and Roman. One pressing issue was the relationship between the law of the Old Testament as observed by Jews and the teachings of Christ, especially for gentile Christians as opposed to those converted from Judaism. At the same time, there was a struggle to classify the relationship between Christian law and Roman law, and the status of Roman law within the Christian belief system.[31]

Issues of the relationship between a claim to divine law and existing patterns of human law also tend to become especially charged and go through a period of development when the temporal power adopts a particular religion. An excellent example of this is in the Buyid dynasty (c. 945–1060) when Shi'i overlords, for the first time, oversaw the power of the Sunni Caliph. This occurrence resulted in a growth of scholarly exploration of how to reconcile the traditional view of the Imámate as the legal authority within Shi'ism with the fact that Shi'is were holding a position of temporal power. The gradual outcome of this new reality was development of Shi'i law and legal thought.[32]

The early history of Bahá'í law reflects this pattern of engagement with issues of the relationship between divine law and human lawmaking. Bahá'í law remains largely discussed and debated in theological terms, and conceived of as an absolute and universally valid law that will eventually reign supreme.[33] This is demonstrated in the largely apologetic character of almost all secondary literature on the topic. However, the early legal history of the Bahá'í Faith shows a unique pattern to the relationship between divine law and human lawmaking.

The legal content of Bahá'u'lláh's revelation appeared almost precisely at the mid-point during the forty years in which He claimed to be the direct recipient of divine guidance. From 1853 until the early

1870s, Bahá'u'lláh provided very little explicit commentary or guidance on legal matters. It is only in 1873 with the appearance of the Kitáb-i-Aqdas that legal themes became significant in His writings.

While explicit laws were absent from Bahá'u'lláh's writings for the first twenty years, there are significant legal implications of the claims Bahá'u'lláh makes in this period. First, the character of Bahá'u'lláh's divine sovereignty as a lawgiver is implied by His claims in relation to Siyyid 'Alí-Muhammad (1819–1850)—known as the Báb. The messianic movement the Báb led in nineteenth century Persia, in which Bahá'u'lláh was a participant and leader, was intertwined with the expectation of the appearance of *Man yuzhiruhu'lláh* (or "He whom God shall make manifest"), a prophetic figure who would bring a message from God after the Báb. The Báb clarified that while He claimed to end the period of Qur'ánic legal authority, His own divine authority would be superceded by *Man yuzhiruhu'lláh*.

Implicit within this was a theme—the contextual and periodic nature of divine law—that Bahá'u'lláh developed extensively in His own writings. Divine legal sovereignty is absolute, but it is expressed to human beings in a relative form. Successive revelations, which are seen in Bahá'í theology as emanations from the same divine source, are expressed relative to the specific collective context of humanity at the time of revelation. Thus, Judaism, Christianity, and Islam, for example, are all expressions of the will of the same God, and each revelation is expressed relative to the context and conditions of the time in which it was revealed. There is an aspect of evolution in this succession that sees later revelations as expanding upon and supplementing older ones with a new relevance and vitality. Thus, just as the Báb expected *Man yuzhiruhu'lláh* to supercede His law, Bahá'u'lláh saw a similar evolution in divine legal sovereignty throughout humanity's religious history.[34]

Second, in addition to these notions of supremacy and evolution in divine law, in the first twenty years of Bahá'u'lláh's revelation, while no real law appears, Bahá'u'lláh does provide explicit commentary and reflection on why there is no law. With the first glimmerings of a distinct

Bahá'í community beginning in 1863 with Bahá'u'lláh's public decla-ration that He was *Man yuẓhiruhu'lláh* bearing a message from God, Bahá'u'lláh began to receive petitions from followers for the laws of the new religion. These requests were not surprising, given the overwhelm-ing emphasis on law in Islam as well as the Báb's focus on political and legal change. While Bahá'u'lláh was in Edirne,[35] a first set of petitions was sent requesting the enunciation of laws. Reportedly, Bahá'u'lláh revealed a letter in Persian laying out a set of laws, but ultimately held it back.[36] In describing this episode, as well as other requests for peti-tions prior to the revelation of the Kitáb-i-Aqdas, Bahá'u'lláh writes, "for a number of years . . . petitions reached the Most Holy Presence [Bahá'u'lláh] from various lands begging for the laws of God, but We held the Pen ere the appointed time had come."[37] In 1873 another set of petitions were sent to Bahá'u'lláh in 'Akká. In the Kitáb-i-Aqdas, Bahá'u'lláh comments:

> Various petitions have come before Our throne from the believers, concerning laws from God, the Lord of the seen and the Unseen, the Lord of all worlds. We have, in consequence, revealed this Holy Tablet and arrayed it with the mantle of His Law that haply the people may keep the commandments of their Lord. Similar requests had been made of Us over several previous years but We had, in Our wisdom, withheld Our Pen until, in recent days, let-ters arrived from a number of the friends, and We have therefore responded, through the power of truth, with that which shall quicken the hearts of men.[38]

The making of laws is often delayed for a variety of reasons such as inefficiency or lack of political will. In relation to a divine law and its universal claims, however, delay is particularly interesting. Above all else, it mediates claims of the absolute and universal character of Bahá'í law by stressing its social and contextual dimension. According to the

Bahá'í concept of manifestationhood, the bearers of divine revelation are not solely channels or mouthpieces of God, nor are they simply incarnations of the divine. Rather, these prophetic figures are emanations of the divine who embody and perfectly mirror the attributes of God. In Bahá'í theology, Manifestations are thought to exist on a plane of existence distinct from human beings and the divine.[39] One implication of this is that the Manifestations are conceived of as having control over the social expression of revelation, of choosing when they will speak, on what matters, and how they will reveal God's will. Thus, the element of response to the collective state of humanity that was seen in the Bahá'í notion of revelation as a progressive and relative reality is mirrored in the internal specifics of each revelation. Bahá'u'lláh revealed His revelation in a manner that was responsive to the specific conditions, requests, and needs He found in the world.

This emphasis on the social dimension of the making of divine law surrounds the Kitáb-i-Aqdas. As was recounted above, the immediate context of the revelation of the Kitáb-i-Aqdas included petitions and requests for the law from the community. Further, after writing the Kitáb-i-Aqdas, Bahá'u'lláh delayed its distribution for a period of time. It is worth noting Bahá'u'lláh's response to one follower, who was especially anxious for the dissemination and implementation of the laws:

Indeed, the laws of God are like unto the ocean and the children of men as fish, did they but know it. However, in observing them one must exercise tact and wisdom. . . . Since most people are feeble and far-removed from the purpose of God, therefore one must observe tact and prudence under all conditions, so that nothing might happen that could cause disturbance and dissension or raise clamor among the heedless. Verily, His bounty hath surpassed the whole universe and His bestowals encompassed all that dwell on earth. One must guide mankind to the ocean of true understanding in a spirit of love and tolerance. The Kitáb-i-Aqdas itself beareth eloquent testimony to the loving providence of God.[40]

In this response, Bahá'u'lláh draws a line between an act of legislation (i.e. the Kitáb-i-Aqdas) and the implementation of that legislation, and He prefers to delay the latter based on general policy considerations of the need for "tact and prudence," the abhorrence of "disturbance and dissension," and the spirit of "love and tolerance." The formalist nature of divine law is thus modulated by the insistence that divine law is operational only in certain requisite conditions, where it is likely to have certain societal effects (at a minimum not causing "disturbance and dissension"). God's sovereignty alone does not legitimize the application of divine law. The application of divine law requires God's law plus something else—a particular context, intention, and environment.

This pattern of the early legal history of the Bahá'í Faith also illustrates crucial differences between Islamic and Bahá'í notions of divine law. These differences have not been well explored in the secondary literature. As Bernard Weiss has commented, there is often a tendency—encapsulated in the image and allusion to prophets, such as Muhammad, and rulers as well—within monotheistic traditions for God to completely dominate the polity,[41] Given these ambitions, it is not surprising that textual exegesis may become a core science and the primary legal methodology may become, as Weiss calls it, textualist and intentionalist.[42] Textualism refers to absolute reliance on a closed set of canonical texts. Within the texts, it is assumed that a specific divine intent exists. Thus, valid law is identified by an act of extrapolation or exegesis from the text. Within this matrix, there is little room for looking at the Qur'án and *hadíth,* or the Torah and the Oral Law, in time and in social context, or viewing it in dynamic terms. As Weiss writes, "[t]he widely accepted contemporary notion that a text has a life of its own apart from its author, that its meaning may continually evolve and change" was foreign to classical Islamic jurists.[43]

The Islamic *sharí'áh* is adjunct to a belief system in which God dominates public and private life in all of its aspects. The five categories of *sharí'áh* extend to cover all potential human behaviors, including everything that lies in between what is legally forbidden (*harám*) and what is obligatory (*wájib*). Actions that are recommended (*mandub*), neutral (*mubáh*), and disapproved (*makrúh*) are all encompassed by the *sharí'áh*.

One of the effects of this concept of divine law is that it makes it very difficult (but not impossible) to ground arguments for so-called progressive legal change within the classical theory of divine law. Within Muslim societies, arguments in favor of changing the status of women or minorities, or altering the treatment of criminals—to cite just a few examples—typically suffer from an appearance of lowered legitimacy. This is because this classical concept of divine law and methodology is innately biased against modes of thought that may appear new. The argument that a legitimate new approach, or way down the path, has been identified inevitably sounds suspect when one's method is to speak of clearly delineated divine intentions.[44]

Secondary literature on Bahá'í law does not reflect much engagement with these issues in the Bahá'í context. Bahá'í notions of progressive revelation appear to be in conflict with many aspects of the textualist and intentionalist methodology of Islamic law. However, despite this, many scholars appear to have adopted aspects of Orientalist interpretations of the Qur'án and Islamic law, and these scholars inserted them into analysis of Bahá'í law—and with them concerns that Bahá'í law might import some of the perceived rigidities of classical Islamic law. Some examples of this Islamicization of Bahá'í law and its effects include the following.

First, there is a tendency to stress the Qur'ánic character of the Kitáb-i-Aqdas. John Walbridge describes the Kitáb-i-Aqdas in the following terms:

In style and content the *Aqdas* is to be compared to the Qur'an, a work in which legislation is often alluded to rather than expounded and in which disparate topics are placed together without obvious logic. In the case of the Qur'an, this might be because it is pieced together from many distinct relations, some very short. The *Aqdas* follows the stylistic conventions of the Qur'an, and thus is not bound to a rigid outline, but it may also have been shaped by similar factors . . . . It seems possible that the text grew gradually from a nucleus of the initial section . . . . According to this theory, Bahá'u'lláh would gradually have added material, probably often in answer to specific questions asked by believers.[45]

Robert Stockman similarly writes: "The style of the *Aqdas* has also been described as Qur'ánic; it, too, contains numerous seemingly unconnected bits of information. An interesting and unanswerable question is whether the style of the *Aqdas* resembles the Qur'án because such a style underscores the claim that the *Aqdas* is the new book of laws or whether the styles of the books resemble each other because each represents concatenated flashes of revelation."[46]

These descriptions are oddly similar to descriptions of the Qur'án by influential scholars of Islamic law. For example, Neil Coulson describes the Qur'án as having "many problems" in its character "as a legislative document" containing "ad hoc solutions for particular problems rather than attempts to deal with any general topic comprehensively."[47] He goes on to explain that:

This piecemeal nature of the legislation follows naturally perhaps from the circumstances in which the Qur'án was revealed; for the official compilation of the Qur'án, which did not appear until some years after the death of the Prophet, represents an arbitrary arrangement of short passages which had been uttered by the Prophet at various times and in various places throughout his life-time—or at least, as far as the legal verses are concerned, during the ten years of his residence at Medina.[48]

Conclusions that have been applied to Bahá'í law mirror those of Coulson even as he makes clear one of the fundamental differences—namely, the post-Prophet compilation of the Qur'án—between the Qur'ánic and the Bahá'í revelation,.

Second, use of the Qur'ánic template has led discussion of Bahá'í law to be framed by typical Orientalist debates. For example, similar to Orientalists who had trouble identifying the legal character of the Qur'án, attempts have been made to minimize the legal nature of the Kitáb-i-Aqdas. Anthony Lee supports a reading of the text as the divine intent to reveal a set of ethical precepts and moral guideposts, but not necessarily law. As Lee states, "It is my contention that Bahá'u'lláh intended by the revelation of the Kitáb-i-Aqdas to offer the 'Choice wine' of upright and ethical conduct embodied in general principles and examples of beneficial law. That Bahá'u'lláh himself regarded these laws as flexible can be demonstrated."[49]

This conclusion, however, appears untenable given the explicit language of legal command and observance one finds in the Kitáb-i-Aqdas.[50] But the rationale for such arguments echoes assumptions abo ut the Islamic nature of Bahá'í law. A fear that Bahá'u'lláh intended a highly textualist method of interpretation, and that rigid schools of interpretation will emerge through this textualism, motivates attempts to minimize the legal nature and content of the Kitáb-i-Aqdas.

These few examples of Islamicization illustrate that the distinctive theology of the Bahá'í Faith—with its emphasis on the relative character of revelation itself—has not been adequately analyzed in the context of Bahá'í law. Analyzing ideals and practices of human lawmaking in Bahá'u'lláh's vision will require exploring this contextually-bound notion of divine will from more perspectives than those that narrowly focus on the Qur'ánic and Islamic analogs for Bahá'í law.

Unity and Positive Law

The role of social context within the Bahá'í concept of divine law becomes even more pronounced when one looks at the issue of succession. Unlike Islam, where the death of the Prophet resulted in two discrete positions concerning proper legal authority—the Sunni position that stressed the role of scholars and *ijtihád,* and the Shí'i position that stressed the need for an Imám, a continuing authoritative legal voice—Bahá'u'lláh explicitly mandated where legal authority was to rest after His passing. He contemplated in the Kitáb-i-Aqdas a system of "Houses of Justice"[51] operating as the legal authorities within society. These houses of justice were to exist at both the international and local levels and were to be elected institutions. 'Abdu'l-Bahá, in His Will and Testament, would later create the institution of secondary (national) houses of justice.[52] Within the institutions, positions of individual authority were to be subsumed to the authority of the institution as a whole, with the houses of justice being able to act only on decisions agreed to by a majority of its members.

This system has now been extensively established. There are over eleven thousand Bahá'í Local Spiritual Assemblies and one hundred eighty Bahá'í National Spiritual Assemblies, all elected annually with nine members. The Universal House of Justice, which is the international governing body of the Bahá'í Faith, was established in 1963 and is elected every five years.

The turn to democratic institutions alone implies a different approach to the basis of legitimacy and role of these institutions, as opposed to the roles of the 'ulamá and caliphate in certain Islamic traditions or the clergy in certain Christian ones. This approach becomes especially clear in the rationale Bahá'u'lláh offers for this system. "Inasmuch as for each day there is a new problem and for every problem an expedient solution," He writes, "such affairs should be referred to the House of Justice that the members thereof may act according to the needs and requirements of the time."[53] 'Abdu'l-Bahá clarifies, "Those matters of major importance which constitute the foundation of the Law of God are explicitly recorded in the Text, but subsidiary laws are left to the House of Justice. The wisdom of this is that the times never remain the same, for change is a necessary quality and an essential attribute of this world and of time and place. Therefore the House of Justice will take action accordingly."[54]

This vision of a dynamic/organic legal institution is complicated by the clear limitation of the powers of the House of Justice in relation to the texts of the revelation of Bahá'u'lláh. The Universal House of Justice has no authority to interpret the texts, and its interpretations can never be accepted as authoritative. This matter is typically discussed through a distinction between interpretation and elucidation. Interpretive authority rested solely with 'Abdu'l-Bahá and His eldest grandson Shoghi Effendi. With the death of Shoghi Effendi, the possibility of authoritative interpretation ended. As the Universal House of Justice explains, "the Guardian [Shoghi Effendi] reveals what the scripture means; his interpretation is a statement of truth which cannot be varied."[55] There is an "absolute prohibition against anyone propounding 'authoritative' or 'inspired' interpretations," which includes the House of Justice.[56] However, within the sphere of its legislative powers on matters not "'expressly revealed in the Bahá'í writings,'"[57] the Universal House of Justice is understood to have the authority to turn toward scripture. This process of using scripture within the context of legislating involves making deductions based on the revealed texts and the authorized interpretations of 'Abdu'l-Bahá and Shoghi Effendi.

This scheme raises questions. What is the relationship between the religious texts and the legislative acts of the Universal House of Justice? Is the law of the Universal House of Justice divine? If the Universal House of Justice is not engaged in interpretation, what is the status and import of its decisions?

There are two points that help resolve these issues.

First, Bahá'u'lláh's writings are not positioned as an explicit source of law to which the Universal House of Justice looks when they are addressing a novel legal question. Unlike the Qur'án, Bahá'u'lláh's writings are not conceived of as all-encompassing legal texts. They do not contain all of the law that is needed for society, either literally or implicitly. The act of lawmaking by the Universal House of Justice thus engages with scripture for only two reasons, both indirect and mediated. The Universal House of Justice will look to the holy text to see if there is an explicit legal injunction on the matter. Its determination of whether this is so is not based on members' own reading, however. It is based upon the interpretations of Bahá'u'lláh's writings provided by 'Abdu'l-Bahá and Shoghi Effendi. Assuming there are no direct injunctions on the issue, the Universal House of Justice will look to the holy text for general principles that should guide its lawmaking on a particular question. Again, this search for guiding principles is mediated by the interpretations of 'Abdu'l-Bahá and Shoghi Effendi.

Within this inquiry, the principles that come to the fore, and are typically reinforced by the Universal House of Justice when it comments on legal matters, are those of dynamism and unity. Following from the conviction that all things are in a constant state of change, Bahá'u'lláh repeatedly applies developmental metaphors to the collective life of humanity. The lens for analyzing the current conditions of political and social life is through the category of social maturation. In a typical restatement of this idea by the Universal House of Justice, "[t]he human race, as a distinct, organic unit, has passed through evolutionary stages analogous to the stages of infancy and childhood in the lives of its individual members, and is now in the culminating period of its turbulent adolescence approaching its long-awaited coming of age."[58]

This vision of social maturation rests upon the idea of unity, which is one of the axes of Bahá'í ontology. "[R]eality" one Bahá'í scholar has argued, "is an integrated whole but . . . this wholeness is a unity in diversity, not a uniformity."[59] Within this integrated whole, there exist four distinct levels of being—God, the Manifestations of God, the human soul, and material reality. Everything in creation—including individual human beings and humanity collectively—is seen as constructed according to patterns of unity in diversity. As 'Abdu'l-Bahá describes:

As difference in degree of capacity exists among human souls, as difference in capability is found, therefore, individualities will differ one from another. But in reality this is a reason for unity and not for discord and enmity. If the flowers of a garden were all of one color, the effect would be monotonous to the eye; but if the colors are variegated, it is most pleasing and wonderful. The difference in adornment of color and capacity of reflection among the flowers gives the garden its beauty and charm. Therefore, although we are of different individualities, . . . let us strive like flowers of the same divine garden to live together in harmony. Even though each soul has its own individual perfume and color, all are reflecting the same light, all contributing fragrance to the same breeze which blows through the garden, all continuing to grow in complete harmony and accord.[60]

Unity and diversity are thus the organizing principle of human life and existence.

This ontology suggests that society needs to evolve to reflect more fully the reality of unity in diversity so as to maximize its potential for social order and organization. The social life of humanity has become more complex and integrated, and thus humanity must develop its ability to organize in patterns of unity in diversity. Society, however, is not static, and it is a human construct. It is the product of human imagination, devotion, and will. While this means that human society can and should change, it does not mean that the form society should take is completely open and anarchic. Social forms, including legal and political institutions, will endure and are most suited to meet the needs of human beings when they are constructed and operate according to the principle of unity in diversity. In fact, the Bahá'í writings argue that a general pattern in the history of the organization of human society illustrates an awareness of the need to construct enlarging patterns of unity: "Unification of the whole of mankind is the hallmark of the stage which human society is now approaching. Unity of family, of tribe, of city-state, and nation have been successively attempted and fully established. World unity is the goal towards which a harassed humanity is striving."[61]

One might surmise, then, that when the Universal House of Justice sets out to legislate, therefore, it turns to the writings of Bahá'u'lláh to reaffirm the ideas of evolution and unity that must guide its decisions. It does not turn to the texts merely to derive a law or glean the divine intention.

One might also surmise that, beyond these uses of the holy text, the Universal House of Justice turns to the sort of information that is typically used in legislative decision-making in liberal democratic societies—the indices of utility and efficiency, studies of impact and effect, and the concerns and opinions of those who might be affected by a particular decision. All of this secondary information, of course, is framed by the higher order principles of evolution and unity.

Second, in addition to the manner in which texts are used and the controlling vision of unity, the legislative act as conceived by Bahá'u'lláh revolves around the political role of changing social meanings and norms. In Sunni Islam, it should be remembered, the discovery of law using the textualist and intentionalist methodology of *ijtihád* is intended to be apolitical in the first instance. Turning to the texts in an attitude of sincerity and striving to glean divine will is perceived of as a nearly sanctified act, and the laws discovered are perceived as pristine expressions of divine intent. To the degree that such lawmaking is political, it is through what the practitioner of *ijtihád* brings to the process, such as his or her human motivations, leanings, and purposes. Bahá'u'lláh's vision for the Universal House of Justice, however, is political in the first instance. By engaging in a legislative act, the Universal House is engaged in politics—specifically, it is aiming to change or engender certain social meanings and norms within the recipient audience. Legislation is to occur only when it will reinforce certain social meanings while rejecting others. Often these political considerations will pre-empt the act of legislating altogether. The existing architecture of social meanings surrounding a particular issue might delay legislation on an issue—even indefinitely—because passing a law on the matter would result in reinforcing undesired behaviors and meanings.[62]

In this preliminary examination, therefore, the early legal history of the Bahá'í Faith illustrates a preoccupation with the relationship between the universal and the relative, and the eternal and the temporal. Divine law is an expression of the eternal and universally valid will of God, but it is also expressed in a contextual, temporal, and relative manner. Issues and meanings of unity are paramount considerations in determining the appropriateness and timeliness of law resting upon divine claims.

Fragmentation, Integration, and World Order

The discussion so far has focused on themes of universalism, relativism, unity, and diversity within the narrow confines of the internal history and operation of Bahá'í law. The next step is to analyze how the Bahá'í writings project these themes onto the analysis of worldwide political, legal, and social affairs generally. Within such an analysis we see an overlap with the units of analysis and categories of Huntington's clash of civilizations thesis and other current approaches in international relations, but they are applied in a different and unique way.

The Bahá'í writings identify two processes underlying the political state of affairs of the world: disintegration and integration. Together these processes explain and reflect the dynamics of collective maturation that Bahá'u'lláh argues is at the epicenter of social and political development.

Disintegration

The Bahá'í vision of internationalism should not be understood as an ideal and utopian vision rooted in the harmonious coming together of the peoples of the world. Underlying Bahá'u'lláh's argument that the world needs to and is moving toward a global order is an understanding that such an order can only emerge through a preliminary process of fragmentation, decay, and division.

The rationale for this is, at least in its first instance, quite simple and revolves around the relationship between unity and diversity in Bahá'í thought. Unity, if it is to exist, must be a conscious choice. This is true in individual relationships, and it is true at the level of international relations. A state in which apparent unity exists on the surface but is supported by elements of coercion or force or is the result of ignorance or willful blindness cannot be deemed a state of unity. In situations where such a facade of unity exists, a change in the conditions that exist—a restructuring of power arrangements or the birth of new knowledge—will quickly lead to collapse.

In addition to the fact that unity is a conscious state, it is also one grounded in a mindset of liberty and equality. Unity presupposes a political culture that primarily affirms individual liberties, social justice, and equality. This culture also includes economic justice, which Bahá'u'lláh discusses both in terms of world politics and in reference to disparities within particular nations and societies.[63] In the absence of such conditions, the conscious choices made to enter into arrangements of unity may be tainted by the dictates of power. Only where liberty and equality coexist can unity, in Bahá'u'lláh's definition, appear.

For such an understanding of unity to become a social and political reality, even in the most rudimentary form, an initial shift must occur at the level of ideas, mental constructs, and associations. While generally this refers to changing the matrix of social meanings, specifically it refers to a shift in the worldview of individual human beings and social institutions. Building unity is, as such, in the first instance, an educative process about shifting the hegemonic idea within social ordering toward unity and away from other, less universal and more specific ideas. Both Bahá'u'lláh and 'Abdu'l-Bahá, for example, speak frequently of destructive social arrangements and the process of changing them in terms of a battle over ideas, meanings, and human processes of learning. For example, 'Abdu'l-Bahá speaks of social prejudices in the following terms: "And the breeding-ground of all these tragedies is prejudice: prejudice of race and action, of religion, of political opinion; and the root cause of prejudice is blind imitation of the past—imitation in religion, in racial attitudes, in national bias, in politics. So long as this aping of the past persisteth, just so long will the foundations of the social order be blown to the four winds, just so long will humanity be continually exposed to direst peril."[64]

This understanding of unity is the foundation for Bahá'u'lláh's explanation of the political and social fragmentation He observed in His lifetime and the basis for His expectation that the world's global affairs would, in essence, become anarchic and destructive in the future. Existing practices, institutions, and theories that are rooted in a mindset and reflect ideas antithetical to a unity-based worldview must decay and deconstruct. This process cannot help but be socially disruptive and threatening to political stability. Moreover, the Bahá'í writings state that the root causes of these disruptions lie in the realm of ideas. As the transformation of human consciousness requires education, these causes have an important cultural dimension. A clash of civilizations rooted in cultural biases and prejudices and reflecting an inability to comprehend diversity except through the construction of "others" is a microcosm of one aspect of the vision of the future Bahá'u'lláh offered.

Shoghi Effendi systematically developed this theme of fragmentation. He described a process that "'tends to tear down, with increasing violence, the antiquated barriers that seek to block humanity's progress towards its destined goal [i.e. unification].'"[65] The specific forms of disintegration and fragmentation which Shoghi Effendi identifies are both attitudinal and structural. He attacks the rise of political ideology generally—with a particular disgust for communism and fascism—but specifically focuses his call to change on ideologies of superiority—in particular, racism and sexism.[66]

It might also be argued that a substantial component of this process of disintegration is the deconstruction of hegemonic theories, histories, and social structures, and indeed of the notion of hegemony itself. Movements that take the form of an intensification of tribalization reflect a growing refusal to accept ideas, practices, or institutions that are perceived to be borrowed, imposed, or foreign. The rise of identity politics within the United States; academic theories such as postmodernism and methods such as revisionism; the intensity of antiglobal-ization protest movements; and the movement away from multiethnic and multireligious states in many parts of the world all reflect a loss of faith in what is established and a movement towards narrower, more local, more traditional, and more intimate sets of relationships and explanations of the world. Claimed universalities—ranging from the inevitability of secularization to the conceits of modernization and Westernization—are all dissembled and dismissed as being partial, local, and particular.

This process of fragmentation as developed in the Bahá'í writings overlaps considerably with the clash of civilizations thesis. The clash of civilizations thesis argues that in the post-Cold War world, the "most important distinctions among peoples are not ideological, political, or economic. They are cultural."[67] Civilizations[68] are considered the larg-est cultural entities. Each civilization is an integrated, comprehensive, enduring, and evolving cultural monolith resting on the sands of time,[69] defined primarily through shared languages, intersubjective understand-ings, and religions. For the first time in history, the world has become "multipolar" and "multicivilizational," rendering traditional theories of world politics, such as realism, insufficient.[70] The cultural dimension of politics that resides within civilizations needs to be understood in order to deal with the complexities of the contemporary world.

Samuel Huntington, for example, argues that the relationship between Western civilization and non-Western civilizations is the defin-ing one of the future,[71] and specifically that the relationships between the West and Islamic and Sinic civilizations are the fault lines that could lead to sustained conflict. In the contemporary world, Islamic civili-zation is seen as a particular source of discontent and destabilization. Huntington writes, "while at the macro or global level of world politics the primary clash of civilizations is between the West and the rest, at the micro or local level it is between Islam and the others." Thus, the terrorist attacks of September 11, 2001 may be seen as part of an "inter-civilizational quasi war" that has been fought between Islam and the

West since the Iranian revolution of 1979.[72] "The underlying problem for the West is not Islamic fundamentalism," Huntington writes, "[i]t is Islam, a different civilization whose people are convinced of the superiority of their culture and are obsessed with the inferiority of their power."[73]

The mindset of the world offered by the clash of civilizations thesis is tribalism, and in this vision, the prospect of a universal civilization is bleak and even undesirable. Assumptions that Western civilization is becoming a universal civilization are seen as false, immoral, and dangerous.[74] Given the strength and endurance of competing civilizations, the universalization of Western civilization could be the product of a tremendous imposition and exertion of Western power in which "universalism legitimates imperialism."[75] Beyond assumptions of Western universality, however, references to a "universal civilization" are seen as substantively empty, false, and immoral.[76] Huntington argues that in the current world of civilizations, clashes and war are the most likely outcome. There is a "thin" veneer of commonalities that exist within all cultures, and in the "multicivilizational world, the constructive course is to renounce universalism, accept diversity, and seek commonalities."[77] Stressing commonalities may limit the clash of civilizations and contribute to intercivilizational understanding.

Like Shoghi Effendi, Huntington acknowledges simultaneous processes of fragmentation within nations that parallel global cultural divisions. Countries that are multicultural run the risk of becoming cleft countries in which different populations see themselves associated with different civilizations. In relation to the United States, Huntington highlights the internal danger of the erosion of what he calls the American creed, which is summed up with the principles of "liberty, democracy, individualism, equality before the law, constitutionalism, [and] private property."[78] Huntington writes that this creed has come under attack by a small number of "intellectuals and publicists" who have "attacked the identification of the United States with Western civilization, denied the existence of a common American culture, and promoted racial, ethnic, and other subnational identities and group-ing."[79] He condemns contemporary politicians and thinkers who pro-mote diversity without promoting American unity and writes that "[a] multicivilizational United States will not be the United States; it will be the United Nations."[80]

Or will it? In Huntington's vision that highlights a process of frag-mentation and disintegration, his conclusions about the centrality of civilizations to global conflict and politics appear compelling. In Bahá'í terms, however, identifying the process of disintegration is only one process among two.

Integration

The Bahá'í writings never speak of the process of fragmentation absent an analysis of a related process of integration. Bahá'u'lláh spoke of the maturation of humanity as a synthesizing process of collective life. It is also a process of the mind. It appears as a shift in the world-view of individuals and institutions, the recalibration of the meanings they associate with phenomena around them, and the basic norms that inform and underlie patterns of behavior. Shoghi Effendi gives a precise description of this process in the following terms:

As we view the world around us, we are compelled to observe the manifold evidences of that universal fermentation which, in every continent of the globe and in every department of human life, be it religious, social, economic or political, is purging and reshap-ing humanity in anticipation of the Day when the wholeness of the human race will have been recognized and its unity estab-lished. . . . [The process of integration] unfolds a System which may well serve as a pattern for that world polity towards which a strangely-disordered world is continually advancing.[81]

The institutions of world order in this vision of integration are seen as evolving gradually through various stages. At the first stage is the construction of the institutions necessary for the implementation of a vision of collective security. Bahá'u'lláh wrote in the Lawḥ-i-Maqṣúd of the establishment of a permanent accord that would have the effect of establishing a transparent and active system of global security:

> The time must come when the imperative necessity for the holding of a vast, an all-embracing assemblage of men will be universally realized. The rulers and kings of the earth must needs attend it, and, participating in its deliberations, must consider such ways and means as will lay the foundations of the world's Great Peace amongst men. Such a peace demandeth that the Great Powers should resolve, for the sake of the tranquility of the peoples of the earth, to be fully reconciled among themselves. Should any king take up arms against another, all should unitedly arise and prevent him. If this be done, the nations of the world will no longer require any armaments, except for the purpose of preserving the security of their realms and of maintaining internal order within their territories. . . . This will ensure the peace and composure of every people, government and nation. We fain would hope that the kings and rulers of the earth, the mirrors of the gracious and almighty name of God, may attain unto this station, and shield mankind from the onslaught of tyranny.[82]

This vision appears to imply areas of agreement that remain sources of debate in the contemporary system of world order, including questions of disarmament; international institutions having autonomous military capacity; and mechanisms for the resolution of border disputes. At the same time, however, many of the institutional forms necessary to implement this first stage of the Bahá'í vision of world order appear to be emerging or already exist.

The second stage, and one that Bahá'u'lláh appears to view as reaching fruition in the distant future, is the emergence of a federal system of global governance. The emergence of this federated system relies upon substantive integration occurring in many spheres of human life, including the formation of individual identity and changes in social meanings and norms related to unity. This process will be slow and gradual, and according to Shoghi Effendi, it is likely to involve severe crises and bloodshed. Using the American Civil War as an analogy, Shoghi Effendi observes the following about the emergence of a federated system:

To take but one instance. How confident were the assertions made in the days preceding the unification of the states of the North American continent regarding the insuperable barriers that stood in the way of their ultimate federation! Was it not widely and emphatically declared that the conflicting interests, the mutual distrust, the differences of government and habit that divided the states were such as no force, whether spiritual or temporal, could ever hope to harmonize or control? And yet how different were the conditions prevailing a hundred and fifty years ago from those that characterize present-day society! It would indeed be no exaggeration to say that the absence of those facilities which modern scientific progress has placed at the service of humanity in our time made of the problem of welding the American states into a single federation, similar though they were in certain traditions, a task infinitely more complex than that which confronts a divided humanity in its efforts to achieve the unification of all mankind.

Who knows that for so exalted a conception to take shape a suffering more intense than any it has yet experienced will have to be inflicted upon humanity? Could anything less than the fire of a civil war with all its violence and vicissitudes—a war that nearly rent the great American Republic—have welded the states, not only into a Union of independent units, but into a Nation, in spite of all the ethnic differences that characterized its component parts? That so fundamental a revolution, involving such far-reaching changes in the structure of society, can be achieved through the ordinary processes of diplomacy and education seems highly improbable. We have but to turn our gaze to humanity's blood-stained history to realize that nothing short of intense mental as well as physical agony has been able to precipitate those epoch-making changes that constitute the greatest landmarks in the history of human civilization.[83]

Various institutions of such a federal system are explicitly mentioned in the Bahá'í writings, but not always in a coherent and consistent manner. For example, within Shoghi Effendi's own writings, one sees reference to a system involving a "world parliament," "international executive," and "supreme tribunal," as well as a system that includes a "world legislature," "world executive," "world tribunal," and "international Force."[84] One also finds reference to a "Universal Court of Arbitration."[85] The general implication appears to be the formation of a world commonwealth in which there is a superstate structure, which has substantive lawmaking, judicial, and administrative functions.

Some of the aspects of the relationship between this process of integration and the Bahá'í world order model are more clearly seen when looked at in light of theories of world politics that compete with the clash of civilizations thesis. In a challenge to neo-realism, Robert Cox[86] has analyzed the world using a critical historicist epistemology. Focusing in on the question of how world order has been transformed, Cox identifies three main forces that alter historical structures—ideas, institutions, and material capabilities. Cox sees the history of world order as the history of movement from one hegemonic pattern to another as new patterns emerge. A particular matrix of ideas, institutions, and material capabilities may lend hegemony to a particular unit—a state, set of states, or even a civilization for a period of time or at a particular juncture.

Coxian theory sees the world as dynamic and changing, and speaks of world order in historical terms. It also highlights the importance of ideas and culture in the evolution of world order, as the transformation from one hegemon to another is viewed as having its genesis at the level of a normative shift, which then encourages the development of particular institutions and attracts material capabilities. This theory raises many questions. Is there any pattern to this transformation? Is it just random? Is it cyclical? The answers to these questions are not always clear. Cox's theory speaks in terms of social forces and means of production, but the strategy/tactics of transformation is not fully worked out in his work,[87] so that overall logic of transformation remains somewhat vague. Some theorists, Cox included, have spoken of a "posthegemonic" world order, which at least implies that the dynamic evolution of world order may plausibly result in a world constructed around points of unity and commonality. As Cox writes, "The prospect of a posthegemonic order implies doubt as to the likelihood that a new hegemony can be constructed to replace a declining hegemony. It suggests doubt as to the existence of an Archimedean point around which a new order could be constructed. Previous hegemonic orders have derived their universals from the dominant society, itself the product of a dominant civilization. A posthegemonic order would have to derive its normative content in a search for common ground among constituent traditions of civilization."[88]

The idea of a posthegemonic world order resonates strongly with Bahá'í thought and the process of integration. As well, Cox's historical method resonates with Bahá'í notions of collective maturation. A Bahá'í reading of history through Coxian theory would suggest that the generative importance of ideas in the appearance of new historical structures places revelation at the epicenter of the emergence of new hegemons. This focus on revelation would not necessarily be inconsistent with the theories of either Cox or Huntington. Consistent with the Bahá'í notion of revelation, however, religion would not be tied to a hegemonic power only when a state or set of states dominating world order were closely aligned with a religious worldview—with the Islamic empire perhaps being a clear example of this.

Rather, each revelation would set the epistemic framework for hegemonic transformation for a long period of time (longue durée), within which there would occur a wide variety of shifts within world order. The progressive and relative nature of revelation from God thus acts at a macro level. Revelation sets a general framework and guidelines within which the superficially chaotic shift from one hegemon to another occurs. There are, thus, macro and micro patterns underlying the history of world order. At the macro level, each revelation alters the set of ideas and mindset for social and political life. The micro pattern involves the specific adjustments of hegemony that occur, perhaps driven by the social forces, institutional configurations, and patterns of material relations Cox identifies. But the micro shifts are contained and contextualized by the revelatory cycle in which they exist and the specific guidance and focus of that revelation.

The resonance of the post-hegemonic idea with Bahá'í beliefs is that it fits well with what Bahá'u'lláh conceived of as the central idea of the current revelatory cycle—the consciousness and appearance of patterns of unity and diversity on a global scale. Encapsulated in the idea of integration is the implication that power arrangements within world politics will increasingly be debated and resolved on terrain where it will become less plausible to speak in terms of hegemonic powers and states and more plausible and coherent, while preserving diversity, to speak the language of unity, universal structures, and international institutions.

One may already see the vivid outlines of this process of integration in the erosion of dichotomous perceptions of international relations, the heightened complexity of world politics, and the reflexive relationship between international political structures and domestic ones. For all of their limitations, weaknesses, and failures, formal international institutions—such as the United Nations—and numerous less formal international arenas of dialogue and action exist and are a sign of a vibrant and deepening process of integration. Within this world, no nation or civilization can maintain an extremely divisive and dichotomous rhetoric and attitude without being constantly challenged, mediated, and changed by the demands and presence of international arenas.

Conclusion

Bahá'í commitments to both a vision of divine law and internationalism represent a distinct attempt at reconciliation of tense universalisms. The desire for God to be the ultimate legislator, and for God's legislation to shape a global and all-encompassing order, are not unique religious claims. However, God's legislation, in Bahá'í teachings, is dynamic, changing, and socially responsive. Divine law is not only to be responded to by humanity; it is also responsive to humanity. This is seen in the Bahá'í focus on themes such as unity, integration, and the changing of social meanings and associations that are applied to social phenomena. The legal institutions within the Bahá'í Faith, as well as the pattern of the unfolding of a system of world order, similarly emphasize the organic, dynamic, and diffuse ways of manifesting divine precepts in the kind of social order that the Bahá'í Faith advocates.

PART 5:

Bahá'í Law and Social Change

7 / Some Reflections on Bahá'í Approaches to Social Change

[FIRST PUBLISHED IN *BAHA'I PERSPECTIVES ON HUMAN RIGHTS*, 2012 (CO-AUTHOR LEX MUSTA)]

Bahá'u'lláh, the founder of the Bahá'í Faith, envisioned a future society with the hallmarks of social peace, equality, and justice. This society's foundation would be the unity of the human race. This vision, animated by a theology and ontology of oneness, will manifest the unity of God, unity of religion, and unity of humanity in the contingent world through patterns of unity in diversity. At all levels of human existence, Bahá'u'lláh, calls for deeper expression of patterns of unity:

The tabernacle of unity hath been raised; regard ye not one another as strangers. Ye are the fruits of one tree, and the leaves of one branch. We cherish the hope that the light of justice may shine upon the world and sanctify it from tyranny. If the rulers and kings of the earth, the symbols of the power of God, exalted be His glory, arise and resolve to dedicate themselves to whatever will promote the highest interests of the whole of humanity, the reign of justice will assuredly be established amongst the children of men, and the effulgence of its light will envelop the whole earth. . . .

Were man to appreciate the greatness of his station and the loft-
iness of his destiny he would manifest naught save goodly character, pure deeds, and a seemly and praiseworthy conduct. If the
learned and wise men of goodwill were to impart guidance unto
the people, the whole earth would be regarded as one country.
Verily this is the undoubted truth. This servant appealeth to every
diligent and enterprising soul to exert his utmost endeavour and
arise to rehabilitate the conditions in all regions and to quicken
the dead with the living waters of wisdom and utterance, by virtue of the love he cherisheth for God, the One, the Peerless, the
Almighty, the Beneficent.[1]

While Bahá'í aspirations to social change have been well represented
in secondary literature, there has been less systematic analysis of the
Bahá'í method of social change. The primary Bahá'í sources—comprising the writings of the Báb, Bahá'u'lláh, 'Abdu'l-Bahá, Shoghi
Effendi, and the Universal House of Justice—are filled with guidance
and teachings about methods and means for effecting change. Indeed,
the Universal House of Justice has recently written of Bahá'ís and
the Bahá'í community as "protagonists of social change" learning "to
apply with increasing effectiveness elements of Bahá'u'lláh's Revelation,
together with the contents and methods of science, to their social reality."[2] However, the primary Bahá'í writings and teachings related to the
means and methods of social change have not been the subject of much
scholarly analysis and consideration.[3] The main exception throughout
Bahá'í history has been a negative statement—that Bahá'ís should not
seek to advance social change through power-seeking within contemporary political processes. This element of Bahá'í doctrine, often labeled
as non-participation in politics, has been the subject of some discussion and in general terms encompasses a critique of existing models of
politics including, but certainly not limited to, the partisanship that
predominates in contemporary democratic models.[4]

A current challenge of the Bahá'í community is to move toward a positive and constructive articulation of how Bahá'ís as individuals and as a community will set out to advance social change toward unity as envisioned by Bahá'u'lláh. Not surprisingly, current answers often focus on the growing Bahá'í community and its efforts to build a pattern of global community life and a system of administration that holds as its starting premise a commitment to unity in diversity, spiritualization of daily life, consultative decision-making, and non-partisan democratic structures. Although there is value and merit in such an answer, it begs the question of whether and how Bahá'ís may be interested in the welfare of humanity as a whole, short of a conversionist paradigm of salvation. Within the Bahá'í community, one finds a very strong ethic and discourse of teaching the Bahá'í Faith to others that leads some to state that the path toward social change is primarily, or perhaps exclusively, through increasing the number of Bahá'ís. From this position, the answer to the question, "What is the Bahá'í method of social change?" would likely include "teaching the Bahá'í Faith," and perhaps "The world will change toward unity when masses of people become Bahá'ís." There is ample evidence within the Bahá'í writings, however, that processes of growth of the Bahá'í community and processes of social change, while interrelated, cannot be conflated and understood as one and the same. To cite but one example, when calling Bahá'ís to "social action," the Universal House of Justice recently stated that "we feel compelled to raise a warning: It will be important for all to recognize that the value of engaging in social action and public discourse is not to be judged by the ability to bring enrollments."[5]

In this short paper we offer some reflections on the Bahá'í method of social change, in particular, how the Bahá'í writings foresee Bahá'ís pursuing social change. These reflections suggest that Bahá'u'lláh expects of His followers dynamic and distinct forms of engagement in the life of society at large that are primarily, though not exclusively, focused on what might be called epistemic social action. At the same time, it is suggested that the

work of building up particular patterns and structures of Bahá'í community life is best conceptualized as part of a broader model of social change
in which Bahá'ís are engaged both externally in the life of society and
internally in their community-building projects. Finally, it is suggested
that a discourse within and about the Bahá'í community would benefit
from a positive shift toward an emphasis on what Bahá'ís can and should
be doing to advance social change, rather than framing discourse about
Bahá'í efforts at social change through what Bahá'ís do *not* do, such as the
limitations on participation in partisan political processes.

Elements of a Bahá'í Approach to Social Change

The following four principles, listed here in logical order and building upon each other, form the foundation for understanding a Bahá'í
method and approach to social change.

1) Social change begins and ends with unity.

Unity, or oneness, is the central concept of Bahá'í theology, ontology,
and social theory; as such, it is also positioned as the central teaching
of Bahá'u'lláh. As Bahá'u'lláh describes His own station and purpose,
"Through Him the light of unity hath shone forth above the horizon
of the world, and the law of oneness hath been revealed amidst the
nations, who, with radiant faces, have turned towards the Supreme
Horizon, and acknowledged that which the Tongue of Utterance hath
spoken in the kingdom of His knowledge."[6] In describing His own revelation, He states:

> I testify that no sooner had the First Word proceeded . . . out
> of His mouth . . . than the whole creation was revolutionized, and
> all that are in the heavens and all that are on earth were stirred to
> the depths. Through that Word the realities of all created things

were shaken, were divided, separated, scattered, combined and reunited, disclosing, in both the contingent world and the heavenly kingdom, entities of a new creation, and revealing, in the unseen realms, the signs and tokens of Thy unity and oneness. Through that Call Thou didst announce unto all Thy servants the advent of Thy most great Revelation and the appearance of Thy most perfect Cause.[7]

Three aspects of the Bahá'í concept of unity are helpful to understanding its social expressions. *First,* unity is a state of knowledge or awareness, as well as a state of action. Bahá'u'lláh often spoke of the need for our vision and perception of the world around us to be firmly rooted in unity. He exhorted human beings to "let your vision be world embracing . . ." and to see with the "eye of oneness."[8] This vision of unity, which reflects the fundamental interconnectedness of social reality, is found throughout the writings of 'Abdu'l-Bahá and Shoghi Effendi that explain social issues and challenges, and include prescriptions for the future. For example, 'Abdu'l-Bahá writes:

Continents remained widely divided, nay even among the peoples of one and the same continent association and interchange of thought were well nigh impossible. Consequently intercourse, understanding and unity amongst all the peoples and kindreds of the earth were unattainable. In this day, however, means of communication have multiplied, and the five continents of the earth have become increasingly interdependent. For none is self-sufficiency any longer possible, inasmuch as political ties unite all peoples and nations, and the bonds of trade and industry, of agriculture and education, are being strengthened every day. Hence the unity of all mankind can in this day be achieved. Verily this is none other but one of the wonders of this wondrous age, this glorious century.[9]

From this perspective, advancing toward unity is not something that human beings blindly stumble toward. Unity must be a consciously chosen and pursued state, expressed as a result of our conscious knowledge of the fundamental interconnectedness of humanity as one human race. Indeed, human beings, absent this conscious knowledge, will often label various conditions as unity when indeed they are not. History is rife with egregious examples of hatred and oppression masquerading as so-called unity. Perhaps most evident in history has been the association of the term *unity* with a limited racial unity, which carries with it an assumption of the inferior, and in some cases subhuman, status of much of humanity standing outside of that limited unification. Because its inclusiveness is limited rather than universal, this false unity, achieved through uniformity, is antithetical to the teachings of Bahá'u'lláh.

Understanding unity also entails a particular orientation to the relationship between oneness and difference (sometimes referred to as the relationship between unity and diversity). Oneness and difference, in this vision, are seen as essential and integrated concepts that are not in conflict as values or constructs. The Bahá'í writings use frequent metaphors to describe this relationship. Bahá'u'lláh states, "Please God, that we avoid the land of denial, and advance into the ocean of acceptance, so that we may perceive, with an eye purged from all conflicting elements, the worlds of unity and diversity, of variation and oneness. . . ."[10] 'Abdu'l-Bahá uses the metaphor of a garden to explain this relationship between unity and diversity:

If the flowers of a garden were all of one color, the effect would be monotonous to the eye; but if the colors are variegated, it is most pleasing and wonderful. The difference in adornment of color and capacity of reflection among the flowers gives the garden its beauty and charm. Therefore, although we are of different individualities, different in ideas and of various fragrances, let us strive like flowers of the same divine garden to live together in harmony. Even though each soul has its own individual perfume and color, all are reflecting the same light, all contributing fragrance to the same breeze which blows through the garden, all continuing to grow in complete harmony and accord. Become as waves of one sea, trees of one forest, growing in the utmost love, agreement and unity.[11]

More than merely an aspiration, this statement is an ontological assertion about the nature and structure of reality. Patterns of distinct entities coming together to form complex unities are understood, in Bahá'í thought, as the most accurate description of the process of creation. As one scholar writes: "According to the Bahá'í view, the nature of reality is ultimately a unity, in contrast to a view that would postulate a multiplicity of differing or incommensurate realities. In a talk delivered in New York City in December 1912, 'Abdu'l-Baha stated that 'oneness is truth and truth is oneness which does not admit of plurality.' In a similar vein, during a talk in Paris in October 1911, 'Abdu'l-Baha stated that 'Truth has many aspects, but it remains always and forever one.'"[12]

Second, unity is a comprehensive concept that carries within it implications not only for individual perceptions, knowledge, and vision but also for political ethics, organization, and our political action as individuals. This comprehensive concept can be seen in one of the foundational themes of Bahá'u'lláh's political ethics—stated in His first public declaration in 1863—that "'in this Revelation the use of the sword is prohibited.'"[13]

As analyzed by Saiedi, Bahá'u'lláh roots this concept in a reinterpretation of *nusrat*, or assisting the cause of God to give it victory.[14] Islamic interpretations of *nusrat*, which have often supported violence and coercion, are challenged by Bahá'u'lláh Who calls His followers to "[a]ssist ye the Lord of all creation with works of righteousness, and also through wisdom and utterance."[15] Saiedi further demonstrates that Bahá'u'lláh's rejection of the sword is not limited to a narrow condemnation of violence; rather, it encompasses a range of social ethics: "The prohibition of killing, violence, and religious coercion; the promotion of love, unity, and fellowship among peoples; the call for peace among the nations; the condemnation of militarism and of the proliferation of arms; the assertion of the necessity for education and productive employment; the condemnation of sedition; the assertion of the need for religion and social justice—all these are presented by Bahá'u'lláh as systematic expressions of the same underlying principle of the removal of the sword."[16]

Employing this principle, Bahá'u'lláh describes how He put an end to Bábí militancy as a means of social change and shifted the Bahá'í community to effecting social change through non-coercive means reflective of the dynamics of unity: "Strife and conflict befit the beasts of the wild. It was through the grace of God and with the aid of seemly words and praiseworthy deeds that the unsheathed swords of the Bábí community were returned to their scabbards. Indeed through the power of good words, the righteous have always succeeded in winning command over the meads of the hearts of men. Say, O ye loved ones! Do not forsake prudence. Incline your hearts to the counsels given by the Most Exalted Pen and beware lest your hands or tongues cause harm unto anyone among mankind."[17]

This new form of politics required by the removal of the sword is one in which unity as an end is privileged over other ends. The practical effects of this shift are far-reaching. To look at one example, consider the role of religion in political discourse. One of the most discussed and analyzed topics in political and legal theory is the proper role (if any) of religion in public discourse. From a Bahá'í perspective, the removal of the sword, which aims to result in unity, places clear limitations on how Bahá'ís can and should engage in political discourse and for what purposes. Politics, in Bahá'u'lláh's vision, is not a legitimate avenue to convince others of the correctness of one's religious beliefs or to try to convince others to convert. A public discourse of conversion would violate the requirement of religious respect and tolerance, the necessity to demonstrate and express love, and the underlying reality of the unity of religion.

Similarly, this limitation on a political discourse of conversion raises broader concerns about the role of religion in politics. The Bahá'í writings are clear in their anti-majoritarian stance. In situations where Bahá'ís might in the future find themselves as a majority population, Shoghi Effendi has articulated a principle of preferential treatment for minorities: "Unlike the nations and peoples of the earth, be they of the East or of the West, democratic or authoritarian, communist or capitalist, whether belonging to the Old World or the New, who either ignore, trample upon, or extirpate, the racial, religious, or political minorities within the sphere of their jurisdiction, every organized community enlisted under the banner of Bahá'u'lláh should feel it to be its first and inescapable obligation to nurture, encourage, and safeguard every minority belonging to any faith, race, class, or nation within it."[18]

While undoubtedly interested in seeing the inculcation of morality and virtues in public life, and believing that religion is an indispensable foundation for civilization, Bahá'u'lláh nonetheless rejects a public virtue that would allow the entrenchment of majority views at the expense of minorities. Shoghi Effendi equates a violation of the rights of nonbelievers with an action that would subvert the essence of the religion itself. He clarifies that a violation of the "legitimate civil rights of individuals in a free society" would effectively reignite "in men's breasts the fire of bigotry and blind fanaticism, cut themselves off from the glorious bestowals of this promised Day of God, and impede the full flow of divine assistance in this wondrous age."[19]

Third, and following from the previous two points, unity is *both* a means and an end. Bahá'u'lláh positions the goal of social relations, communities, and structures as expressing and reflecting the fundamental unity of humanity. The individual and collective purposes and potentialities of humanity can best be accomplished and achieved through recognition of this fundamental unity and by learning to express it in action. Through this lens, human social history is understood as humanity's long effort to construct social patterns where an encompassing unity is increasingly recognized and actualized. Shoghi

Effendi describes this view of history: "Unification of the whole of mankind is the hall-mark of the stage which human society is now approaching. Unity of family, of tribe, of city-state, and nation have been successively attempted and fully established. World unity is the goal toward which a harassed humanity is striving."[20] This vision of history is understood to be a dynamic and ongoing process. It is also a contingent one, rooted in humanity's conscious knowledge and effort.

The Bahá'í teachings make clear that the process of building social unity must take place in a manner that reflects the principles of unity. Simply stated, the ends do not justify the means; indeed, from a Bahá'í perspective, the nature of unity that is sought as an end cannot be achieved through means that violate unity. As Bahá'u'lláh states in paragraph 160 in the Kitáb-i-Aqdas, "We have assigned to every end a means for its accomplishment. . . ." With respect to unity, one could impose "unity" on diverse peoples through coercion and the threat of force. Indeed, from ancient to contemporary times one can find examples of human beings using force to create a coerced unity. From a Bahá'í perspective, such coercion is not a legitimate means for creating unity, nor is that end a true state of unity in diversity. Rather, such a forced state is understood as a state of oppression. Relatedly, one finds clear statements throughout the Bahá'í writings to the effect that the genesis of conflict is due to a lack of established unity in diversity. This perspective has been summarized as follows: "Only through the dawning consciousness that they constitute a single people will the inhabitants of the planet be enabled to turn away from the patterns of conflict that have dominated social organization in the past and begin to learn the ways of collaboration and conciliation. 'The well-being of mankind,' Bahá'u'lláh writes, 'its peace and security, are unattainable unless and until its unity is firmly established.'"[21]

Unity through uniformity, in Bahá'í terms, is both unjust and unsustainable. It is not a state of unity born out of conscious knowledge of human beings and of how difference and oneness interact. Unity through uniformity does not give expression to actions that promote justice or equality for all.

2) Bahá'ís should privilege action at the level of social meanings, as distinct from social forms and social norms, in their efforts to effect social change in the broader society.

The positioning of unity as both the means and end of social change frames the central challenge, and analytical lens, for thinking about *how* Bahá'ís may legitimately pursue social change. What are methods of social change that may be consistent with the means of unity in diversity?

To develop an answer to this question, it is necessary to provide a framework for organizing and thinking about different approaches to social change. One useful framework is to think about efforts at social change as potentially focused on three distinct but interrelated levels: social forms, social norms, and social meanings.

Social forms, in this framework, do not refer to any particular sociological theory of forms. Rather, in this context, the term refers to public, outward, and shared phenomena that play roles in structuring and ordering the life of society. Most obviously, these are institutions and organizations, including public and government institutions. The term *social forms* also refers to the central tools such entities use to perform their ordering functions, including, for example, laws and policies. It might also be said that social forms are constructs through which formal public power is organized and exercised within society, including through the institutions of government.

Social forms are distinct from *social norms*, which generically can be described as the shared principles of behavior within a group or society. In any given group or society, there will be certain shared rules or principles of behavior that express the expectedness or unexpectedness of behaviors and associated attitudes and values. These shared principles of behavior—which may be implicit or explicit—constitute a type of group infrastructure, where certain modes of acting and engaging in relation to others may be pursued or avoided.

Social meanings remove us from the realm of shared institutions and structures (social forms) and shared rules and principles of behavior (social norms) and are focused on the shared mental constructs within a particular society or group. In this understanding, social meanings might be defined as the "semiotic content attached to various actions, or inactions, or statuses, within a particular context."[22] Such meanings may be consciously constructed by social actors, including governments, corporations, or groups of individuals, in order to reinforce sets of behaviors, understandings, or outcomes. The most powerful meanings are those that appear most natural and are taken for granted—uncontested—and such meanings will have the most significant impact on shaping the contexts within which individuals act and relate. Legal scholar Lawrence Lessig states three propositions with respect to social meanings and their strength: ". . . first, that social meanings exist; second, that they are used by individuals, or groups, to advance individual or collective ends; and third, that their force in part hangs upon their resting upon a certain uncontested, or taken-for-granted, background of thought or expectation—alternatively, that though constructed, their force depends upon them not seeming constructed."[23] Furthermore, Lessig writes, "If social meanings exist, they are also used. They not only constitute, or guide, or constrain; they are also tools—means to a chosen end, whether an individually or collectively chosen end. They are a resource—a semiotic resource—that society provides to all if it provides to any. They are a way 'for hitting each other and coercing one another to conform to something [one has] in mind'; or for inspiring another or inducing another to do, or believe, or want, in a certain way."[24]

As Lessig describes, social meanings may be contested or uncontested, foregrounded or backgrounded. Where a social meaning is uncontested and in the background—meaning it is almost subconsciously taken for granted and assumed—it has the most power. These social meanings shape our choices and behaviors with little conscious cognitive intermediation. Conversely, when social meanings are contested and foregrounded, they have the least power in dictating our choices and behaviors. In such a context, various competing meanings are the subject of ongoing public debate. The process of changing social meanings is ultimately a process of social meanings being moved from being contested to uncontested and from foreground to background.

Change at the level of social meanings can be distinguished from change at the level of social norms, as well as from change at the level of social forms. As distinct from the cognitive association ascribed to a particular action, social norms refer to the behavioral expectations that indicate the established and accepted ways of acting. Where meanings are about mental associations, norms are preoccupied with behavioral choices. Social forms, however, refer to the actual institutions and structures that are given social expression and are the most transparent, directly observable influencers of social action. Implicit with social forms is that, for the purposes of adherence, they are capable of harnessing and utilizing social coercion and force.

In its efforts to advance broad social change in the contemporary world at large, the Bahá'í community prioritizes action to effect change at the level of social meanings. Specifically, the Bahá'í community privileges action at the level of meanings that will increase awareness, understanding, consciousness, and shared associations that reinforce the realities of unity and its associated concepts of equality and justice.

The privileging of action at the level of meanings is done for a number of reasons. First, action at the level of meanings fits the Bahá'í emphasis on the paradigm of unity. The idea of unity as a conscious, deliberate state and the necessity that it be advanced in a noncoercive manner require that it emerge at the levels of our perception and knowledge, as well as in our actions, relationships, and collective life. Social unity is the shared outward expression of a consciousness of the diverse, interrelated, and mutually interdependent dimensions of our existence in relation to others. Certain architectures of social meanings will reinforce such a reality of unity—and concomitantly encourage behaviors that reflect it—while others will be in conflict with it. As these architectures increasingly reflect and reinforce unity-centered ones, the potentiality for unity-centered social norms and forms will deepen and in some respects accelerate. The Bahá'í International Community describes this process in its identification of how social forms for a global age will only emerge once collective shifts in consciousness take place:

> Laying the groundwork for global civilization calls for the creation of laws and institutions that are universal in both character and authority. The effort can begin only when the concept of the oneness of humanity has been wholeheartedly embraced by those in whose hands the responsibility for decision making rests, and when the related principles are propagated through both educational systems and the media of mass communication. Once this threshold is crossed, a process will have been set in motion through which the peoples of the world can be drawn into the task of formulating common goals and committing themselves to their attainment.[25]

The Bahá'í method of focusing at the level of social meanings is seen throughout Bahá'í history. It finds its genesis in Bahá'u'lláh's emphasis on focusing on individuals' "hearts." We see examples of such an approach to social action throughout the life of 'Abdu'l-Bahá, a particularly powerful one being His approach to the question of racial equality and unity. An illustrative example took place during 'Abdu'l-Bahá's journey to the United States in 1912. He attended a dinner at the home of Morgan Shuster with leading social and political figures of the Washington, DC area, which was the location of the temporary office of the Iranian government in America. After witnessing the seating and the company, He rearranged the seating so that Louis George Gregory, a prominent African-American attorney, would be placed at His right hand. This action was taken at a time when only one restaurant in all of Washington, DC would permit white and black Americans to sit together. In undertaking this action, 'Abdu'l-Bahá was challenging the conventional and predominant meanings of skin color that pervaded American society—and in particular the association of dark skin with inferiority. At the same time, He was reinforcing the meanings of unity—and in particular, that unity meant demonstrating a universal love for humanity and honoring the qualities and capacities of all individuals rather than drawing false and arbitrary distinctions based on, for example, race and gender—that were the direct subject matter of many of His talks throughout His journey. In *Century of Light,* a connection is drawn between this episode and 'Abdu'l-Bahá's method of changing social meanings:

Appreciating these limitations on the part of His hearers, 'Abdu'l-Bahá did not hesitate to introduce into His relations with Western believers actions that summoned them to a level of consciousness far above mere social liberalism and tolerance. One example that must stand for a range of such interventions was His gentle but dramatic act in encouraging the marriage of Louis Gregory and Louise Mathew—the one black, the other white. The initiative set a standard for the American Bahá'í community as to the real meaning of racial integration, however timid and slow its members were in responding to the core implications of the challenge.[26]

Another example of this privileging of social meanings is seen in how the Universal House of Justice and the worldwide Bahá'í Community sought to make contributions to the cause of peace during the height of the Cold War. The Universal House of Justice wrote a document called *The Promise of World Peace,* which was then distributed globally to leaders, thinkers, and populations at large. At the heart of the document was an argument for the shared meanings of peace to be associated with a positive state of unity (as distinct from, for example, an absence of war) and relatedly to serve as a pathway for individuals and communities to play a constructive role in the building of a peaceful global civilization. The message opens by associating meanings of peace with meanings of unity:

> The Great Peace towards which people of good will throughout the centuries have inclined their hearts, of which seers and poets for countless generations have expressed their vision, and for which from age to age the sacred scriptures of mankind have constantly held the promise, is now at long last within the reach of the nations. For the first time in history it is possible for everyone to view the entire planet, with all its myriad diversified peoples, in one perspective. World peace is not only possible but inevitable. It is the next stage in the evolution of this planet—in the words of one great thinker [Teilhard de Chardin], "the planetization of mankind."[27]

It goes on to locate the genesis of change as an expression of people's minds—the way we understand and perceive: "The endowments which distinguish the human race from all other forms of life are summed up in what is known as the human spirit; the mind is its essential quality. These endowments have enabled humanity to build civilizations and to prosper materially."[28]

Building on this theme, the message argues that the failure to achieve peace is ultimately tied to a "paralysis of will." Among other things, overcoming this paralysis requires a fundamental shift in the arena of the mind—a shift in consciousness. In particular, the message states:

> [w]orld order can be founded only on an unshakeable consciousness of the oneness of mankind, a spiritual truth which all the human sciences confirm. Anthropology, physiology, psychology, recognize only one human species, albeit infinitely varied in the secondary aspects of life. Recognition of this truth requires abandonment of prejudice—prejudice of every kind—race,

class, colour, creed, nation, sex, degree of material civilization, everything which enables people to consider themselves superior to others.

Acceptance of the oneness of mankind is the first fundamental prerequisite for reorganization and administration of the world as one country, the home of humankind. Universal acceptance of this spiritual principle is essential to any successful attempt to establish world peace. It should therefore be universally proclaimed, taught in schools, and constantly asserted in every nation as preparation for the organic change in the structure of society which it implies.[29]

This statement is a call to shared meanings of unity and oneness; and it puts forward the argument that through such changes in shared meanings, individuals and groups of individuals will be propelled toward, and find openings for, new forms of social action.

Bahá'u'lláh's elevation of change at the level of social meanings is a direct reflection of His positioning of unity as central to ontology and as the fundamental force in existence. Focusing on change at the level of these meanings is fundamentally an epistemic vision of social action. It is one in which shared mental associations and understandings come into existence and then act as a social force to shape different patterns of old social norms and the evolution of new social forms. When primacy is placed on unity as the centrifugal element of social change, it is the only such epistemic vision that could manifest the change while remaining true to the vision and reality of unity. By contrast, promoting social change primarily through changes in social forms fundamentally involves the use of coercion and ultimately is a source of social conflict because inherent within it is the exercise of social power. Similarly, placing primary focus on changes in behavioral norms, absent the requisite change in meanings, often results in the emergence of and ethic of division and difference. Focus comes to be placed on those who do or do not follow the new behavioral norms. In religious terms, what often appears is a litmus test for those who believe (or are pure or saved) and those who do not believe and are not saved. Conversely, when focus is placed on social meanings, the commitment is that, as the architecture of social meanings increasingly emerges as one conducive to the development of patterns of unity, a context is thus created in which movement toward changing social norms and social forms can take place in a manner that is increasingly less coercive and more organic in nature.

By targeting change at the level of social meanings, the constructive principle of social action also frames and gives limits and definition to the Bahá'í principle of non-participation in politics.[30] As mentioned earlier, this principle can be understood as speaking to the issue of involvement by Bahá'ís and the Bahá'í community in existing political processes and structures, and to the question of whether to focus energies on acquiring power within or on reforming existing systems. Bahá'u'lláh's teachings on the non-participation of politics indicate His view that emphasis was not to be placed on these existing systems because the methods used to secure power in existing systems and the institutions in place for the exercise of this power do not reflect the primacy of unity. Furthermore, attempting to impose a religious program, including through contemporary political methods and institutions, is antithetical to unity.[31] It is thus not surprising to find in the Bahá'í writings statements that clearly distinguish the Bahá'í Administrative Order from existing political institutions. As Shoghi Effendi states:

It would be utterly misleading to attempt a comparison between this unique, this divinely-conceived Order and any of the diverse systems which the minds of men . . . have contrived. . . . Such an attempt would in itself betray a lack of complete appreciation of the excellence of the handiwork of its great Author. . . . The divers and ever-shifting systems of human polity, whether past or present, whether originating in the East or in the West, offer no adequate criterion wherewith to estimate the potency of its hidden virtues or to appraise the solidity of its foundations.[32]

3) Bahá'ís should also seek to effect social change by building a global pattern of Bahá'í community life that ever increasingly reflects unity at the level of social meanings, norms, and forms.

While there is a logical privileging of action at the level of social meanings in Bahá'í efforts to effect social change in society at large, the Bahá'í community is also directly active at the level of social forms and social norms. It goes without saying that the patterns of community organization and life within the Bahá'í community are based on a conscious effort to reflect the teachings of Bahá'u'lláh in action. This effort to actualize the Word in a collective community is also projected and understood as an experiment in expressing the fundamental principles and teachings of human equality, justice, and unity, and this effort is expressed through all levels of how the Bahá'í community organizes and governs itself. For instance, the Bahá'í Administrative Order, which has both elected and appointed institutions, is rooted in an ethic of equality and is an effort to create patterns of engagement that are not power-based in orientation between the leaders and the population.[33] Shoghi Effendi has emphasized the relationship between the administrative order and its basis in unity, justice, and equality:

The vitality which the organic institutions of this great, this ever-expanding Order so strongly exhibit; . . . the high courage, the . . . resolution of its administrators . . . the . . . unquenchable enthusiasm . . . the heights of self-sacrifice . . . the breadth of vision, the confident hope, the creative joy, the inward peace, the uncompromising integrity, the exemplary discipline, the unyielding unity and solidarity . . . the degree to which its moving Spirit has shown itself capable of assimilating the diversified elements within its pale, of cleansing them of all forms of prejudice and of fusing them with its own structure—these are evidences of a power which a disillusioned and sadly shaken society can ill afford to ignore.

Compare these splendid manifestations of the spirit animating this vibrant body of the Faith of Bahá'u'lláh with the cries and agony, the follies and vanities, the bitterness and prejudices, the wickedness and divisions of an ailing and chaotic world. Witness the fear that torments its leaders and paralyzes the action of its blind and bewildered statesmen. How fierce the hatreds, how false the ambitions, how petty the pursuits, how deep-rooted the suspicions of its peoples! How disquieting the lawlessness, the corruption, the unbelief that are eating into the vitals of a tottering civilization![34]

In this effort to create a pattern of community organization and life on a global scale—which includes in its membership the full panoply of human diversity, experience, and background—a particular experiment is taking place at the level of social forms, norms, and meanings. Specifically, the Bahá'í community can be understood as a testing ground in which the social expressions of unity, cutting across a global audience, are being advanced, tested, and refined. These collective efforts include the community's developing, maturing, and changing certain social meanings, striving to adopt certain social norms, and seeking to build institutional and organizational forms that exemplify unity.

The fact that within the Bahá'í community experimentation is taking place at all of these levels is explicit and clear from the Bahá'í writings. When Bahá'u'lláh first expressed the formation of His community in the Najíbíyyih Garden in the outskirts of Baghdad in 1863, He immediately began the project of contesting existing architectures of social meanings while foregrounding the new social meanings of which people were to become conscious. This contesting of social meanings is seen, as discussed earlier, in His calling for the "removal of the sword," the implications of which include a warning to "Beware lest ye shed the blood of any one. Unsheathe the sword of your tongue from the scabbard of utterance, for therewith ye can conquer the citadels of men's hearts. We have abolished the law to wage holy war against each other.

God's mercy hath, verily, encompassed all created things, if ye do but understand. "[35] But beyond this admonition, it is woven into the very fabric of Bahá'í community life that social meanings that reinforce and point toward unity are to be preferred over all others. This turn toward social meanings that reflect unity is seen in how the project of the Bahá'í community has been described by the Universal House of Justice:

> The experience of the Bahá'í community may be seen as an example of this enlarging unity. It is a community of some three to four million people drawn from many nations, cultures, classes and creeds, engaged in a wide range of activities serving the spiritual, social and economic needs of the peoples of many lands. It is a single social organism, representative of the diversity of the human family, conducting its affairs through a system of commonly accepted consultative principles, and cherishing equally all the great outpourings of divine guidance in human history. Its existence is yet another convincing proof of the practicality of its Founder's vision of a united world, another evidence that humanity can live as one global society, equal to whatever challenges its coming of age may entail. If the Bahá'í experience can contribute in whatever measure to reinforcing hope in the unity of the human race, we are happy to offer it as a model for study.[36]

At the same time, the Bahá'í community makes efforts to advance new patterns of social norms and social forms. From His earliest days, Bahá'u'lláh reinforced the call to construct new norms of conduct, as well as new conceptions of law. These efforts are seen in numerous examples, including how the Bahá'í community of Iran challenged and broke established patterns that limited the educational opportunities and public roles of women in governing institutions. It is also seen in, as has been discussed elsewhere,[37] how Bahá'u'lláh changed established understandings and attitudes of divine law, and in particular expected certain levels of individual understanding and social cohesion to have emerged prior to His laws becoming applicable. Indeed, the entire pattern of Bahá'í elections and consultative decision-making can be seen as an effort to simultaneously change meanings of democracy, inculcate a new set of normative behaviors for public officials, and create new institutional structures of participatory democracy.

4) Although the Bahá'í community's external and internal programs of social change are distinct, they interact and reinforce each other in dynamic and evolving ways, and ultimately form part of one dynamic process.

So far, we have outlined two distinct efforts to effect social change pursued by the Bahá'í community—one focused externally on the world at large, and one focused internally within the Bahá'í community. Externally, action at the level of social meanings is privileged, while internally, actions at the levels of social forms, norms, and meanings are all pursued. Across both external and internal spheres of activity, the essential nature of unity stands firm. Given that unity is the central theological, ontological, and social construct of the Bahá'í Faith, all efforts at progress and change are to be focused on building and deepening patterns of unity.

While these external and internal efforts at social change are distinct, they ultimately can be seen as forming part of one multifaceted process of advancing humanity toward unity. Specifically, the two processes should be understood as intersecting and interacting with one another in dynamic and increasingly complex ways. The Bahá'í writings are full of descriptions of a future where processes internal to the Bahá'í community will eventually exert degrees of influence on society at large. As the Universal House of Justice states, quoting Shoghi Effendi:

That this process [development of the global Bahá'í Community] will continue to gain in scope and influence and the Administrative

Order demonstrate in time "its capacity to be regarded not only as the nucleus but the very pattern of the New World Order" is clear from his writings. "In a world the structure of whose political and social institutions is impaired, whose vision is befogged, whose conscience is bewildered, whose religious systems have become anaemic and lost their virtue," he asserted so emphatically, "this healing Agency, this leavening Power, this cementing Force, intensely alive and all-pervasive," is "taking shape," is "crystallizing into institutions," and is "mobilizing its forces."[38]

One way of understanding these statements is that as social meanings continually become unity-centered in the world at large, and as the Bahá'í community continually develops and matures in its expressions of unity at the levels of meanings, norms, and forms, the interaction between internal and external processes will increase. For example, as unity-centered social meanings take root, there will be greater receptivity and demand for ideas about how social norms and forms may emerge to reflect the dynamics of unity. Thus, the experiment and learning of the Bahá'í community at the level of social forms may be of more relevance. The Bahá'í community may become a model for emerging patterns of unity. For example, the National Spiritual Assembly of the Bahá'ís of the United States has described the experience of that community in dealing with race relations in the following terms:

From its inception in 1863 the Bahá'í community was dedicated to the principle of the unity of humankind. Bahá'ís rely upon faith in God, daily prayer, meditation, and study of sacred texts to effect the transformation of character necessary for personal growth and maturity; however, their aim is to create a world civilization that will in turn react upon the character of the individual. Thus the concept of personal salvation is linked to the salvation, security, and happiness of all the inhabitants of the earth and stems from the Bahá'í belief that "the world of humanity is a composite body" and that "when one part of the organism suffers all the rest of the body will feel its consequence."

Guided and inspired by such principles, the Bahá'í community has accumulated more than a century of experience in creating models of unity that transcend race, culture, nationality, class, and the differences of sex and religion, providing empirical evidence that humanity in all its diversity can live as a unified global society. Bahá'ís see unity as the law of life; consequently, all prejudices are perceived as diseases that threaten life. Rather than considering that the unity of humankind can be established only after other problems afflicting it have been solved, Bahá'ís believe that both spiritual and material development are dependent upon love and unity.[39]

This increased interaction between internal and external efforts at social change raises another set of more complex questions. As the two efforts interact, does this create an increased legitimate role for Bahá'í social forms in social affairs and governance at large? This matter has been written about at some length elsewhere, in the context of Bahá'í teachings about the relationship between religious and political institutions, as well as the meaning of world order in the Bahá'í writings.[40] The Universal House Justice, in commenting on this matter, seems to contemplate the possibilities of increased interaction between Bahá'í and civil political institutions, as well as an increased role for Bahá'í institutions, but the form of this interaction is somewhat open and dynamic:

The second fundamental principle which enables us to understand the pattern towards which Bahá'u'lláh wishes human society to evolve is the principle of organic growth which requires that detailed developments, and the understanding of detailed developments, become available only with the passage of time and with the help of the guidance given by that Central Authority in the Cause to whom all must turn. In this regard one can use the simile of a tree. If a farmer plants a tree, he cannot state at that moment what its exact height will be, the number of its branches or the exact time of its blossoming. He can, however, give a general impression of its size and pattern of growth and can state with confidence which fruit it will bear. The same is true of the evolution of the World Order of Bahá'u'lláh.[41]

Conclusion

The four elements of the Bahá'í approach to social change outlined above highlight a diffuse, grassroots, creative, and epistemic process. This approach, at heart, relies on changing how individuals and groups of individuals work to think in new ways and, stemming from those new ways of thinking, work to inculcate new patterns of behavior and ultimately new patterns of social organization. The centrality of unity to this approach demands that the Bahá'í community pursue external social change at the level of social meanings. Within the Bahá'í community, the action for social change is more integrative, focused simultaneously on the levels of meanings, norms, and forms.

Similar to any other method of social change, this particular rendering of the Bahá'í approach has certain challenges. The model will work best in certain conditions when certain parameters are adhered to, but it will be less successful in other contexts. Although it will be for future papers to examine and assess the relative successes or failures of this model as it has been implemented by the Bahá'í community to date, one can see generally where the challenges lie within such a model.

First, it is vitally important, as was noted in the introduction, to ensure that internal means/ends and external means/ends are not conflated and confused. Bahá'ís must strive to have a sincerity of motive in their efforts at social change, and, as indicated by the Universal House of Justice, the value of social action is not to be measured through statistics of conversion. Rather, the ultimate motivating force must be that of service which stems from a conscious recognition of the fundamental unity of all humanity: "That one indeed is a man who, today, dedicateth himself to the service of the entire human race. The Great Being saith: Blessed and happy is he that ariseth to promote the best interests of the peoples and kindreds of the earth. In another passage He hath proclaimed: It is not for him to pride himself who loveth his own country, but rather for him who loveth the whole world. The earth is but one country and mankind its citizens."[42]

This sustained focus on unity demands personal vigilance from each and every Bahá'í and by the entire community of Bahá'ís, to maintain a sincerity of purpose and motive when engaging in efforts at social change. As the Universal House of Justice stated, ". . . we feel compelled to raise a warning: It will be important for all to recognize that the value of engaging in social action and public discourse is not to be judged by the ability to bring enrollments. Though endeavors in these two areas of activity may well effect an increase in the size of the Bahá'í community, they are not undertaken for this purpose. Sincerity in this respect is imperative."[43]

Second, the epistemic and long-term approach to social change requires caution in measuring success or failure through fixed or near-term criteria and standards. Envisioning social change as a process of changing social meanings implies a commitment to an epistemic and long-term vision of how social change occurs. Such change ultimately stems from alterations in how people perceive phenomena and the architecture of those perceptions in relation to each other. While some changes may happen quite quickly, this transformation ultimately is a gradual process where fundamental shifts in the perceptions of masses of human beings and human communities take place over the long term. One of the challenges of such an approach, especially when it is undertaken by a diverse and disparate (and ever-changing) community of people, is mobilizing and the deepening of an understanding of the long-term and epistemic nature of this process—and more pointedly, that the process of change is often experienced in the first instance in something intangible (how people think) as opposed to something tangible (such as new social forms).

Throughout Bahá'í history, one sees Bahá'í leaders reinforcing this orientation toward the lengthy process of change, whether speaking about the processes within the Bahá'í community or outside of it. Bahá'u'lláh, when describing both the internal and external aspects of social change, constantly encouraged His followers to recognize the long-term epistemic nature of the process in which He was engaged. For example, in relation to the internal processes of the Bahá'í community, Bahá'u'lláh was met frequently by requests from His followers for new social forms—laws and institutions in particular. In response to these requests, Bahá'u'lláh called upon His followers to see the process of change in different terms. For example, in the Kitáb-i-Aqdas, in addition to focusing on hearts and minds, Bahá'u'lláh also specifically positioned shifts in knowledge, understanding, and motivation as being the linchpins for the further development and application of new norms and forms within the Bahá'í community.[44] Similarly, while He spoke of His Order and created its embryonic institutions, efforts were not made to begin building these institutions in earnest until later in Bahá'í history. When Shoghi Effendi fully inaugurated the development of institutions, he similarly emphasized how this transition was part of a lengthy process that stretches from new perceptions and knowledge to new forms.[45]

'Abdu'l-Bahá describes this long-term process, in somewhat metaphorical terms, in the following way:

Development and progression imply gradual stages or degrees. For example, spiritual advancement may be likened to the light of the early dawn. Although this dawn light is dim and pale, a wise man who views the march of the sunrise at its very beginning can foretell the ascendancy of the sun in its full glory and effulgence. He knows for a certainty that it is the beginning of its manifestation and that later it will assume great power and potency. Again, for example, if he takes a seed and observes that it is sprouting, he will know assuredly that it will ultimately become a tree. Now is the beginning of the manifestation of the spiritual power, and inevitably the potency of its life forces will assume greater and greater proportions. Therefore, this twentieth century is the dawn, or beginning, of spiritual illumination, and it is evident that day by day it will advance. It will reach such a degree that spiritual effulgences will overcome the physical, so that divine susceptibilities will overpower material intelligence and the heavenly light dispel and banish earthly darkness. Divine healing shall purify all ills, and the cloud of mercy will pour down its rain. The Sun of Reality will shine, and all the earth shall put on its beautiful green carpet. Among the results of the manifestation of spiritual forces will be that the human world will adapt itself to a new social form, the justice of God will become manifest throughout human affairs, and human equality will be universally established.[46]

A third challenge to this vision of social change would be a failure to prioritize unity at all times and in all contexts. The constant litmus test for individual and collective efforts to effect change is the measure and standard of unity, which includes our own thoughts and actions in relation to others—such as, for example, whether in one's own mind one draws distinctions between categories of individuals within the Bahá'í community, in society, or in the world as a whole. It also is the measure for community life as a whole. To the degree that community life is fractured, divided, uninspired, or apathetic, one will ultimately find weaknesses and misunderstandings in the nature and substance of unity that has been and must be created. Finally, in terms of external efforts at social change, it is sometimes hard to navigate the line between action at the level of social meanings to advance unity and involvement in activities that may reinforce other social meanings or social norms, and forms that are not conducive to the appearance of unity.

Ultimately, it is through ever-increasing consciousness of Bahá'í methods of social change and frank, truthful, transparent, and open assessment of the challenges to meaningfully advancing those approaches (including the inevitable failures that can and must occur) that real social change will occur. Moving from a largely negative discourse of social change (non-participation in politics) or a conflation of conversion and social change to an epistemic vision that emphasizes what Bahá'ís can and must do will ultimately advance the Bahá'í community and its historic and world-changing enterprise.

PART 6:

Discourses and the Study of Bahá'í Law

8 / Imagining Bahá'í Law

[FIRST PUBLISHED IN *BAHÁ'Í STUDIES REVIEW*, VOL. 14, NO. 1, 2007.]

Very little has been written about Bahá'í law, and even less about how it may be understood, expanded, and applied in the future. In the Bahá'í Faith, a discussion of the principles of legal interpretation and methodology has yet to begin. What we do know is that individuals are encouraged to interpret scripture for themselves.[1] Also, it is absolutely clear that such individual interpretations are not authoritative or binding[2] and that there exists a legislative body for the expansion of Bahá'í law—the Universal House of Justice. But the principles that will govern the legislative enterprise have not been explicated or analyzed. Furthermore, beyond what appears to be a rejection of the strict principles of *stare decisis*,[3] and as such the prioritizing of a contextual approach, it is almost wholly unknown how a future Bahá'í judiciary might function or interpret the law.

While scholarship concerning Bahá'í law is in its infancy, it will likely begin to develop further in the near future. Increased interaction between religion and state has historically spurred the development of religious law and legal systems. This is true, for example, in the evolution of both Islamic law and canon law. In Islam, the emergence of Muslim rulers in historically non-Muslim territories contributed to the emergence of a body of Islamic law to be applied to the population. In the Middle Ages, the development of canon law was in support of papal claims to public power, as can most clearly be seen in the eleventh and twelfth centuries.

For very different reasons, Bahá'í communities around the globe are increasingly interacting with the state and becoming involved in public life. Historically, the main rationale for state–Bahá'í interaction outside of Iran was to secure legal status for local communities or support for persecuted Bahá'í communities elsewhere, but this is beginning to change. Bahá'í communities are now sometimes asked to take on a more explicitly public role. Such public roles are largely a by-product of community growth and the recognition of the Bahá'í Faith as an independent religion. However, the comfortable existence of Bahá'í communities within liberal democratic states in Europe and North America may face challenges in the near future, particularly concerning how Bahá'í law and the law of the state will interact. One example of this is seen in the increasing number of governments legalizing, or considering legalizing, same-sex marriage. A Bahá'í marriage, under Bahá'í law, is limited to two individuals of the opposite sex. It is unclear if these changes in marriage law (which can reflect changing constitutional norms) could impact aspects of the civil legal recognition of Bahá'í institutions and, for example, the role of Bahá'í marriage officers, who may also be agents of the state.[4]

Of course, historical examples of how religion-state interaction instigates a period of development of religious law are often much more stark than the forms of increased interaction that are currently seen in state–Bahá'í relations. In the Bahá'í context, there is no current claim or issue of public power. Rather, the current questions are preoccupied with how the Bahá'í community might assist the state in particular policy areas, or in the legal organization and status of the Bahá'í community within the state. But these narrower questions are sufficient to require significant discussion and debate concerning Bahá'í law. Thus, one may expect that individuals and institutions will intensify the study and development of Bahá'í law in the near future.

Udo Schaefer's paper "An Introduction to Bahá'í Law: Doctrinal Foundations, Principles and Structures" is a logical starting point for exploring directions in which discussions of legal interpretation and methodology might develop within the Bahá'í community, in particular as a result of Bahá'í–state interaction. As the first overview of Bahá'í law to be published in a major legal journal, Schaefer's paper represents one of the most likely entryways into Bahá'í law for individuals, scholars, and institutions, both within and outside of the Bahá'í community. It is instructive, therefore, to review the approach Schaefer takes to Bahá'í law, some of the choices and assumptions he makes, and the image a reader may be left with concerning the fundamentals of Bahá'í law.

Schaefer's Text-Centric Construction of Bahá'í Law

Schaefer explains the purpose of his paper in the following terms:

> The present study aims to provide an overview of the revealed law of the Bahá"i Faith, which is of interest for students of both legal history and religious studies. We are entering virgin territory here, as no attempt has yet been made at a systematic jurisprudence, nor has a tradition of Bah'a'í jurisprudence been established that might compare with the Islamic *Usúlu'l-fiqh*. Since the foundations and principles of this law can be understood only within their theological context, and knowledge of this context is rare outside the Bah'a'í community, some basic background information about the faith will be provided first.[5]

Within this purpose, one finds a text-centric approach toward Bahá'í law. The task of providing an overview of Bahá'í law primarily involves identifying and organizing the rules stated in Bahá'í scripture. As Schaefer writes, "The Bahá'í community is in the possession of a revealed Law, a *ius divinum* [divine law], whose source is the entire body of sacred texts emanating from the pen of Bahá'u'lláh, which together constitute the 'Book' (*al-kit b*)."[6] Specifically, in Schaefer's text-centric approach, an understanding of Bahá'í law comes from placing it within its theological framework and thus within the Bahá'í religious system as a whole. As a result, the paper is basically constructed around three broad topics. It opens with a discussion of the historical, religious, and theological context of Bahá'í law—including Bahá'í concepts of religion, the state, and justice.[7] This topic is followed by a discussion of the core constructs of a religious law: sources, how the law is brought into force, and temporal validity.[8] Finally, the bulk of the paper outlines some of the rules that Schaefer suggests form the corpus of the Bahá'í *ius divinum*, organized in categories of penal, family, marriage, inheritance, and community constitutional law.[9]

Schaefer's approach results in a particular form of presentation of Bahá'í law—a presentation that is familiar to legal academics and scholars of religious law. This is a rule-oriented, formal, and positivistic body of law. Use of the term *ius divinum* connotes a set of clearly prescribed rules, which can be organized and categorized according to the general categories of either common or civil legal systems. Further, Bahá'í law is also considered to be embedded within the logic of theology—the law is understood to exist within and reflect fundamental norms and principles concerning the nature of God, and the relationship between God and human beings. Thus, as Schaefer describes, the expansion of the body of law must reflect these theological norms, and in a Bahá'í context, this means that all Bahá'í law is elevated to the category of divine law. Schaefer discusses the legitimate sources of Bahá'í law as follows: "Finally, the Bahá'í community has a supplementary divine law that is also in the category of *ius divinum positivum*, namely the legislation made by the Universal House of Justice, the supreme administrative body, which is democratically elected by the world community. The published laws established by this body are therefore also sources of law. Thus, the Bahá'í divine law is a *ius divinum positivum* with the subcategories of *ius divinum scripturae* and *ius divinum supplementum*, which together constitute the Bahá'í sacred law."[10]

While other justifications for the law might be offered, the ultimate
one is positivistic in nature—legitimacy is innate because the law is
mandated by God, either through the intermediary of His Manifestation (Bahá'u'lláh), or through the institutions He created and inspires
as the lawgiver.

By providing an explication of the rules of the religion, the norms
and principles that inspire them, and the affirmation of their status as
being of God, Schaefer provides what one would expect from an early
work on a religion's laws. Indeed, Schaefer's paper is somewhat similar
to projects of scholars of Islamic law in Europe and North America in
the 1960s and 1970s that were intended to provide broad overviews of
Islamic law and organize and systematize vast bodies of material. For
example, Joseph Schacht, in his seminal work *An Introduction to Islamic
Law*, focused on the historical context of Islamic law, its status as a
sacred law, and the statement of legal rules for which he (like Schaefer)
used categories heavily drawn from Western legal traditions.

Ultimately, Schaefer leaves the reader with the image of Bahá'í law as
a new *shari'a*—as Bahá'í scripture providing a clearly delineated set of
rules, which in various ways and to various degrees challenges, reforms
or overturns scriptural rules of the past. Indeed, the Qur'án is the main
point of reference for Schaefer as he seeks to present Bahá'í laws. Furthermore, Schaefer places these new scriptural rules into a rational–legal
structure that lays the foundation for future codifications of the law:

> The Law revealed by Bahá'u'lláh (like all revealed law) is not a
> consistent legal system, let alone a systematic code. It is rudimen-
> tary, calculated for further development. The Kitáb-i Aqdas (like
> the Qur'án) only regulates certain aspects of law, such as matters
> concerning personal status (e.g. family law and inheritance law)
> and penal law. The latter includes only a few norms which, in
> combination with statements on the theology of law and on the
> purpose of punishment, are intended to form the basis of a future

criminal code. The Kitáb-i Aqdas and the Testament of 'Abdu'l-Bahá comprise the constitutional law of the community.[11]

Questioning a Text-Centric Approach

While Schaefer's text-centric approach meets general expectations concerning the treatment of religious law, it is precisely in setting out to meet these expectations—to prioritize a text-centric approach—that certain issues arise.

The treatment of Bahá'í law, and in particular core legal-scriptural texts such as the Kitáb-i-Aqdas, has been a point of controversy in Bahá'í history.[12] Bahá'í law was consciously backgrounded by Bahá'u'lláh in a pattern that was largely maintained through the ministries of 'Abdu'l-Bahá and Shoghi Effendi, and that continues to be maintained by the Universal House of Justice. This backgrounding was partially a function of the realities of a religious system in its early stages of development, especially for a community as small and dispersed as the Bahá'í community. But more significantly, from the days of Bahá'u'lláh, the backgrounding was positioned as one expression of the nature of Bahá'í law itself. While the laws "must be faithfully obeyed by all," in "observing them one must exercise tact and wisdom" "so that nothing might happen that could cause disturbance or dissension or raise clamor among the heedless."[13] In these statements, and the backgrounding of his law, Bahá'u'lláh is both affirming the normative validity—indeed the essentiality—of His law for the well-being of humanity while at the same time distinguishing the fact of normative validity from the political dimension of law, and specifically how the coercive force of law is used as a force for both individual and social change.

This recognition of the political dimensions of law innately frees the law from some of the implications of the positivist assumptions that often accompany assertions of divine law. While the fact that the laws come from the voice of God may legitimize the law, God's voice alone does not *de facto* legitimize the application of that law. In terms of placing Bahá'í law within its own history, this means that the story is not one of revelation, interpretation, and application. Rather, the story of Bahá'í law is one of of gradualism, a prioritizing of individual conscience and choice over coercion, the acceptance of a diversity of practices in certain contexts, and a focus on the construction of social conditions in which the wider applications of a religious law may be a positive force for change. This characteristic of gradualism is distinct from many traditions of religious law where the unquestionable validity of a divine legal sanction encourages a drive to immediately apply the laws and to starkly sanction their violation. This gradualistic approach is also foreign to aspects of modern traditions of positive law, in which law cannot be said to exist apart from the power of the state.

Schaefer notes this particular feature of Bahá'í law when he writes:

A peculiar feature of Bahá'ism is that most norms of the revealed law (including the ordinances of ritual) do not come into force *ipso iure* upon their promulgation, but have to be formally enacted by introductory acts of the supreme legislative body with global responsibility, the "Universal House of Justice" (*Baytu'l 'adl al-a'zam*). This gradual process of bringing laws into force derives from the founder of the religion himself, who did not want the break with the customary order of life to be too abrupt; instead, it should be fitted to the capacity of people to accept it. Moreover, the socially relevant legal norms, especially the regulations concerning criminal justice, presume the existence of a society already shaped by the revelation, a "society destined to emerge from the chaotic conditions that prevail today." A further reason for the need for formal enactment of the revealed laws is that they are valid for a period of at least one thousand years. As social conditions on earth are subject to constant change, legal norms that regulate specific details once and for all are in danger of leading to rigid legal casuistry and to the petrification of the law. Bahá'u'lláh has eliminated this danger by providing the legal system "with an essential element of flexibility." The divine law regulates only "matters of major importance." Moreover, the legal norms have been revealed at a high level of abstraction. They are so general and leave so much unregulated that they need to be specified and adapted to the conditions of the time. They are in need of detailed sub-regulations. In the Bahá'í community, these sub-regulations—the development of the legal system—do not result from authoritative *interpretation* by the religious scholars, "the learned ones" (as the Rabbis in Judaism and the *"ulam"* in Islam), but from supplementary *legislation.* The institution of a supreme legislature that has been "freed from all error" allows for constant adaptation of the law to changing social conditions, since this legislature can amend its own laws, through *ius divinum,* and thus take account of altered circumstances.

Certain legal norms were (at least for the eastern Bahá'ís) considered binding from the start, others were declared universally valid by 'Abdu'l-Bahá, and later by Shoghi Effendi and eventually by the Universal House of Justice. As far as the institutions and structures of community order are concerned, implementation of law began during the office of 'Abdu'l-Bahá. It is self-evident that revealed legal norms are effective in the community as ethical guidelines even before they come into force.[14]

This excellent description of how Bahá'í law operates points to the tension found in Schaefer's text-centric approach. The fact that the laws revealed by Bahá'u'lláh are not automatically binding, are subject to another legislative act to be brought into force, and are contingent on the construction of certain social conditions would suggest that a text-centric approach is only appropriate for limited and certain ends.[15] An approach that focuses on delineating rules within their theological context to demonstrate their internal logic within the Bahá'í system— and as such their normative validity within the Bahá'í belief system—is perfectly appropriate to illustrate Bahá'í theology, or the Bahá'í visions of a future state of society. However, this approach is limited as a method to illustrate the nature of Bahá'í law or to provide the foundations for a systematic jurisprudence—which is Schaefer's stated goal. Unlike *usul al-fiqh*, the Bahá'í system is specifically designed to not create an elaborate apparatus of laws and doctrines that exist apart from (and often in conflict with) the acts of legislative authority and formal institutions.[16] As such, it would make sense to emphasize how Bahá'í law may operate and be applied early on in the process of developing approaches to Bahá'í jurisprudence. Focusing primarily on text-based rules found in scripture is not as useful. Bahá'u'lláh, as well as Bahá'í legal authorities, has emphasized the method of Bahá'í law, as well as its substance.[17] Scholars should be attentive to this fact when outlining the nature of Bahá'í law.

A text-centric approach also runs the risk of misconstruing issues of authority, enforceability, and coercion in respect to Bahá'í law. One illustration of this is in the very choice to use familiar legal categories, born out of the Western legal tradition, to organize and delineate the rules found in Bahá'u'lláh's writings. These categories are not neutral but rather carry with them assumptions and connotations that may or may not be appropriate for understanding the nature and function of Bahá'í law.

For example, Schaefer's use and discussion of Bahá'í "penal law" raises many issues concerning how Bahá'í law is being presented. Schaefer is not explicit about the way in which he uses the term *penal*. His discussion appears to suggest that he is using the term in the sense of the term *criminal* as opposed to the more general meaning of *involving a penalty* or *punishment*. The significance of Schaefer's interpretation is that there are qualitative differences between different offenses. What a society agrees constitutes a criminal offense carries with it the full weight of social stigma and opprobrium, as well as the full coercive power of the state to do violence to offenders. On the other hand, there are vast ranges of penalties that are understood socially and are treated legally as being distinctly different from pure criminal offenses in nature. One example are offenses that might be deemed regulatory or statutory.[18]

Schaefer begins his discussion of penal law by noting that "The Kitáb-i Aqdas contains some provisions of penal law, but these are expressed in a very general and abstract way, allowing for the later specification of offenses. There is no legal definition of elements of an offense. The details of penal laws were not specified by Bahá'u'lláh."[19] This raises a red flag, however. Bahá'u'lláh undoubtedly identifies many offenses in the Kitáb-i-Aqdas. But what constitutes a criminal offense, as opposed to an offense that we should understand in other terms, is not clearly identified in scripture and cannot be identified at this point in the development of Bahá'í law.[20] This is a matter to be clarified by the Universal House of Justice, in the context of the social norms and realities of the societies in which it is required to legislate and bring law into force. By lumping such a wide range of offenses into the category of penal law—including murder, arson, theft, homosexuality, adultery, and backbiting—Schaefer has imposed a current legal category, which carries with it significant weight and connotations, onto a mixed bag of offenses that may not all fit into the same categories as Bahá'í law develops. What constitutes a crime in a Bahá'í legal order, and how legal authorities might enforce the law and punish offenders, remains wholly unknown. In other words, it is too soon, and too unclear, to speak of a Bahá'í penal law, especially in the criminal law sense, and particularly a penal law that lumps together everything that has the appearance of being an offense in the Kitáb-i-Aqdas.

Further, penal law is a public law that is supported by the coercive power of the state. There does not exist a penal law in the absence of such authority, except in the hypothetical or theoretical sense. Moreover, penal laws, especially as they connote a criminal offense by their very nature, are representative of and embedded within the social meanings and norms of the society in which they emerge. In this respect, Bahá'í penal law is the quintessential example of how divine law is subject to processes of social construction. Bahá'u'lláh's assertion of the validity of His laws for all of humanity must be read in the context of His assertion of the dynamic, gradual, and contingent nature of His law.

One example of the effect of this may be found with the issue of adultery. While it is possible that sexual relations outside of marriage (or *ziná*) could, in a future Bahá'í order, constitute a penal (criminal) offense as Schaefer posits (though this is not indicated in the texts), at the same time, it can be legitimately asserted that within contemporary Bahá'í communities, adultery is not understood or treated as a penal (criminal) offense, but rather individuals are encouraged to strive to be examples in their sexual conduct, to be tolerant and loving, and to accept that they will be subject to failures and tests. Consider the following statements from the Bahá'í writings, all of which relate to how some of the offenses that fall under the term *ziná* are to be treated:

The world today is submerged, amongst other things, in an over-exaggeration of the importance of physical love, and a dearth of spiritual values. In as far as possible the believers should try to realize this and rise above the level of their fellow-men who are, typical of all decadent periods in history, placing so much over-emphasis on the purely physical side of mating. Outside of their normal, legitimate married life they should seek to establish bonds of comradeship and love which are eternal and founded on the spiritual life of man, not on his physical life. This is one of the many fields in which it is incumbent on the Bahá'ís to set the example and lead the way to a true human standard of life, when the soul of man is exalted and his body but the tool for his enlightened spirit. Needless to say this does not preclude the living of a perfectly normal sex life in its legitimate channel of marriage.[21]

We must struggle against the evils in society by spiritual means, and by medical and social ones as well. We must be tolerant but uncompromising, understanding but immovable in our point of view.[22]

It is the challenging task of the Bahá'ís to obey the law of God in their own lives, and gradually to win the rest of mankind to its acceptance.

In considering the effect of obedience to the laws on individual lives, one must remember that the purpose of this life is to prepare the soul for the next. Here one must learn to control and direct one's animal impulses, not to be a slave to them. Life in this world is a succession of tests and achievements, of falling short and of making new spiritual advances. Sometimes the course may seem very hard, but one can witness, again and again, that the soul who steadfastly obeys the law of Bahá'u'lláh, however hard it may seem, grows spiritually, while the one who compromises with the law for the sake of his own apparent happiness is seen to have been following a chimera: he does not attain the happiness he sought, he retards his spiritual advance and often brings new problems upon himself.[23]

In this example, one can see the implications of Schaefer's text-centric methodology for the image of Bahá'í law it creates. The understanding of Bahá'í law one gains from Schaefer is one that emphasizes rules over method, and the absolute validity of those laws as a *ius divinum*. In contrast, Bahá'í law may be framed in terms of the ways in which it is applied, used, and enforced. One then finds a deemphasis of positive authority, an enlightened and diffuse perspective on methods of social change, and a practical illustration of how unity cannot be achieved through coercion, such as the coercive applications of legal norms in social situations where individuals are not prepared for such norms.

Law as Text / Law in Practice

Ultimately, the example above is intended to draw a distinction between "Law as Text" as contrasted with "Law in Practice," and to illustrate that these two different discourses will create quite different perceptions and understandings of the same subject matter. The key contrasts of these two approaches, in the context of a religious law, can be summarized as follows in Table 1:

	Law as Text	Law in Practice
Focuses on the	Word	word in action
In order to identify	statements of rules	ways in which statements of rules are used or applied
Which are part of	the *ius divinum*	political and social institutions, and thus embedded within particular social meanings and norms
And advances our understanding of	the theology of law	the realities of how religious legal systems develop and change, and in particular how the Baha'i system might evolve
And demonstrates	the absolute validity of the rules.	the contingent/contextual validity of rules, and the political and social processes needed for the application of the rules.

To be clear, the main emphasis of this brief comment is not necessarily to argue for the objective or normative superiority of one image of law over another. Rather, the main assertion is that different legal discourses will interpret and treat a legal subject in a different manner, and the conclusions reached concerning that legal subject may thus vary widely. Students of law will also recognize that the general categories outlined in the table could be situated within contemporary jurisprudential thought—and quite familiar debates between, for example, formalism and realism.

What has been put forward throughout this short comment, is that a "Law in Practice" discourse is essential for meaningful discussion of Bahá'í law, especially where the stated purpose is to contribute to the project of forming a systematic jurisprudence, or otherwise understanding Bahá'í law in its legal character and dimensions. Schaefer's more formal approach also has much to contribute, but at this stage in the development of Bahá'í law, privileging an image of Bahá'í law as a new (updated) *shari'a*—especially to the exclusion of a "Law in Practice" image—is problematic. Schaefer's portrayal of Bahá'í law, while continuous with strong traditions within the study of religious law, and demonstrating continuity with scriptural legal traditions, is somewhat at odds with the history of Bahá'í law. Indeed, the law as found in the texts is subsumed by a legal practice which—while maintaining the integrity and authority of the texts, and the rules stated therein—accepts that the application and expansion of Bahá'í law is subject to a progressive and gradual process of social change. As valuable as Schaefer's work is, it puts forward an image of Bahá'í law that is incomplete. Without the balance of a "Law in Practice" discourse, Bahá'í law is distorted in favor of a positivistic and formalistic portrayal which betrays the contextual underpinnings of the system. A "Law in Practice" image is needed as a guidepost for future scholars as they build on the pathways Schaefer has laid.

9 / Themes in the Study of Bahá'u'lláh's Kitáb-i-Aqdas: Emerging Approaches to Scholarship on Bahá'í Law

[FIRST PUBLISHED IN *JOURNAL OF BAHÁ'Í STUDIES*, VOLUME 27, NUMBER 4, 2017]

Abstract

A quarter century has passed since the publication of the authorized translation of Bahá'u'lláh's Kitáb-i-Aqdas from Arabic to English. In that time, English language scholarship on the Kitáb-i-Aqdas, especially its legal content, has grown. This essay reviews the emerging body of scholarship surrounding the Kitáb-i-Aqdas and Bahá'í law, identifies core themes and approaches, and suggests directions which future study of this topic might encompass.

Introduction

The year 2017 marks the twenty-fifth anniversary of the publication of the authorized translation from Arabic into English—and subsequently into other languages—of the full text of the Kitáb-i-Aqdas (The Most Holy Book), the central book of scripture of the Bahá'í Faith.[1] Prior to 1992, the full text was accessible only to those who read Arabic or through a few translations of questionable quality that were generally not used by members of the Bahá'í community.[2]

Written while Bahá'u'lláh was in exile in Palestine in 1873, the Kitáb-i-Aqdas is a relatively short work comprised of 190 paragraphs in its English translation. Known as the "Mother Book" of the Bahá'í Faith,[3] it is also routinely referred to as Bahá'u'lláh's "Book of Laws"[4] because it discusses the nature and concept of law and provides some of the foundational laws of the Bahá'í Faith.[5]

The release of the authorized translation in 1992 was a marked shift in access and availability of the Kitáb-i-Aqdas to adherents of the Bahá'í Faith, as well as to scholars and the general public. While portions of the work had been the subject of authorized translation by Shoghi Effendi and a synopsis and codification of the work had been available since 1973, studying excerpts and summaries is significantly different than studying a work of scripture as a whole.

It is worth reflecting on how the Kitáb-i-Aqdas has been studied and commented on over the past twenty-five years, what trends have emerged in scholarship, and what patterns might occur in the future study of the work. In this paper, an examination of the English-language emerging scholarship on the Kitáb-i-Aqdas provides a window into contemporary approaches to the academic study of the Bahá'í Faith, as well as into the first wave of scholarly writing on a tradition of religious legal scholarship. Perhaps unsurprisingly, a predominant observation is how dependent this nascent English-language scholarship is on importing constructs from the study of other religious systems—in particular Islam—as well as making relatively unexamined assumptions about the meaning of law in the Bahá'í context that may actually be in conflict with indigenous elements of primary Bahá'í legal texts.

Themes in the Study of the Kitáb-i-Aqdas

The publication of the translation of the Kitáb-i-Aqdas in 1992 was accompanied by a significant sense of anticipation within the Bahá'í community. The central Bahá'í governing institution, the Universal

House of Justice, drew a direct correlation between the accessibility of the text and the evolution of the Bahá'í community itself: "The accessibility to Western readers of the Kitáb-i-Aqdas in full authorized text, for the first time in one of their major languages, enormously extends the sphere of its influence, opening wider the door to a vast process of individual and community development which must certainly exert an increasingly powerful, transformative effect on peoples and nations as the Book is translated further into other languages."[6]

The Universal House of Justice also emphasized the unique status of the Kitáb-i-Aqdas within the canon of Bahá'u'lláh's writings: "A Book of such indescribable holiness is itself a symbol of the incomparable greatness of the Revelation of Bahá'u'lláh and is, indeed, a potent reminder of the high respect which is due to all that has flowed from His prodigious, truth-bearing pen. May the friends of God ever be mindful of its exalted rank among the sacred texts of the Faith; treasure it as the bread of life; regard possession of it as a sacred honor, as a priceless legacy from the Pen of the Most High, as a source of God's greatest bounty to His creatures; place their whole trust in its provisions; recite its verses; study its contents; adhere to its exhortations; and thus transform their lives in accordance with the divine standard."[7]

At various levels within the Bahá'í community, the release of the translation was accompanied by dialogue and study. In some local communities, study sessions took place both before and after the release of the text so that members could explore together the significance and meaning of the book. In various countries, Bahá'í schools held special study sessions on the text. During its conference in Montreal in 1993, the Association for Bahá'í Studies held a special one-day symposium on the Kitáb-i-Aqdas at McGill University.[8] Parallel to these opportunities for study and dialogue, some initial commentaries on the work were made accessible to the broader Bahá'í population. For example, in 1993, the Bahá'í World Center produced and distributed the monograph "The Kitáb-i-Aqdas: its place in Bahá'í Literature," which placed the book in a broader social and historical context while commenting on main themes of justice, government, law, liberty, belief, learning, family, and the advancement of civilization. Importantly, the release of the translation and these early commentaries was accompanied by reminders to the Bahá'í community of the critical fact that the laws of the Kitáb-i-Aqdas were explicitly written by Bahá'u'lláh to envision a social order for the future and were not, in many instances, designed for immediate use and application.

Around this time, the growth of scholarship on the Kitáb-i-Aqdas began to accelerate. While there had been some scholarly work prior to 1992—particularly in Persian, but also in other languages—one sees an increase and a broader diversity of works appear following the English translation and publication. To give a few examples, in addition to broad commentaries[9] and descriptions or explanations of rules,[10] works have been published on the style of language,[11] on organizing themes and key concepts,[12] on the Bahá'í concept of law,[13] and on its associated philosophical themes.[14] As well, there have been a growing number of commentaries on the book in academic journals other than those focused on Bahá'í, Islamic, or Middle Eastern studies.[15]

Six emerging trends may be identified based on a review of the secondary literature on the Kitáb-i-Aqdas since 1992: 1) the Kitáb-i-Aqdas has primarily, though not exclusively, been considered for its legal content; 2) the legal content of the Kitáb-i-Aqdas has been approached in a multiplicity of ways reflecting different perspectives on the nature of Bahá'í law; 3) analogies between the Kitáb-i-Aqdas and the Qur'án or shari'a law have been common; 4) there has been very limited consideration of the Kitáb-i-Aqdas from scholars who are not members of the Bahá'í community; 5) there are challenging issues with some of the legal content of the Kitáb-i-Aqdas with which scholars have not yet widely grappled but that will likely become an increasing area of study; 6) and reflecting the priorities of the Bahá'í community, the relationship between law and social change from a Bahá'í perspective will become an increasing area of focus in analyses of the text.

1) The Kitáb-i-Aqdas has primarily, though not exclusively, been considered for its legal content.

As one would expect, a particular focus of the study of the Kitáb-i-Aqdas to date has been its legal content. In this regard, secondary literature mirrors the emphasis on the legal dimensions of the work made explicit in Bahá'í primary literature. For example, as the Universal House of Justice describes:

The Law of God for this Dispensation addresses the needs of the entire human family. There are laws in the Kitáb-i-Aqdas which are directed primarily to the members of a specific section of humanity and can be immediately understood by them but which, at first reading, may be obscure to people of a different culture. Such, for example, is the law prohibiting the confession of sins to a fellow human being which, though understandable by those of Christian background, may puzzle others. Many laws relate to those of past Dispensations, especially the two most recent ones, those of Muḥammad and the Báb embodied in the Qur'án and the Bayán. Nevertheless, although certain ordinances of the Aqdas have such a focused reference, they also have universal implications. Through His Law, Bahá'u'lláh gradually unveils the significance of the new levels of knowledge and behaviour to which the peoples of the world are being called. He embeds His precepts in a setting of spiritual commentary, keeping ever before the mind of the reader the principle that these laws, no matter the subject with which they deal, serve the manifold purposes of bringing tranquility to human society, raising the standard of human behaviour, increasing the range of human understanding, and spiritualizing the life of each and all. Throughout, it is the relationship of the individual soul to God and the fulfilment of its spiritual destiny that is the ultimate aim of the laws of religion. "*Think not*," is Bahá'u'lláh's own assertion, "*that We have revealed unto you a mere code of laws. Nay, rather, We have unsealed the choice Wine with the fingers of might and power."* His Book of Laws is His *"weightiest testimony unto all people, and the proof of the All-Merciful unto all who are in heaven and all who are on earth."*[16]

This focus follows a long tradition in the Bahá'í Faith of associating the Kitáb-i-Aqdas with its legal content, while another book of Bahá'u'lláh—the Kitáb-i-Íqán (The Book of Certitude), written in 1861—is viewed as His central doctrinal work.

Within this context, the secondary literature presents a mix of both descriptive and analytical works. Some of the full monographs examining the Kitáb-i-Aqdas have compared it to other religious texts.[17] Shorter pieces have also tended to offer a range of analytical and critical perspectives on legal aspects of the work including, for example, its treatment of equality.[18]

At the same time, the Kitáb-i-Aqdas is not merely a book of laws but reveals a complex spiritual universe. As the term "Mother Book" suggests, the Kitáb-i-Aqdas may be thought of as encapsulating core concepts and themes that run throughout Bahá'u'lláh's revelation. From this perspective, the Kitáb-i-Aqdas contains fundamental teachings on theological, epistemological, and social themes. Some of these themes are expressed through legal statements, and others are communicated through spiritual exhortation, ethical precepts, messages to rulers and leaders, and descriptions of the nature of God, the Manifestation, and human reality. For example, the Kitáb-i-Aqdas opens with five short paragraphs discussing the nature of God, the station of the Manifestation of God, the spiritual nature of human beings, and the relationship between human beings and the Divine. This is immediately followed in paragraphs 6 to 19 by a discussion of how to live the spiritual life—which includes the laws regarding prayer, meditation, and fasting—as well as the foundations for social relations, such as the importance of not speaking or acting in ways that are harmful to others.

It is worth highlighting this broad content of the Kitáb-i-Aqdas because the focus placed on the legal dimensions of the book necessarily results in a concentration on the place of law within the Bahá'í revelation that may limit the scope of its analysis. Certainly, as in past scriptures, law does have a central role. But the role of law in the Bahá'í Faith has distinct elements as well. These include (1) the sharp break from the legal traditions in Islam that emphasized the primacy of rules covering all aspects of life and the necessity for blind obedience (*taqlíd*); (2) the historical pattern of application of law, which in the case of the Bahá'í Faith involves the conscious and purposeful delay in the application of the law; (3) the role of individual knowledge and love in relation to obedience to the law; and (4) the emphasis on law in practice as a dynamic and contextual phenomenon.[19]

It should be expected that broader approaches to the study and consideration of the Kitáb-i-Aqdas will be encouraged and continue to emerge. Indeed, such a broadening of perspective would aid in the understanding of the book as a legal text because it would deepen our knowledge of the distinct nature of the Bahá'í concept of law itself. Too often a legal orientation to the text translates into a narrow focus on rules and a discourse about the book as being a set of rules. As has been discussed in some secondary literature, appropriate consideration given to the social and political theory elements, in addition to the theological and ontological ones, helps inform a more nuanced understanding of the concept of law itself in the Bahá'í Faith and highlight some of its distinctive elements while correcting the tendency to be overly focused on rules.[20]

2) The legal content of the Kitáb-i-Aqdas has been approached in a multiplicity of ways, reflecting different perspectives on the nature of Bahá'í law.

The approach to the translation and dissemination of the Kitáb-i-Aqdas has created significant space for diverse discourses about Bahá'í law to emerge organically and begin to develop in terms of their sophistication and complexity. This, in turn, has encouraged a dynamic in the Bahá'í community where there does not appear to be overly rigid or fixed notions of the law, its meaning, and its application. Generally, Bahá'í community life has not adopted a particularly rigid and legalistic focus.

When the Universal House of Justice released the translation of the Kitáb-i-Aqdas in 1993 it was made clear that the release did not indicate a change in the applicability of the laws.[21] As well, the release of the Kitáb-i-Aqdas was not accompanied by an increase in legislative activity by Bahá'í institutions.[22] The Universal House of Justice has authority to determine if or when laws in the Kitáb-i-Aqdas may come into force and to devise and enact new laws to supplement them. There has been no demonstrable or measureable increase in the use of that authority over the past quarter century. Similarly, there has not been any significant change in the roles and responsibilities of other Bahá'í institutions regarding their legal functions. For example, the range of laws and the scope of the role of Bahá'í institutions currently remains somewhat limited.[23] At the same time, guidance on how these roles are to be fulfilled has maintained a focus on flexibility and the importance of context.[24]

As a result, a number of distinct narratives and approaches to understanding and using Bahá'í law have emerged in the scholarly literature on the Kitáb-i-Aqdas. This, in some ways, reflects Bahá'u'lláh's own encouragement for individuals to seek out their own study and understanding of the text: "In such a manner hath the Kitáb-i-Aqdas been revealed that it attracteth and embraceth all the divinely appointed Dispensations. Blessed those who peruse it! Blessed those who apprehend it! Blessed those who meditate upon it! Blessed those who ponder its meaning! So vast is its range that it hath encompassed all men ere their recognition of it. Erelong will its sovereign power, its pervasive influence and the greatness of its might be manifested on earth."[25]

In terms of the various discourses that have developed (though all are in their relative infancy), Bahá'í law has been analyzed from the following perspectives:

- as a religious law building upon previous scriptures;[26]
- as a set of rules for individual conduct and social organization that are critical for human salvation;[27]
- as a distinct concept of law that challenges predominant religious and secular concepts of law;[28]
- and as having a particular role in social change.[29]

This focus on the legal dimensions of the text and the diversity of approaches is not without some tensions. For example, some of the scholarly discourse reflects the differences between textualist approaches that emphasize how the Kitáb-i-Aqdas establishes new sets of rules, and other approaches that underscore the importance of how Bahá'í law has been used in practice and how this practice affects our understanding of law, legal processes, and legal structures. In some respects, this debate mirrors elements of the next trend regarding analogies between Bahá'í and Islamic law.

3) Analogies between the Kitáb-i-Aqdas and the Qur'án or Shari'a law have been common.

It is worth highlighting the particular insistence of much of the secondary literature on drawing analogies between the Qur'án or shari'a law and the Kitáb-i-Aqdas. There are some foundations in the primary literature for drawing such a comparison. For example, in regard to the nature of divine revelation generally, Shoghi Effendi states, "the Qur'án should be to some extent studied by the Bahá'ís but they certainly need not seek to acquire a mastery over it, which would take years, unless they really want to. All Divine Revelation seems to have been thrown out in flashes. The Prophets never composed treatises. That is why in the Qur'án and our own Writings different subjects are so often included in one Tablet. It pulsates, so to speak. That is why it is 'Revelation.'"[30]

A number of works discuss how the structure of the Kitáb-i-Aqdas is apparently similar to that of the Qur'án and how the articulation of laws is analogous to the way shari'a law is expressed. For example, John Walbridge writes:

In style and content the Aqdas is to be compared to the Qur'an, a work in which legislation is often alluded to rather than expounded and in which disparate topics are placed together without obvious logic. In the case of the Qur'an, this might be because it is pieced together from many distinct revelations, some very short. The Aqdas follows the stylistic conventions of the Qur'an, and thus is not bound to a rigid outline, but it may also have been shaped by similar factors. . . . It seems possible that the text grew gradually from a nucleus of the initial section. . . . According to this theory, Bahá'u'lláh would gradually have added material, probably often in answer to specific questions asked by believers.[31]

Other studies observe stylistic analogies between the Qur'án and the Kitáb-i-Aqdas. For example, Bushrui comments on these similarities and the fact that they are perhaps more pronounced in the Kitáb-i-Aqdas than in some of Bahá'u'lláh's other writings.[32]

Another example of using the Qur'án as a reference point is the effort to understand the laws of the Kitáb-i-Aqdas through comparisons to shari'a law or, more broadly, Islamic legal traditions.[33] In some respects, this is a necessary part of uncovering some of the meanings and implications of the work, as Bahá'u'lláh makes both explicit and implicit references to the Islamic context in which He lived and in which the Kitáb-i-Aqdas was revealed. For example, Bahá'u'lláh uses Quran'ic allusions and metaphors from the outset of the text—from the story of Joseph to the meaning of "wine."[34] Moreover, a number of the laws are specifically expressed in contrast to Islamic traditions, such as His statement that He has "relieved" the faithful from the more onerous obligatory prayer requirements that existed in previous dispensations.[35] Thus, explanations of this context are vital to understanding aspects of this work. This is reflected in Shoghi Effendi's injunction that the Kitáb-i-Aqdas be heavily annotated when translated and published,[36] thus resulting in the "notes" that accompany the text, many of which concern Quran'ic or Islamic context.

Concurrent to this Quran'ic line of focus in the secondary literature is the emergence of some scholarship that points to the significant limitations of using Quran'ic and Islamic touchstones for the study of the Kitáb-i-Aqdas. For example, I have argued elsewhere that the Bahá'í concept of law represents a fundamental deviation from the Islamic one and, indeed, a radical rejection of predominant Islamic legal traditions.[37] This includes an explicit rejection of the tradition of development of law by scholars (*usul al-fiqh*), a new emphasis on conscious knowledge and love as the rationale for adherence to the law, and a contextual imperative for the application of divine laws in human lives and communities. From this perspective, rather than relying upon an Islamic analog, Bahá'u'lláh's intent is to transform conceptions of law. He does this both by speaking explicitly to His most immediate audience familiar with the Qur'án and by addressing more broadly and generally—through religious, philosophical, social, and historical references—humanity's understanding, use, and experience of law. This line of reasoning suggests that, perhaps inadvertently, elements of the legalistic orientation found in predominant Islamic traditions are being imported into the study and analysis of Bahá'í law—a tendency that should be challenged.

4) There has been very limited consideration of the Kitáb-i-Aqdas from scholars who are not members of the Bahá'í community.

The scholarship produced on the Kitáb-i-Aqdas has almost exclusively been the fruit of work by members of the Bahá'í community, and, as such, much of it has the tenor of apologetics. There are some references to aspects of the Kitáb-i-Aqdas in literature by non-Bahá'í scholars—particularly from the disciplines of Iranian, Middle Eastern, and Islamic studies—but there has been little in-depth analysis or commentary.[38]

It is perhaps surprising that in a quarter century, the central written work of the Bahá'í religious system has not garnered broader scholarly attention outside the Bahá'í community. From one perspective, this lack of attention might be considered symptomatic of the fact that the study of the Bahá'í Faith generally remains in its infancy. It reflects a range of demographic and contextual factors, including the fact that the Bahá'í community is relatively small and generally does not attract significant attention from, nor is a source of public conflict with, the state—outside of its Iranian homeland, where the Bahá'í community is subject to ongoing persecution—since its teachings enjoin adherence to domestic laws and pose serious limitations to seeking political roles and power.

From another perspective, this lack of attention could also be partially accounted for by the general pattern of backgrounding, or giving limited attention to, the application of Bahá'í law within the Bahá'í community—a pattern that has been evident since the founding of the religion and is a reflection of the Bahá'í concept of law. As has been documented in detail elsewhere, the rationale for this backgrounding includes the commitment to the establishment of certain social contexts and forms of both individual and shared knowledge and understanding before the coercive force of law becomes applicable.[39] For example, there are laws (such as those related to dowry and length of engagement before marriage) that currently apply to Bahá'ís of Iranian heritage—the majority of whose families have been part of the Bahá'í community for multiple generations—but not to Bahá'ís of non-Iranian heritage. Furthermore, Bahá'u'lláh Himself raised caution about how the laws are used and advised that they must be observed with "tact and wisdom" so that "nothing might happen that could cause disturbance and dissension."[40]

The delay in making the Kitáb-i-Aqdas widely accessible, as well as the delay in the application of the laws, are reflections of this pattern of backgrounding. With such a pattern in place, it is no surprise that the small amount of secondary literature by scholars outside the Bahá'í community would focus on matters other than Bahá'í law.

One might expect that, at some point, the study of the central text of the Bahá'í religion will attract more scholarly interest as the study of the Bahá'í Faith continues to grow and evolve. We might anticipate that, specific to Bahá'í law, the growth of scholarly attention to Islamic societies and the increasing interest in the political, religious, and social trends that have led to contemporary realities may eventually engender some interest in the Bahá'í Faith and its particular legal tradition. Setting aside the specifics of theological claims, the Bahá'í Faith historically, culturally, and socially represents a distinct religious movement that emerged from within an Islamic society at a time of great significance to the understanding of geopolitical trends and currents today. The Bahá'í Faith's commitment to democratization and globalism, its rejection of religious fanaticism and clerical power, and its system of grassroots governance focused on the empowerment of local communities further adds to the Faith's contemporary relevance. The shift one sees in the Bahá'í legal imagination from the predominant strands of thought and practice within Islamic legal orthodoxy is a central element and expression of the distinctive Bahá'í response to political, social, and cultural challenges of the day. It can be said that the study of the Bahá'í Faith, and the place of law within the Bahá'í order, will increasingly provide a unique perspective that is valuable for understanding current realities, challenges, and opportunities.

However, there are, as suggested in the next section, issues that may give rise to tensions with public and legal discourses. Also, it remains uncertain when the study of the Kitáb-i-Aqdas will broaden into a subject matter of scholarly interest beyond the Bahá'í community itself.

5) There are challenging issues with some of the legal content of the Kitáb-i-Aqdas with which scholars have not yet widely grappled, but which will become an increasing area of study.

One result of the lack of an extensive culture of study of and inquiry into the Kitáb-i-Aqdas is that significant potential challenges and flashpoints with the content of the book have not yet been explored, analyzed, or understood in much depth. The most well-known of these issues involve Bahá'í standards of sexual morality (in particular, though not solely, related to homosexuality),[41] gender equality (especially concerns that some elements of the text might be interpreted as reinforcing male dominance),[42] and harsh punishments (such as the potential for the death penalty for crimes such as murder).[43] More generally, to the contemporary reader in many parts of the world, the text of the Kitáb-i-Aqdas can be quite disorienting, with implicit and explicit allusions to a vast range of other scriptures primarily from Islamic and Bábí traditions. One aspect of these references is that the text appears to spend significant time (for a very short work) on seemingly obscure and insignificant matters. This combination of covering vast terrain—including many high-profile issues for both individuals and society—in a condensed style, one that uses an economy of diction within the span of a short book, creates an extremely challenging text to use and understand, particularly with respect to subject matter that is potentially controversial in the contemporary world.

Certainly these and other challenging issues are matters of interest to the broader discourse within Bahá'í community life and to those who are inquiring about the Bahá'í Faith. Most commonly, they are debated and discussed through the lens of contemporary standards, modes of discourse, and mores.

Having said that, some of the challenging or controversial issues raised in the Kitáb-i-Aqdas have been approached in the secondary literature. For example, the issue of gender equality in the Bahá'í Faith has received scholarly attention—some of which is on the specific dimensions of gender equality in the Kitáb-i-Aqdas—producing many distinct understandings of the Bahá'í concept of equality and its relationship to contemporary ideas and practices. It is not clear, at this point, whether there is a predominant approach to defining or conceptualizing the Bahá'í understanding of gender equality and how that incontrovertible aspect of Bahá'u'lláh's teachings may be squared with apparent gender preferences in Bahá'í law (such as in the context of Bahá'í inheritance law in cases of intestacy). At the same time, particularly helpful analyses have been developed about the general approach to equality—such as the vision of complementarity described by John S. Hatcher or the focus on changing legal and institutional structures presented by Schweitz—and about how specific laws, such as inheritance laws, might be understood in ways that challenge assumptions that they reflect a form of gender inequality. Bahá'í sexual ethics, including teachings about homosexuality, have received limited scholarly attention, and the majority of the studies remain somewhat descriptive of the teachings instead of being analytical and conceptual in nature.[44] Bahá'í concepts of criminal punishment, including the death penalty, have been the subject of only a few commentaries.[45]

The literature on these challenging topics is minimal, and it is also fair to observe that the modes of inquiry they represent are somewhat limited. As would be expected, there is some focus on how Bahá'u'lláh's writings on these subjects relate to, reflect, or deviate from norms of the nineteenth-century Islamic context in which the Bahá'í Faith was born, as well as contemporary norms in various societies. Needless to say, there is a need for more analysis that interprets and locates these issues within the framework of Bahá'u'lláh's teachings as a whole and that considers them in relation to His concept of law, in relation to how

Bahá'í law operates and is understood, and, more broadly, in relation to Bahá'u'lláh's vision of the future.[46]

Bahá'u'lláh explicitly envisions many of His laws for a future society that has the understanding and the capacity to apply them and a social context that is receptive and conducive to their use.[47] For this reason, He also mandates that the laws contained in the Kitáb-i-Aqdas do not apply unless the Universal House of Justice explicitly states that they do.[48]

In-depth analysis may reveal very different perspectives on how these issues can be coherently located within the overarching and unyielding commitment of the Bahá'í Faith to advancing conditions of social justice, equality, and peace for all citizens of the world as part of an expression of the central Bahá'í teaching of the oneness of humanity. Regardless of the specific topic, we can expect that greater attention will be paid by the emerging scholarship to these and other significant and far-reaching issues contained in the Kitáb-i-Aqdas. We can also foresee how some of these topics may lead to conflicts with contemporary perspectives and norms. To better understand these potential areas of tension, there is a need to expand the diversity of approaches to the analysis of the Kitáb-i-Aqdas with respect to these issues, including grounding analysis in the particular and distinct Bahá'í concept of law and its approach to operation and implementation. As noted earlier, this includes considering the implications of having a divine model of law that is contingent on certain social contexts and environments for its application, as well as the requirement that law be followed out of conscious knowledge and active love. Such a focus may well provide a different understanding of the nature of these teachings, their implications for the daily lives of individuals and communities, and their coherence with other Bahá'í writings and teachings.

6) Reflecting the priorities of the Bahá'í community, the relationship between law and social change from a Bahá'í perspective will become an area of increasing focus in understanding the text.

The ways in which law is a force for advancing or inhibiting social change is one common lens through which law is thought about and analyzed. This is true historically in religious contexts—where we see the implementation of new laws as a foundation for engendering religious norms in individuals and societies—and in liberal democracies today where the enactment, implementation, and interpretation of law can be significant factors in struggles around matters of equality, fairness, and justice. Law can be used to shape and bind the actions of individuals, groups, organizations, corporations, and governments; and in various ways it can be a source for reinforcing or changing existing patterns.

While there will always be a relationship between law and social change, the way law plays this role, and the degree to which law is utilized in this regard, is a matter of choice and design. Law may be the leading driver in ensuring a particular social reality, or it may be a late actor, following the emergence of a particular context or set of understandings. As well, the degree to which we explicitly and consciously consider how laws may shape, impact, or change social realities may vary. Sometimes we may focus quite explicitly on how a particular law may be used to form a specific social condition. At the same time, however, our decision to enact laws may be motivated by a whole host of other interests unconnected to their capacity to shape a particular social reality, from particular and special interests, to otherworldly considerations, to desired collateral objectives.

As noted earlier, in the Bahá'í community, the historic pattern of backgrounding Bahá'í law relates to a particular conception of the relationship between law and social change. In particular, it suggests— unlike, for example, the Islamic legal context—a deemphasis of the role of law in shaping a spiritualized society. Instead of having a focus on law to effect change in different societies, Bahá'ís focus on systems of knowledge and understanding and systems of social awareness and cohesion, and they strive to ensure that these systems are in place before Bahá'í laws have an extensive role to play.

This pattern reflects a broader and increasingly popular orientation in the Bahá'í community to creating the epistemic infrastructure that leads to the emergence of particular social patterns. This approach is distinct from the development of sets of laws and the imposition of those laws. For example, a major thrust of Bahá'í activity today is engagement in social action and participation in influencing and deepening people's understanding of how the principles of unity, equality, and justice may be applied to various public discourses on matters of key interest to the welfare of humanity:

> Effective social action serves to enrich participation in the discourses of society, just as the insights gained from engaging in certain discourses can help to clarify the concepts that shape social action. . . . [I]nvolvement in public discourse can range from an act as simple as introducing Bahá'í ideas into everyday conversation to more formal activities such as the preparation of articles and attendance at gatherings, dedicated to themes of social concern—climate change and the environment, governance and human rights, to mention a few. It entails, as well, meaningful interactions with civic groups and local organizations in villages and neighbourhoods.[49]

The Bahá'í focus on influencing and participating in discourses as a mechanism for social change is quite different, for example, than having a religious community advocate for particular changes in laws that might reflect its social teachings. It is also different from engaging in the world at large for the purpose of achieving converts: "It will be important for all to recognize that the value of engaging in social action and public discourse is not to be judged by the ability to bring enrolments. Though endeavours in these two areas of activity may well effect an increase in the size of the Bahá'í community, they are not undertaken for this purpose. Sincerity in this respect is an imperative."[50]

This particular construction of the relationship between law and social change in the Bahá'í Faith suggests an approach to the study of the Kitáb-i-Aqdas that is largely unexplored. In some respects, the fact that much of the Kitáb-i-Aqdas is aimed at a social order that is in the distant future has perhaps limited exploration into what the text, particularly in its treatment of Bahá'í law, has to say about how change toward new patterns of social order may emerge, including implications for contemporary social debates and how law and its coercive power are employed or withheld on the path of progress.

Conclusion

To students of law and religion, a topic of great importance is how a religious community interacts with its laws, develops modes of legal interpretation and practice, and evolves its understandings of the role of law in religious life. In the case of the Bahá'í Faith, we are seeing the earliest stages of these processes, with the last quarter century being the first period of time when the Bahá'í community and scholarly attention in the West have turned to the question of Bahá'í law in any demonstrable way. What has emerged to date is an eclectic and diverse set of understandings and approaches to the study of Bahá'í law that reflects a community in which law is still only a gradually emerging preoccupation. At the same time, the upcoming decades will probably see an acceleration of legally focused dialogue and development and the emergence of approaches to understanding Bahá'í law that are more indigenous in character and that uniquely address and contribute to the prevailing, but highly varied, public and legal discourses about the needs of human societies.

Notes

1 / Some Reflections on the Concept of Law in the Bahá'í Faith

1. While the Bahá'í Faith emerged in nineteenth-century Iran and is to-day one of the most geographically widespread religions, its number of adherents remains quite small, estimated in the five-to-six million range.

2. For a discussion of this pattern of backgrounding, see Roshan Danesh, "The Politics of Delay—Social Meanings and the Historical Treatment of Bahá'í Law."

3. For example, the preeminent English-language academic journal on the relationship between law and religion—the *Journal of Law and Religion*—has published only three articles (by two authors) on Bahá'í law even though the journal has been looking to publish more articles on this subject.

4. Two influential historical studies of Islamic law are: Joseph Schacht, *An Introduction to Islamic Law* (Oxford: Oxford University Press), 1982, and Noel Coulson, *A History of Islamic Law* (Edinburgh: Edinburgh University Press), 1964. A recent overview text is Wael B. Hallaq, *An Introduction to Islamic Law* (Cambridge: Cambridge University Press), 2009. Generally, fewer works are specifically focused on Shi'i law, though academic literature on that subject has been growing. An overview work is Hossein Modarressi, *An Introduction to Shi'i Law: A Bibliographical Study* (London: Ithaca Press), 1984.

5. For a good overview of key concepts of Islamic law, such as *ijtihád*, particularly in the Sunni context, see Frank Vogel, *Islamic Law and Legal System: Studies of Saudi Arabia.*

6. In the form of Shi'ism that is predominant in Iran, it is believed that the twelfth Imam, Muhammad Ibn al-Hasan, disappeared from human

229

view by going into occultation (*ghayba*). Shi'ites refer to the twelfth Imam as the Mahdi and await his reappearance as the savior for humanity. Bahá'ís consider the Báb to be the Mahdi.

7. For a general overview of Shi'ism and its history and theology, see Moojan Momen, *An Introduction to Shi'i Islam* (New Haven: Yale University Press), 1987. There is an extensive and growing body of writing about *ijtihád*. For an analysis of *ijtihád* in Shi'i Islam, including contemporary debates, see Esmat al-Sadat Tabatabei Lotfi, *Ijtihád in Twelver Shiism: The Interpretation and Application of Islamic Law in the Context of Changing Muslim Society,* PhD thesis, University of Leeds, 1999.

8. Shoghi Effendi refers to the revelation of the Kitáb-i-Aqdas as perhaps "the most signal act" of Bahá'u'lláh and describes it as the "Charter of the future world civilization" (Shoghi Effendi, *God Passes By,* 337–38).

9. Bahá'u'lláh, The Kitáb-i-Aqdas, 3, 18.

10. Bahá'u'lláh, The Kitáb-i-Íqán, ¶15.

11. This does not mean there is not a veneration of learning. Bahá'u'lláh praises those who are learned in His religion.

12. Danesh, "The Politics of Delay—Social Meanings and the Historical Treatment of Bahá'í Law," *World Order* 35.3.

13. Shoghi Effendi began a "Synopsis and Codification" of the Kitáb-i-Aq das, which was completed after his passing and published in 1973. The Universal House of Justice published the first authorized translation into English in 1992. Translations into other languages were completed based on the English translation.

14. Letter dated October 7, 1993, written on behalf of the Universal House of Justice to an individual.

15. Bahá'u'lláh, The Kitáb-i-Aqdas, ¶2, ¶7, ¶36.

16. Ibid., ¶5.

17. Saiedi, "An Introduction to 'Abdu'l-Bahá's *The Secret of Divine Civilization,*" *Converging Realities,* 1.1. https://bahai-library.com/saiedi_introduction_sdc. March 21, 2014.

18. 'Abdu'l-Bahá, *The Secret of Divine Civilization,* ¶2, ¶6, ¶175.

19. Ibid., ¶175, ¶185.

20. Bahá'u'lláh, The Kitáb-i-Aqdas, ¶1.

21. *Usul al-fiqh* is the study of the principles in Islamic jurisprudence that outlines the legitimate sources of law and how those sources may be used to derive rules. There are some differences between the science of

law in Sunni and Shi'i Islam which are in part responsible for the legal diversity within Sunnism and Shi'ism.

22. Bahá'u'lláh, The Kitáb-i-Aqdas, ¶2.

23. Ibid., ¶5.

24. Ibid., ¶5.

25. Ibid., ¶5.

26. Research Department at the Bahá'í World Center. Memorandum to the Universal House of Justice dated August 14, 1996, quoted in Schaefer, *Bahá'í Ethics in Light of Scripture,* vol. 2, 696–97.

27. Bahá'u'lláh, The Kitáb-i-Aqdas, ¶3, ¶4.

28. 'Abdu'l-Bahá, *Selections from the Writings of 'Abdu'l-Bahá,* no. 12.1.

29. Bahá'u'lláh, The Kitáb-i-Aqdas, ¶4, ¶125.

30. Ibid., ¶160.

31. The Huqúqu'lláh or "The Right of God" is considered a spiritual bounty and obligation and involves paying a certain percentage on accumulated wealth, but only when one has accrued wealth in excess of a base amount after all other financial obligations have been discharged.

32. Some examples are specific details regarding the law of marriage, which have been applied to differing degrees at various times to Bahá'ís of Iranian descent.

33. Some examples of this are abortion and use and choice of contraceptives.

34. Research Department at the Bahá'í World Center. Memorandum to the Universal House of Justice dated August 14, 1996, quoted in Schaefer, *Bahá'í Ethics in Light of Scripture* vol. 2, 698.

35. Baháu'lláh, The Kitáb-i-Aqdas, ¶99.

36. Ibid., p. 98.

37. Ibid., note 74.

38. Bahá'u'lláh, quoted in Bahá'u'lláh, The Kitáb-i-Aqdas, 6.

39. Baháu'lláh, quoted in Bahá'u'lláh, The Kitáb-i-Aqdas, 6–7.

40. Approaches to academic study of Bahá'í law are discussed in Roshan Danesh, "Imagining Bahá'í Law," *Bahá'í Studies Review* 14.1 (2007): 97–105.

2 / Some Reflections on the Structure of the Kitáb-i-Aqdas

1. One example of an exception to the view that the Kitáb-i-Aqdas is unstructured is provided by Nader Saiedi in *Logos and Civilization.* Saiedi

challenges the assumption that the Kitáb-i-Aqdas is a "random listing of unrelated laws" and suggests that the laws have "meaningful connections" (266). He provides a relatively detailed scheme for the organization of the paragraphs of the book, around a number of core principles.

2. Walbridge, "Kitab-i Aqdas, The Most Holy Book." https://bahai-library.com/walbridge_encyclopedia_kitab_aqdas.

3. Schaefer, "An Introduction to Bahá'í Law: Doctrinal Foundations, Principles, and Structures," *Journal of Law and Religion* 18, no. 2 (2002–2003): 308–69.

4. Taherzadeh, *The Revelation of Bahá'u'lláh, Volume 3: 'Akká, The Early Years, 1868–77,* 277.

5. Walbridge, "Kitab-i Aqdas, The Most Holy Book." https://bahai-library.com/walbridge_encyclopedia_kitab_aqdas.

6. See Danesh, "Some Reflections on the Concept of Law in the Bahá'í Faith," *Journal of Bahá'í Studies* 24.1–2 (2014).

7. Bahá'u'lláh, The Kitáb-i-Aqdas, ¶1.

8. Bahá'u'lláh's concept of law, including His legal language, and the relationship of law to the human soul, as well as to Bahá'í teaching regarding unity, are discussed in some detail in Roshan Danesh, "Some Reflections on the Concept of Law in the Bahá'í Faith," *Journal of Bahá'í Studies* 24.1–2. This article is a companion to that previous piece.

9. 'Abdu'l-Bahá, Lawh-i-Aflak (Tablet of the Universe). Provisional translation. Mar. 2014. https://bahai-library.com/abdulbaha_lawh_aflakiyyih.

10. 'Abdu'l-Bahá, *Selections from the Writings of 'Abdu'l-Bahá,* no. 103.4.

11. Bahá'u'lláh revealed three obligatory prayers. Each prayer has specific observances to be followed, such as the time at which it is to be recited. Bahá'ís may choose which one of the three prayers to say daily. On the last month of the Bahá'í calendar, fasting is enjoined from sunrise to sunset. Fasting is intended to serve a number of purposes, including providing a time of heightened consciousness on one's spiritual being. Bahá'ís are also instructed to repeat "Alláh-u-Abhá" (God is Most Glorious) ninety-five times a day (Bahá'u'lláh, Kitáb-i-Aqdas, ¶18).

12. Taherzadeh, *The Revelation of Bahá'u'lláh, Volume 3: 'Akká, The Early Years, 1868–77,* 276–77.

13. Hatcher, "Unsealing the Choice Wine at the Family Reunion," 28.

14. Saiedi, *Logos and Civilization: Spirit, History, and Order in the Writings of Bahá'u'lláh,* 264.

15. Bahá'u'lláh, The Kitáb-i-Aqdas, ¶19.
16. Universal House of Justice, in Bahá'u'lláh, The Kitáb-i-Aqas, 3.
17. Research Department, Memorandum to the Universal House of Justice dated August 14, 1996, in Schaefer, *Bahá'í Ethics in Light of Scripture*, vol. 2, 697.
18. Saiedi, *Logos and Civilization: Spirit, History, and Order in the Writings of Bahá'u'lláh*, 242.
19. Bahá'u'lláh, *Gleanings from the Writings of Bahá'u'lláh*, no. 139.5.
20. Bahá'u'lláh, *Tablets of Bahá'u'lláh*, 85.
21. Bahá'u'lláh, *Gleanings from the Writings of Bahá'u'lláh*, no. 111.1.
22. Saiedi, *Logos and Civilization: Spirit, History, and Order in the Writings of Bahá'u'lláh*, 243–44.
23. Ibid., 244.
24. It is important to note that Bahá'u'lláh often employs the metaphor of the "sword" to refer to the human tongue.
25. Saiedi makes a similar observation about paragraph 19. He states that "we can see that what is common among all of the acts prohibited in this verse is the violation of the sanctity and dignity of the human being: murder, adultery, and backbiting involve treating human beings as inferior or as objects" (Saiedi, *Logos and Civilization: Spirit, History, and Order in the Writings of Bahá'u'lláh*, 267). It should also be noted that Saiedi interprets the reference to prohibitions in paragraph 19 as being a reference to laws and prohibitions in other religious Holy Books.
26. Saiedi, *Logos and Civilization: Spirit, History, and Order in the Writings of Bahá'u'lláh*, 267.
27. Universal House of Justice, in Bahá'u'lláh, The Kitáb-i-Aqdas, 1–2.
28. Ibid., 7.
29. Ibid., 9.
30. Research Department at the Bahá'í World Center. Memorandum dated August 14, 1996 to the Universal House of Justice, in Schaefer, *Bahá'í Ethics in Light of Scripture*, vol. 2, 697.
31. Ibid., 696.
32. Ibid, 698.
33. Bahá'u'lláh, The Kitáb-i-Aqdas, ¶5.
34. Research Department at the Bahá'í World Center. Memorandum dated August 14, 1996 to the Universal House of Justice, in Schaefer, *Bahá'í Ethics in Light of Scripture*, vol. 2., 696.

35. Alai, "Kitáb-i-Aqdas as Described and Glorified by Shoghi Effendi," 23.
36. Bahá'u'lláh, The Kitáb-i-Aqdas, ¶99.

3 / The Politics of Delay—Social Meanings and the Historical Treatment of Bahá'í Law

1. Siyyid 'Ali-Muhammad, known as the Báb (1819–50), is considered by Bahá'ís to be an independent Manifestation of God bearing an independent revelation from God, the central message of which is concerned with the impending appearance of Bahá'u'lláh. Bahá'ís consider the revelation of the Báb to have the status of scripture and view the Bábí Faith as a precursor to the Bahá'í Faith. Historically, the vast majority of early Bahá'ís were Bábís. Today, no Bábí community remains.
2. Ficicchia, *Der Bahaismus-Weltreligion der Zukunft? Geschichte, Lehre und Organisation in kritischer Anfrage* [Bahá'ísm = Religion of the Future? History, Doctrine and Organization: A Critical Inquiry] (Stuttgart, Germany: Evangelische Zentralstelle fur Weltanschauungsfragen, 1981).
3. Ficicchia, quoted in Schaefer, "Ficicchia's Portrayal Bahá'í law," in Udo Schaefer, Nicola Towfigh, and Ulrich Gollmer, *Making the Crooked Straight: A Contribution to Bahá'í Apologetics,* 324.
4. Schaefer, "Ficicchia's Portrayal," in *Making the Crooked Straight,* 334.
5. See Schaefer, "Ficicchia's Portrayal," in *Making the Crooked Straight,* 337.
6. Ibid.
7. Ibid., 337–338.
8. Ibid., 338.
9. Ibid., 340–342.
10. Schaefer, "Ficicchia's Portrayal," in *Making the Crooked Straight,* 341.
11. See Schaefer, "Ficicchia's Portrayal," in *Making the Crooked Straight,* 343–44.
12. Ibid. In the Kitáb-i-Aqdas, Bahá'u'lláh states, "Beware that ye take not unto yourselves more wives than two. Whoso contenteth himself with a single partner from among the maidservants of God, both he and she shall live in tranquility" (The Kitáb-i-Aqda, ¶63). 'Abdu'l-Bahá and Shoghi Effendi clarified that the Bahá'í law, in fact, enjoined monogamy (see the memorandum from the Research Department of the Universal House of Justice dated June 27, 1996, titled "Monogamy, Sexual

Equality, Marital Equality, and the Supreme Tribunal," to the Universal House of Justice (https://bahai-library.com/uhj_equality_monogamy_uhj)). In this same memo, the Research Department explains this movement to a strict law of monogamy in the following terms:

The progressive clarification of the details of the laws of the Faith has been accompanied by a gradual implementation of their provisions. This principle is exemplified in relation to the law of monogamy.

It should be noted that the gradual introduction and application of certain laws which require followers to abandon their time-honored laws and practices to which they have been accustomed is not new in this Dispensation. This gradual introduction of laws may be found also in earlier religions. For example, the consumption of alcohol was common among the Arabs during the days of Muhammad. The Qur'an decrees prohibition of drinking alcohol in stages. Muhammad introduced the prohibition of alcohol in a progressive manner. At first, He said that there are advantages and disadvantages in drinking, but that the disadvantages outweigh the advantages (see Qur'an 2:219). Some time later, He counselled His followers not to perform obligatory prayers if they were intoxicated (see Qur'an 4:43), and finally, when people became accustomed to these restrictive measures, He forbade drinking altogether (see Qur'an 5:89).

13. See Schaefer, "Ficicchia's Portrayal," in *Making the Crooked Straight*, 352–62.
14. Schaefer, "Ficicchia's Portrayal," in *Making the Crooked Straight*, 337–338.
15. See Schaefer, "Ficicchia's Portrayal," in *Making the Crooked Straight*, 338–339.
16. Schaefer, "Ficicchia's Portrayal," in *Making the Crooked Straight*, 338.
17. Saiedi describes, in *Logos and Civilization: Spirit, History, and Order in the Writings of Bahá'u'lláh*, 232, the steps leading to the revelation of the Kitáb-i-Aqdas as the following:

If we look at the different tablets of Bahá'u'lláh referring to the revelation of the Kitáb-i-Aqdas, we can clearly distinguish three stages leading to that event. The first stage is the arrival, during the Edirne period, of many petitions from His followers requesting laws. In response to this first set of petitions, at the end of His stay in Edirne, Bahá'u'lláh revealed a short tablet in Persian concerning laws, but He never released the Tablet. The second stage was the arrival of further petitions, as Bahá'u'lláh says in His tablet, in "recent days." The third stage is the revelation of the Kitáb-i-Aqdas in Arabic in response to the second set of petitions.

18. See Saiedi, *Logos and Civilization*, 232.
19. Bahá'u'lláh first instructed that the Kitáb-i-Aqdas be published in 1891 in Bombay.
20. Adib Taherzadeh, a scholar of the Bahá'í Faith, observes that "from the beginning He [Bahá'u'lláh] stressed to His followers the need to be discreet and wise in the implementation of its laws" (Taherzadeh, *The Revelation of Bahá'u'lláh: 'Akka, The Early Years 1868–77*, Vol. 3, 279).
21. For example, more laws apply to Bahá'ís of Persian descent than to Bahá'ís in other parts of the world. In addition, the application of certain laws has been suspended in some contexts and for certain populations, while remaining in force for others.
22. This is made clear by the Universal House of Justice in its Introduction to the Kitáb-i-Aqdas. (See the Universal House of Justice, Introduction to Bahá'u'lláh, The Kitáb-i-Aqdas, 7).
23. The Universal House of Justice, Introduction to Bahá'u'lláh, The Kitáb-i-Aqdas, 5, quoted in Schaefer, "Ficicchia's Portrayal," in *Making the Crooked Straight*, 345.
24. Schaefer et al., *Making the Crooked Straight*, 345.
25. Some readers may resist the emphasis on the social and political aspects of the historical treatment of Bahá'í law, given the doctrine of infallibility in the Bahá'í Faith, and, in particular, in relation to the Universal House of Justice. Such resistance is misplaced. To comprehend a particular body of law, it is necessary to look at the law in action—how it is applied by institutions; how it is used by institutions, communities and individuals; and how it is understood and related to by those subject to it. While Bahá'í law in action may be impacted by the doctrine of infallibility when the Universal House of Justice is engaged in particular functions, the vast potential panorama of Bahá'í law in action in the future will not be subject to this doctrine. This is true when local,

regional, or national Bahá'í institutions are applying Bahá'í law, when individual Bahá'is interpret and strive to follow the law, and when communities establish and reinforce legally based norms.

26. Bahá'u'lláh, quoted in Universal House of Justice, Introduction to Bahá'u'lláh, The Kitáb-i-Aqdas, 6.

27. The phrase "classical Islamic legal theory" is primarily a reference to the predominant role ijtihád comes to play in Sunni Islam as early as the eighth century, and in Shi'ih Islam beginning in the thirteenth century.

28. See Weiss, The Spirit of Islamic Law, 53.

29. Vogel, Islamic Law and Legal System: Studies of Saudi Arabia, 26.

30. 'Abdul-Bahá, quoted in Universal House of Justice, Introduction to Bahá'u'lláh, The Kitáb-i-Aqdas, 5.

31. 'Abdu'l-Bahá, The Will and Testament of 'Abdu'l-Bahá, 14–15.

32. Bahá'u'lláh, The Kitáb-i-Aqdas, 87.

33. There has been an increasing amount of debate concerning the translation and meaning of Bahá'u'lláh's statement that "all matters of state should be referred to the House of Justice." For example, Juan R. I. Cole, a history professor at the University of Michigan, has argued that it has been mistranslated and that the phrase umúr-i-siyásiyyih should be translated as referring to leadership and setting punishments as opposed to the political role implied in the use of the term state. (See Juan R. I. Cole, Modernity and Millennium: The Genesis of the Baha'i Faith in the Nineteenth-Century Middle East, 96–97). Cole's translation, however, is questionable. The term siyása has a long and complicated history. The metaphor underlying the term is of a man on a horse as a symbol of effective power. Gradually, over the course of hundreds of years siyása became the term for politics in all Middle Eastern languages. See Bernard Lewis, The Political Language of Islam, 11.

Even as early as the eleventh and twelfth centuries one finds derivations on siyása with significant political connotations. In this period, the Islamic jurists intensified their attention to the public and constitutional realm. While usúl al-fiqh spoke volumes about private law, it had little to say about public law, power, and authority until al-Máwardí (972–1058) set out, in response to the erosion and demise of the Abbasid Caliphate, to incorporate public law, policy, and administration explicitly into the realm of fiqh, or Islamic jurisprudence. By the later medieval period, the principles of siyása shar'iyya, or the incorporation of public law, policy, and administration into the realm of Islamic jurisprudence, became more fully established. *Siyása shar'iyya* eventually became a central theme in Sunni Islamic thought.

34. The Universal House of Justice, letter dated July 21, 1968 to the National Spiritual Assembly of the Bahá'ís of the United States, quoted in the Universal House of Justice, Department of the Secretariat, letter dated April 27, 1995 to an individual, http://bahai-library.com/uhj/theocracy.html. Bahá'ís remain largely aloof from public debate on most political issues. For example, in North America, one would not typically find either Bahá'í institutions or individual Bahá'ís offering public opinions on how the current regulatory schemes concerning abortion, capital punishment, or same-sex marriage, to cite just a few examples, should be treated.

   Yet noninvolvement in preexisting forms of current political debate is a temporary injunction, for the Universal House of Justice states that "with the passage of time, practices in the political realm will definitely undergo the profound changes anticipated in the Bahá'í writings. As a consequence, what we understand now of the policy of non-involvement in politics will also undergo a change" (letter dated June 23, 1987 written on behalf of the Universal House of Justice to an individual, in "Prominent People: Extracts from the Bahá'í Writings and Letters Written by or on Behalf of Shoghi Effendi and the Universal House of Justice," no. 1878, in *The Compilation of Compilations: Prepared by the Universal House of Justice 1963–1990,* vol. 2.

   Restrictions on Bahá'í involvement in contemporary political institutions is not rooted in an antinomian or anti-institutional bias with Bahá'í doctrine. Rather Bahá'ís have been active in constructing an "administrative order" that, while focused on governing the internal affairs of the Bahá'í community, is expected to increasingly interact with the civil institutions in the future.

35. See Lessig, "The Regulation of Social Meaning," *The University of Chicago Law Review,* 62, no. 3 (1995): 943–1045.

36. Bahá'u'lláh, *The Seven Valleys and The Four Valleys,* 18; Bahá'u'lláh, *Tablets of Bahá'u'lláh revealed after the Kitáb-i-Aqdas,* 67.

37. Bahá'u'lláh, "Súriy-i-Haykal," in *The Summons of the Lord of Hosts,* ¶173.

38. Shoghi Effendi, *Bahá'í Administration: Selected Messages 1922–1932,* 131, 132.

39. See, for example, the work of John Rawls and Jurgen Habermas.

40. For example, Jeffery Simmonds writes, "the ultimate goal of the Bahá'í faith is the establishment of a completely Bahá'í society which means a Bahá'í state or a theocracy where religion and politics, or church and state are not separate. The Universal House of Justice will be the governing body of the world or of those states which become Bahá'í." ("The Relationship of the Laws [of the] *Kitáb-i-Aqdas* to the Laws of the Bayán of the Báb," unpublished manuscript, quoted in Sen McGlinn, "Church and State in the World Order of Bahá'u'lláh," https://bahai-library.com/mcglinn_church_state_order, unpublished manuscript on file with the author).

41. A dualistic approach is evident in the work of Sen McGlinn on church and state in the Bahá'í Faith. For example, see McGlinn, "Church and State in the World Order of Bahá'u'lláh"; McGlinn, *Church and State: A Postmodern Political Theology.*

42. Juan Cole has argued in *Modernity and Millennium* (46) that Bahá'u'lláh and 'Abdu'l-Bahá were "surely among the first major religious figures in the region" to "embrace . . . the principle of the separation of religion and state."

4 / Hegemony and Revelation: A Bahá'í Perspective on World Order

1. 'Abdu'l-Bahá, *Some Answered Questions*, no. 12.4.

2. Bahá'u'lláh, quoted in Shoghi Effendi, *The World Order of Bahá'u'lláh*, 169.

3. Shoghi Effendi, *The World Order of Bahá'u'lláh*, 168.

4. Bahá'u'lláh, The Kitáb-i-Aqdas, ¶181.

5. Shoghi Effendi, *The World Order of Bahá'u'lláh*, 203.

6. For an overview of the Bahá'í writings discussing the lesser peace, please see the letter dated April 19, 2001, written on behalf of the Universal House of Justice and the accompanying memorandum from the Research Department also dated April 19, 2001. https://www.bahai.org/library/authoritative-texts/the-universal-house-of-justice/messages/20010419_001/1#604877079.

7. Letter dated July 29, 1996 from the Universal House of Justice to an individual believer. See also the Research Department, "Attainment

of the Unity of Nations and the Lesser Peace." https://www.bahai.
org/library/authoritative-texts/the-universal-house-of-justice/messag-
es/20010419_001/1#604877079.

8. For a statement of Robert Cox's approach to world order see Cox, *Approaches to World Order.*

9. Cox, Robert and Timothy Sinclair, *Approaches to World Order.*

10. Ibid., 151–52.

11. For a discussion of the concept of "Manifestation" see Cole, *The Concept of the Manifestation in the Bahá'í Writings,* 1982.

12. In Bahá'í terminology, the recurrence throughout history of Manifestations of God bearing divine revelation is referred to as "progressive revelation."

13. The Universal House of Justice. Introduction to Bahá'u'lláh, The Kitáb-i-Aqdas: The Most Holy Book, 5

14. Shoghi Effendi, *The World Order of Bahá'u'lláh,* 202.

15. Ibid., 42.

16. 'Abdu'l-Bahá, *Selections from the Writings of 'Abdu'l-Bahá,* no. 225.24–25.

17. Bahá'u'lláh, quoted in Shoghi Effendi, *The World Order of Bahá'u'lláh,* 41.

18. Bahá'u'lláh, The Kitáb-i-Aqdas, ¶7.

19. Bahá'u'lláh, *Prayers and Meditations,* no. 176.29.

20. Ibid., no. 116.1.

21. Bahá'u'lláh, quoted in Shoghi Effendi, *The World Order of Bahá'u'lláh,* 25.

22. Bahá'u'lláh, *Gleanings from the Writings of Bahá'u'lláh,* no. 27.2.

23. Shoghi Effendi, *The World Order of Bahá'u'lláh,* 19.

24. This is seen most concretely in 'Abdu'l-Bahá's prescriptions for the reform of Iran, as outlined in *The Secret of Divine Civilization.*

25. Shoghi Effendi, *The World Order of Bahá'u'lláh,* 44.

26. Ibid., 44–45.

27. Shoghi Effendi, *The World Order of Bahá'u'lláh,* 163–64.

28. Saiedi, *Logos and Civilization: Spirit, History, and Order in the Writings of Bahá'u'lláh,* 243–44.

29. Gollmer, "Bahá'í Political Thought," in Udo Schaefer, Nicola Towfigh, and Ulrich Gollmer, *Making the Crooked Straight: A Contribution to Bahá'í Apologetics,* 438.

30. Abizadeh, "Politics Beyond War: Ulrich Gollmer's Contribution to Bahá'í Political Thought," 21.
31. Bahá'u'lláh, The Kitáb-i-Aqdas, ¶144.
32. Lessig, "The Regulation of Social Meaning," in The University of Chicago Law Review 62, no. 3: 943–1045.
33. Bahá'u'lláh, The Seven Valleys and the Four Valleys, 29.
34. Taherzadeh, The Covenant of Bahá'u'lláh, 389–90.
35. For example, Juan Cole has argued that Bahá'u'lláh and 'Abdu'l-Bahá were "surely among the first major religious figures in the region" to "embrace . . . the principle of the separation of religion and state" (Modernity and the Millennium: The Genesis of the Bahá'í Faith in the Nineteenth-Century Middle East, 46).
36. The Universal House of Justice discusses the issues related to religion and order in a letter dated April 27, 1995, available at https://www.bahai.org/library/authoritative-texts/the-universal-house-of-justice/messages/19950427_001/1#985937741. See also Danesh (2004, 2008–9). Please see fuller discussion of these themes in Chapter 5 of this book.
37. Shoghi Effendi, Directives from the Guardian, 79.
38. Bahá'u'lláh, The Kitáb-i-Aqdas, note 189.
39. Universal House of Justice, "Establishment of Regional Councils." https://www.bahai.org/library/authoritative-texts/the-universal-house-of-justice/messages/19970530_001/1#812063594.
40. Danesh, "The Politics of Delay: Social Meanings and the Historical Treatment of Bahá'í Law," World Order 35, no. 3: 34–37.

5 / Church and State in the Bahá'í Faith: An Epistemic Approach

1. Taherzadeh, The Covenant of Bahá'u'lláh, 143–44) (including a full translation of Bahá'u'lláh's Book of the Covenant into English). See also Bahá'u'lláh, Tablet of the Branch. https://www.bahai.org/library/authoritative-texts/bahaullah/days-remembrance/6#107577136.
2. See Shoghi Effendi, God Passes By, chs. 14–21 for details on 'Abdu'l-Bahá's life.
3. Bahá'u'lláh, The Kitáb-i-Aqdas, ¶30.
4. Ibid., ¶42.
5. Bahá'u'lláh, The Mystery of God, note 1, 204–7.
6. 'Abdu'l-Bahá, Will and Testament of 'Abdu'l-Bahá.
7. Shoghi Effendi, The World Order of Bahá'u'lláh, 9, 19, 143–157.

8. The Universal House of Justice currently comprises nine members elected for a five-year term. In accordance with Bahá'í electoral principles, there are no political parties or campaigns. The members of the Universal House of Justice are elected by the members of the National Bahá'í elected institutions, which are currently called National Spiritual Assemblies. For a discussion of Bahá'í elections, *see* Arash Abizadeh, "Democratic Elections Without Campaigns? Normative Bahá'í Foundations of National Bahá'í Elections," *World Order* 37 (2005): 7–49.

9. The writings of Bahá'u'lláh are considered by Bahá'ís to be revealed by God. The writings of 'Abdu'l-Bahá and Shoghi Effendi are considered authoritative interpretations of Bahá'u'lláh's revelation. The Universal House of Justice was not invested by Bahá'u'lláh with interpretative authority. However, its statements on certain matters are considered infallible and embody the highest Bahá'í institutional authority. For the purposes of this article, the writings of Bahá'u'lláh, 'Abdu'l-Bahá, Shoghi Effendi, and the Universal House of Justice are collectively considered to constitute the primary Bahá'í literature.

10. Such terms appear in the writings of Shoghi Effendi, which include writings on his behalf. See text accompanying notes 89–94 (giving quotes of such statements).

11. Letter dated April 18, 2001 from the Universal House of Justice to anonymous (on file with author).

12. Bahá'u'lláh, *Tablets of Bahá'u'lláh Revealed After the Kitáb-i-Aqdas*, 129.

13. Bahá'u'lláh, *Gleanings from the Writings of Bahá'u'lláh*, no. 115.3.

14. The term "church and state" increasingly appears in secondary literature in reference to the Bahá'í Faith. It is a problematic term for a range of reasons, including the fact that there exists no priestly class, power, or function in the Bahá'í Faith, while this term adopts a Christian frame of reference. In this article, the phrase "church and state" is used for symmetry with the secondary literature on which the article comments. The reader will note, however, that "church and state" is used interchangeably with references to religious and civil institutions.

15. Robarts, "A Few Reminiscences about Shoghi Effendi Taken from Pilgrim Notes of January 1955, from the Canadian National Spiritual Assembly Film Retrospective, and from Some Other Words of the Beloved Guardian," in *The Vision of Shoghi Effendi*, 174. This description is a pilgrim note, meaning a statement recorded by an individual on

pilgrimage from a conversation or utterance of Shoghi Effendi. Pilgrim notes are not considered authoritative, and their use is not widely encouraged in the Bahá'í community.

16. Latimer, "The Social Teachings of the Bahai Movement," *Star of the West* 7 (1916): 139. It should be noted Latimer's discussion is not entirely clear as to whether he foresees the Bahá'í institutions as having judicial, legislative, and executive powers, or only judicial and legislative ones. See note 18 and accompanying text (discussing a perspective that limited this power to the judicial and legislative sphere).

17. John A. Robarts, *A Few Reminiscences about Shoghi Effendi,* 173–74. The idea of evolutionary stages does appear in a number of places in Bahá'í primary literature—and particularly in the writings of Shoghi Effendi.

18. See, for example, Keith Ransom-Kehler, "A World at Peace: Bahá'í Administration as Presented to a Group of Free Thinkers," *The Bahá'í Magazine* 24 (1933): 216 (stating that the "International House of Justice has only a legislative function; it alone can enact those universal laws that apply to all mankind" and that "[a]ny nation refusing to submit to its commands must be immediately suppressed by a combination of all other nations").

19. Juan Cole has argued that Bahá'u'lláh and 'Abdu'l-Bahá "surely were among the first major religious figures in the region" to "embrace . . . the principle of the separation of religion and state." Juan R. I. Cole, *Modernity and the Millennium: The Genesis of the Bahá'í Faith in the Nineteenth Century,* 46.

20. Ibid., 191.

21. McGlinn, "A Theology of the State from the Bahá'í Teachings," 41. In 2005, McGlinn self-published his master's thesis *Church and State: A Postmodern Political Theology, Book One* (self-published, 2005), which includes many of the conclusions reached in the 1999 article. Unless otherwise indicated, the citations in this article are taken from the 1999 article.

22. Ibid., 708.

23. Ibid., 709.

24. See Ulrich Gollmer, Udo Schaefer, and Nicola Towfigh, *Making the Crooked Straight: A Contribution to Bahá'í Apologetics.*

25. See Ficicchia, *Religion der Zukunft? Geschichte, Lehre und Organisation in kritischer Anfrage.*

26. Schaefer et al., *Making the Crooked Straight*, 423 (emphasis omitted).
27. Ibid., 425–27.
28. Ibid., 439.
29. Ibid.
30. Schaefer, in a footnote, comments as follows:

> Ficicchia, who evidently does not understand my thesis, then refers to another passage of my thesis, in which I present the theocratic structural elements of the order of the Bahá'í community: "Hence, the administrative order is theocratic in character: God himself governs his people— not through a Delphic Oracle but through a revealed Book and through legal institutions that have been granted the charisma of infallibility" (Ibid., 191).

31. The authors of *Making the Crooked Straight* did not clearly advocate a particular form or address the question of institutional forms.
32. See Harold J. Berman, *Law and Revolution: The Formation of the Western Legal Tradition*, which discusses the evolution of the relationship between law and religion in Europe, including an excellent discussion of the Papal Revolution.
33. Bahá'u'lláh, The Kitáb-i-Aqdas, ¶83.
34. Ibid., ¶82.
35. Bahá'u'lláh, *Gleanings*, no. 115.3.
36. Bahá'u'lláh, The Kitáb-i-Aqdas, ¶2.
37. The concept of the Manifestation of God is at the core of Bahá'í prophetology and central to understanding the Bahá'í concept of the relation between the Divine and human beings. See Juan R. I. Cole, *The Concept of the Manifestation in the Bahá'í Writings*, 9.
38. McGlinn, *A Theology of the State from the Bahá'í Teachings*, 701.
39. Ibid., 702.
40. See Buck, *Symbol and Secret: Qur'án Commentary in Bahá'u'lláh's Kitáb-i-Íqán*.
41. There are a number of works written on the life of the Báb and the rise of His religious movement. See Amanat, *Resurrection and Renewal: The Making of the Babi Movement in Iran, 1844–1850*; Hasan M. Balyuzi, *The Báb, Herald of the Day of Days*; 'Abdu'l-Bahá, *A Traveller's Narrative: Written to Illustrate the Episode of the Báb*.

42. The Báb's writings frequently refer to "He Whom God Shall Make Manifest," a reference to a Manifestation of God to come after the Báb.
43. Bahá'u'lláh, The Kitáb-i-Íqán, ¶1.
44. Ibid., ¶102.
45. McGlinn, A Theology, 701.
46. Bahá'u'lláh, Gleanings, no. 27.4.
47. Bahá'u'lláh, The Kitáb-i-Aqdas, ¶1.
48. Saiedi, Logos and Civilization: Spirit, History, and Order in the Writings of Bahá'u'lláh, 144–45, 154.
49. Bahá'u'lláh, The Kitáb-i-Íqán, ¶57–65.
50. Ibid., ¶146–49.
51. McGlinn, A Theology, 702.
52. Bahá'u'lláh, The Kitáb-i-Íqán, ¶114 (emphasis added).
53. Ibid., ¶103.
54. Ibid., ¶113.
55. Ibid., ¶112.
56. Saiedi, Logos, 133.
57. Ibid., 157.
58. Schaefer et al., Making the Crooked Straight, 592–93.
59. Ibid., 701.
60. Bahá'u'lláh, The Kitáb-i-Aqdas, ¶162.
61. Bahá'u'lláh, The Kitáb-i-Íqán, ¶117.
62. Ibid.
63. 'Abdu'l-Bahá, The Secret of Divine Civilization, ¶130.
64. Ibid., ¶135.
65. Letter dated April 18, 2001 from the Universal House of Justice to anonymous (on file with author).
66. Bahá'u'lláh, The Kitáb-i-Aqdas, 87.
67. The original words of this phrase are "umúr-i-siyásiyyih kull rájí ast bih bayt-i-'adl."
68. Cole, Modernity, 96–97.
69. Ibid.
70. In this period, the Sunni Islamic jurists intensified their attention to the public and constitutional realm. While usúl al-fiqh (the sources and science of law as developed by the ulama) spoke volumes about private law, it had less to say on public power and authority until scholars such as al-Máwardí (AD 972–1058) set out to reflect on public law

and power and incorporate it into the realm of *fiqh* as developed by the *ulama*. Therefore, we see the emergence of the use of the term *siyása*, combined with *sharí'áh*, to indicate the extension of *sharí'áh* and *fiqh* into the political (e.g., *siyása*) realm.

71. *See* Coulson, *A History of Islamic Law* (giving a classical introduction to the history and evolution of Islamic law, including a good discussion of the terminology and themes mentioned in this article).

72. Bahá'u'lláh, *Tablets of Bahá'u'lláh,* 128–29.

73. Because the Universal House of Justice is specifically empowered to legislate general laws, it is distinguished from institutions in classical Islamic legal theory.

74. Bahá'u'lláh, *Tablets of Bahá'u'lláh,* 12.

75. Coulson, *A History of Islamic Law,* 71.

76. Ibid.

77. Vogel, *Islamic Law and Legal System: Studies of Saudi Arabia,* 26.

78. Coulson, *A History of Islamic Law,* 71.

79. 'Abdu'l-Bahá, quoted in the Introduction to Bahá'u'lláh, The Kitáb-i-Aqdas, 5–6. Bahá'u'lláh made it explicit that the laws He described in His writings cannot be repealed or altered by the Universal House of Justice. They can only be altered by a future Manifestation of God. These laws number approximately ninety-five. As a general principle, however, these laws require an act of implementation by the Universal House of Justice to become operative.

80. 'Abdu'l-Bahá, *Will and Testament of 'Abdu'l-Bahá,* 14.

81. Ibid., 19.

82. Ibid., 20.

83. Ibid., 14–15.

84. Ibid., 20.

85. See Schaefer, "Infallible Institutions?", *Bahá'í Studies Review* 9 (1999/2000): 17–45 (available at http://bahai-library.org/bsr/bsr09/9B1_schaefer_infallibility.htm, discussing the infallibility in the Bahá'í Faith).

86. Ibid.

87. For example, William S. Hatcher has argued for a broader scope of the infallibility of the Universal House of Justice, than, for example, Schaefer has. See Hatcher, "Reflections on Infallibility," (*Journal of Bahá'í Studies,* vol. 17, Issue 1/4, 2007). The Universal House of Justice

stated in a letter written on its behalf dated April 7, 2008 that "Nevertheless, it should be mentioned that, while there are explicit passages in the authoritative texts that make reference to the infallibility of the House of Justice in the enactment of legislation, the argument that it is free from error only in this respect is untenable."

88. See, for example, notes 15–20 and accompanying texts.

89. A National Spiritual Assembly, quoted in a letter dated April 27, 1995 from Universal House of Justice to anonymous. https://www.bahai. org/library/authoritative-texts/the-universal-house-of-justice/messages/19950427_001/1#985937741.

90. Letter dated November 30, 1930 written on behalf of Shoghi Effendi to an individual believer.

91. Letter dated November 19, 1939 written on behalf of Shoghi Effendi to an individual believer.

92. Letter dated April 19, 1941 written on behalf of Shoghi Effendi to an individual believer.

93. Shoghi Effendi, *World Order of Bahá'u'lláh*, 6–7.

94. Shoghi Effendi, *Messages to the Bahá'í World, 1950–1957*, 155.

95. Letter dated April 7, 1999 from the Universal House of Justice to all National Spiritual Assemblies. Bahá'í Reference Library at https://www.bahai.org/library/.

96. McGlinn, *A Theology*, 713.

97. McGlinn, "Theocratic Ideas and Assumptions in Bahá'í Literature: An Inquiry," in *Reason and Revelation: New Directions in Bahá'í Thought*, 39–82.

98. Ibid., 59–64.

99. Ibid.

100. Ibid.

101. See text accompanying notes 10–14. A number of authors, including Cole and McGlinn, place reliance on 'Abdu'l-Bahá's Risáliy-i-Siyásiyyih (Treatise on Politics) to support separationist readings of the primary literature. The Universal House of Justice responded to this interpretation of the treatise by stating that it does not represent a commentary on the appropriate relationship between Bahá'í and civil institutions:

You have referred also to a number of extracts from Risáliy-i-Siyásiyyih, in which 'Abdu'l-Bahá describes the damaging effects of the interference of religious teachers in political affairs. The inapplicability of these passages to the future role of the democratically elected Houses of Justice is clarified by study of the Bahá'í Writings on the World Order of Bahá'u'lláh. (Ltr. from the Universal House of Justice dated April 18, 2001 from the Universal House of Justice to anonymous (on file with author)).

To date, there has not been an authorized translation of the Risáliy-i-Siyásiyyih. The Universal House of Justice has provided a translation of some excerpts, and a few scholars have produced their own translation of the Risáliy-i-Siyásiyyih. For example, Mcglinn provides his translation under the chosen title "Sermon on the Art of Governance." (McGlinn, *Church and State*, 379–401).

102. For example, Shoghi Effendi, in describing the emergence of a world "Super-State," refers to it in the context of a "Commonwealth of all the nations of the world" including "federated representatives" and "federated units." Shoghi Effendi, *World Order of Bahá'u'lláh*, 40–41.

103. Letter dated October 1985 from the Universal House of Justice to the peoples of the world. This letter has been widely published as Universal House of Justice, *The Promise of World Peace* (available at http://info.bahai.org/article-1-7-2-1.html).

104. Dann J. May, *The Bahá'í Principle of Religious Unity and the Challenge of Radical Pluralism*, (unpublished master's thesis in Interdisciplinary Studies, U. N. Tex. 1993), http://bahai-library.com/theses/religious.unity/.

105. Shoghi Effendi, *World Order of Bahá'u'lláh*, 202.

106. 'Abdu'l-Bahá, *The Promulgation of Universal Peace*, 33.

107. 'Abdu'l-Bahá, quoted in a letter dated April 19, 2001 from the Universal House of Justice to anonymous. https://www.bahai.org/library/.

108. Bahá'u'lláh, *The Seven Valleys and the Four Valleys*, 29.

109. The emphasis on human response and choice was seen in a number of instances in Bahá'u'lláh's lifetime. For example, Bahá'u'lláh drew a connection between the lack of response of the world's kings and rulers to letters that Bahá'u'lláh addressed them, and humanity's pathway toward world peace. Specifically, the rulers' lack of response was a loss of the opportunity for the world to emerge into a new pattern of civi-

lization—a "Most Great Peace"—in the foreseeable future. Bahá'u'lláh wrote that "[n]ow that ye have refused the Most Great Peace, hold ye fast unto this, the Lesser Peace, that haply ye may in some degree better your own condition and that of your dependants." Letter dated April 19, 2001 from the Universal House of Justice to anonymous. https://www.bahai.org/library/.

110. Saiedi, *Logos,* 62–66, 322–24.
111. Ibid., 243–44.
112. Danesh, "The Politics of Delay—Social Meanings and the Historical Treatment of Bahá'í Law," *World Order* 35 (2004): 33.
113. Bahá'u'lláh, The Kitáb-i-Aqdas, 6–7.
114. For example, Shoghi Effendi writes:

We should—every one of us—remain aloof, in heart and in mind, in words and in deeds, from the political affairs and disputes of the Nations and of Governments. We should keep ourselves away from such thoughts. We should have no political connection with any of the parties and should join no faction of these different and warring sects.

Absolute impartiality in the matter of political parties should be shown by words and by deeds, and the love of the whole humanity, whether a Government or a nation, which is the basic teaching of Bahá'u'lláh, should also be shown by words and by deeds. . . .

According to the exhortations of the Supreme Pen and the confirmatory explanations of the Covenant of God Bahá'ís are in no way allowed to enter into political affairs under any pretense of excuse; since such an action brings about disastrous results and ends in hurting the Cause of God and its intimate friends. (*Directives of the Guardian,* no. 94).

115. Bahá'u'lláh, *Gleanings from the Writings of Bahá'u'lláh,* no. 115.3.
116. Saiedi discusses at some length Bahá'u'lláh's rejection of coercion in public and social life. *See* Saiedi, *Logos,* 362–70.
117. Shoghi Effendi, *World Order of Bahá'u'lláh,* 152.
118. Saiedi, *An Introduction to 'Abdu'l-Bahá's The Secret of Divine Civilization, Converging Realities* §1.1 http://bahai-library.com/file.php5?file=-saiedi_introduction_sdc&language=.
119. 'Abdu'l-Bahá, *Secret of Divine Civilization,* ¶11–18.
120. Ibid ¶20.

121. Ibid ¶24–32.
122. This is seen in how, for example, 'Abdu'l-Bahá emphasizes the centrality of mass education, democratization, and the end of imitation as keys to social change.
123. "Mirrors for Princes" refers to the tradition of writing practical guides giving advice and instructions for rulers on their conduct.
124. 'Abdu'l-Bahá, *The Secret of Divine Civilization*, ¶29–41.
125. Ibid.
126. Ibid., ¶30.
127. Ibid., ¶31.
128. Ibid.
129. Ibid., ¶32.
130. Ibid., ¶41.
131. For example, 'Abdu'l-Bahá states that "if religion becomes the source of antagonism and strife, the absence of religion is to be preferred. Religion is meant to be the quickening life of the body politic; if it be the cause of death to humanity, its nonexistence would be a blessing and benefit to man." 'Abdu'l-Bahá, *Foundations of World Unity*, 22.
132. I am using this term narrowly and cautiously. I am not implying the adoption or incorporation of any particular strand of so-called postmodernist philosophy or thought. Rather, I am simply referring to the fact that certain points of emphasis in 'Abdu'l-Bahá's argument are not ones that were stressed by modernity but rather are ones that have been stressed in political debate in response to and looking back on modernism.
133. Browne, *Selections from the Writings of E.G. Browne on the Bábí and Bahá'í Religions*, 430.
134. Ibid.
135. For example, the Universal House of Justice, in explaining the Bahá'í avoidance of politics states "the aim of the Bahá'ís is to reconcile viewpoints, to heal divisions, and to bring about tolerance and mutual respect among men, and this aim is undermined if we allow ourselves to be swept along by the ephemeral passions of others." Letter dated January 3, 1982 from the Universal House of Justice to anonymous (on file with author). https://www.bahai.org/library/authoritative-texts/the-universal-house-of-justice/messages/19820103_001/1#003634893.
136. See Balyuzi, *'Abdu'l-Bahá*, 171–339.
137. See Shoghi Effendi, *World Order of Bahá'u'lláh*, 9, 19, 143–157.

138. This has been an issue of discussion at certain periods within Bahá'í history and among academics. A few have suggested that the move to institutionalization, in particular under Shoghi Effendi, was a co-optation of an original vision that was more diffuse, informal, and open. This was seen most directly after 'Abdu'l-Bahá's passing, when a very few Bahá'ís questioned the authenticity of His Will and Testament, the establishment of the Guardianship, and the move toward institutionalization that took place. There is historical and textual evidence, however, which illustrates that Bahá'u'lláh intended for some degree of institutionalization. For example, as discussed earlier, Bahá'u'lláh specifically contemplated the creation of "houses of justice."

139. The term *theocracy* literally means *rule of God*. Such rule is to be distinguished, for example, from the term *hierocracy*, which means *rule by clerics*. In common and contemporary usage, however, *theocracy* has come to typically mean *rule by religious entities* and is conceived of as implying a necessary contradiction to democracy. This implied contradiction is rooted in the idea, for example, that it is inherently undemocratic for the members of one religious community to have all political power in contexts of diversity. Given the strong commitment to democracy and the removal of the sword in the Bahá'í Faith, one would expect different social meanings—definitions that may require more consideration of the literal meanings of the term—to be associated with the term *theocracy* as used in the Bahá'í context. Similar arguments could be made concerning the term *Bahá'í state*, which, for example, might be understood as not necessarily implying institutional integration but harmony among the principles guiding the conduct and objectives of political and religious institutions.

140. Letter dated April 27, 1995 from the Universal House of Justice to anonymous. https://www.bahai.org/library/authoritative-texts/the-universal-house-of-justice/messages/19950427_001/1#985937741.

141. Ibid.

142. Ibid.

143. Ibid.

144. A question with respect to this particular letter on theocracy concerns how the term "political" is defined and used. The Universal House of Justice states that the Bahá'í Faith is political in the sense of "the science of government and of the organization of human society." (Letter dated April 27, 1995 from the Universal House of Justice to anonymous.

http://bahai-library.com/uhj/theocracy.html). At the same time, it states that the Bahá'í Faith "denies being a 'political' organization," and Bahá'ís are not to be involved in "'political' matters." (Ibid.) It would be helpful to know precisely what distinguishes the first and second uses of the term. If building the Kingdom of God is political, presumably it includes allowance for certain types of political action—action that fits with the Bahá'í vision of how that Kingdom is to happen.

145. Letter dated April 27, 1995 from the Universal House of Justice to anonymous. https://www.bahai.org/library/authoritative-texts/the-universal-house-of-justice/messages/19950427_001/1#985937741.

146. Ibid.

147. Ibid.

148. Ibid.

6 / Internationalism and Divine Law: A Bahá'í Perspective

1. Bahá'u'lláh, *Gleanings from the Writings of Bahá'u'lláh*, no. 117.1.

2. Schaefer, "An Introduction to Bahá'í Law: Doctrinal, Foundations, Principles, and Structures," 307.

3. Bahá'u'lláh, The Kitáb-i-Aqdas, ¶12.

4. Ibid., ¶20. Note: Bahá'ís are enjoined to write a will, and this verse applies only to cases of intestacy.

5. Ibid., ¶155.

6. Ibid., ¶188.

7. Ibid., ¶2.

8. Ibid., ¶121, ¶174.

9. 'Abdu'l-Bahá, *Will and Testament of 'Abdu'l-Bahá*.

10. Bahá'u'lláh, The Kitáb-i-Aqdas, ¶37.

11. Ibid., ¶99.

12. Ibid., ¶7.

13. Ibid., ¶1.

14. Ibid., ¶2.

15. Ibid., ¶29.

16. Ibid., ¶4.

17. Ibid., ¶5.

18. Saiedi discusses some of the implications of the term "mother book" in Saiedi, *Logos and Civilization: Spirit, History, and Order in the Writings of Bahá'u'lláh*, 235.

19. Bahá'u'lláh, The Kitáb-i-Aqdas, 1–2.
20. Ibid., 2–3.
21. Ibid., ¶75.
22. Ibid., ¶83.
23. Ibid., ¶81.
24. Ibid., ¶82.
25. Ibid., ¶84.
26. At the core of the Bahá'í administrative system are local, national, and international elected bodies. The local and national bodies are currently called "spiritual assemblies," though it is expected they will evolve into "houses of justice." Spiritual assemblies are currently made up of nine individuals elected to one-year terms. The international body is called the "Universal House of Justice," and its nine members are elected to five-year terms. It was first elected in 1963, and it is housed on Mt. Carmel, Haifa. The Universal House of Justice is the supreme institution in the Bahá'í system, and it has the authority to pass laws on matters not explicitly addressed by Bahá'u'lláh. Organized along these lines, the contemporary Bahá'í community is established in 190 countries, and its members represent over two thousand indigenous tribes, races, and ethnic groups.
27. Bahá'u'lláh, quoted in Schaefer, "An Introduction to Bahá'í Law: Doctrinal, Foundations, Principles, and Structures," 30.
28. Ibid., 91.
29. 'Abdu'l-Bahá, *The Secret of Divine Civilization*.
30. Shoghi Effendi, *The World Order of Bahá'u'lláh*, 26–47.
31. The early outgrowth of these debates was an emerging distinction between kanon and nomos, which partially contributed to a delay in the substantive development of legal methodologies and theories rooted in Christianity for 1100 years, when such development was prompted by the need to reform the Church and achieve a degree of autonomy from the temporal ruler. For a discussion of these issues see Charles Donahue, Jr., "A Crisis of Law? Reflections on the Church and the Law over the Centuries," *The Jurist*).
32. Unlike Sunni Islam, there are very few works exploring the evolution of Shi'i legal thought. For one of the best discussions, see Hossein Modarressi Tabátabá'i, *An Introduction to Shí'í Law: A Bibliographical Study*.

33. A good example of such literature is Adib Taherzadeh, *The Revelation of Bahá'u'lláh: 'Akká, The Early Years 1868–77* vol. 3, 275–399.

34. Udo Schaefer explains the Bahá'í idea of progressive revelation, and its legal implications, in the following terms:

> "Every religion has at some point been faced with the question of its relationship to preceding religions. They are all set in the continuum of a particular tradition, whether this be of the Abrahamic or Middle Eastern religions or of the religions of Asia. The relationship of a religion to the tradition in which it stands, and to the religions outside of that tradition, is deduced from the concept of revelation as defined by the faith in question.
>
> The doctrine of progressive, cyclically recurring divine revelation and the mystical unity of the religions is the theological keystone of the Bahá'í Faith, the new theological paradigm. The historical revealed religions, the chain of Prophets from Adam to Bahá'u'lláh, constitute 'the one and indivisible religion of God,' the 'changeless Faith of God, eternal in the past, eternal in the future.' The revelation of Bahá'u'lláh is, as 'Abdu'l-Bahá expressed it, 'not a new path to salvation,' but the 'ancient Path,' cleared of the historical baggage inevitably accumulated by the religions in the course of history. It is the new 'Book of God,' the 'unerring Balance' on which 'whatsoever the peoples and kindreds of the earth possess must be weighed,' and through which 'truth may be distinguished from error.' . . . This viewpoint provides the criteria for assessing the role of the historical religions. Their claim to truth is recognized and accepted. They are of divine origin and are manifestations of the divine Word. . . . Neither have these religions been 'done away with' as a result of the new revelation, nor has a time limit been set on their claim to truth. The testimony of the Torah, the Gospel and the Qur'án remains the truth. These books of God are an integral part of scripture in the broadest sense of the word; all religious truths contained in them are 'facets' of an ultimate truth whose immense depths always remain unfathomable to humankind. Only to the extent that time alters the social condition of humankind does the 'old law' lose its validity—i.e. revelation takes account of the changing conditions of human society so that each new religion is appropriately fashioned by its founder to foster laws that best advance society. In other words, revealed religious

law has a type of historical apparel whereby instead of destroying the 'old law,' it fulfils it. Whereas the 'horizontal' dimension of revelation (that sphere which is concerned with the development of a constantly changing world and with forms of worship—law and ritual) is, so to speak, the variable, the 'vertical' dimension, the eternal nucleus of the religion of God that 'does not change nor alter' is the constant."

(Udo Schaefer, Nicola Towfigh, & Ulrich Gollmer, *Making the Crooked Straight: A Contribution to Bahá'í Apologetics,* 279–282).

35. Bahá'u'lláh was in Edirne from 1863 to 1868.
36. Saiedi describes the steps leading to the revelation of the Kitáb-i-Aqdas as the following:

If we look at the different tablets of Bahá'u'lláh referring to the revelation of the Kitáb-i-Aqdas, we can clearly distinguish three stages leading to that event. The first stage is the arrival, during the Edirne period, of many petitions from His followers requesting laws. In response to this first set of petitions, at the end of His stay in Edirne, Bahá'u'lláh revealed a short tablet in Persian concerning laws, but He never released the Tablet. The second stage was the arrival of further petitions, as Bahá'u'lláh says in His tablet, in "recent days." The third stage is the revelation of the Kitáb-i-Aqdas in Arabic in response to the second set of petitions. (Saiedi, *Logos and Civilization,* 232).

37. Bahá'u'lláh, The Kitáb-i-Aqdas, note 126.
38. Ibid., ¶98.
39. Juan Cole summarizes the concept of the manifestation in the following terms:

The Bahá'í concept of the intermediary between God and humankind expresses itself most paradigmatically in the term "manifestation of God" or "theophany" (mazhar-i iláhí, zuhúr). This idea emphasizes simultaneously the humanity of that intermediary and the way in which he shows forth the names and attributes of God. According to the Bahá'í writings, the manifestation of God is not an incarnation of God, as the transcendent Godhead can never incarnate itself in a mere mortal frame. But neither is the manifestation of God an ordinary, sinful mortal. He acts as a pure mirror to reflect the attributes of the Deity into this temporal plane. The term "manifestation of God" is not the only name the Bahá'í scriptures apply to this figure. They refer to him as prophet, messenger, prophet endowed with constancy, Primal Will, Word of God, Universal Intellect, and Primal Point. It should be clear that the concept of the manifestation of God in Bahá'í thought involves many elements. In some ways, the Bahá'í writings affirm the validity of terms and ideal which appear in past scriptures, theologies and philosophical systems. Much terminology, for instance, derives from the Qur'án (which Bahá'ís regard as authentic revealed scripture) and ultimately reflects the Judaic religious heritage. For example, in the Bahá'í writings the Jewish insistence on the oneness and transcendence of God are consistently present. One also finds terminology similar to that of John's Gospel, especially to those passages where John explicates the Logos concept. But in the Bahá'í writings, these past terms are integrated into a new vision, and sometimes endowed with new significances. Although perhaps none of the terms and concepts which Bahá'í scripture employs to describe God's envoy to humankind appear there for the first time, including that of the manifestation of God (an epithet used by Shí'í thinkers), the Bahá'í scripture's use of these terms and concepts creates a new theology. It differs from the conventional Imámi Shí'í prophetology in some respects, and often has more in common with the prophetology of the Muslim philosophers.

(Cole, "The Concept of the Manifestation in the Bahá'í Writings," *Bahá'í Studies* 9 (1982): 1, 2.)

40. Bahá'u'lláh, The Kitáb-i-Aqdas, 6–7.
41. Weiss, *The Spirit of Islamic Law.*
42. Ibid., 53.
43. Ibid.
44. Fiqh theory and the practice of ijtihád are, of course, dynamic and allow for a degree of diversity and change. However, recent attempts to theorize approaches to Islamic law that would have more liberal or progressive results have not been widely successful.

45. Walbridge, *Kitab-I Aqdas, the Most Holy Book,* 1–2 (unpublished manuscript, on file with the author and available at https://bahai-library. com/walbridge_encyclopedia_kitab_aqdas).

46. Stockman, "Revelation, Interpretation, and Elucidation in the Baha'i Writings," in Momen, ed., *Scripture and Revelation,* 53, 67, n. 5.

47. Coulson, *A History of Islamic Law,* 11–13, 17.

48. Ibid., 13.

49. Lee, Presentation at Fifth Annual Colloquium on Scriptural Studies, Choice Wine: The Kitáb-i-Aqdas and the Development of Bahá'í Law, Address at Fifth Annual Colloquium on Scriptural Studies, Bahá'í Stud. Inst. 2 (transcript on file with author).

50. For example, Bahá'u'lláh uses the term avámir (commandments) to refer to the laws of the Kitáb-i-Aqdas, implying their status as rules that are to be followed, as opposed to flexible ethical precepts.

51. Bahá'u'lláh, The Kitáb-i-Aqdas, ¶30.

52. 'Abdu'l-Bahá, *Will and Testament of 'Abdu'l-Bahá,* 14.

53. Bahá'u'lláh, The Kitáb-i-Aqdas, 87.

54. Ibid., 5.

55. The Universal House of Justice, Messages from the Universal House of Justice: 1963–1986, no. 23.20.

56. Ibid.

57. Shoghi Effendi, quoted in ibid.

58. Letter dated October, 1985 from the Universal House of Justice to the peoples of the world, (on file with author and available at https:// www.bahai.org/library/authoritative-texts/the-universal-house-of-justice/messages/19851001_001/1#883867984). This letter is known in the Baha'i community as the "The Peace Message."

59. Hatcher, "The Kitáb-i-Aqdas: The Causality Principle in the World of Being," in *The Law of Love Enshrined,* 114.

60. 'Abdu'l-Bahá, *The Promulgation of Universal Peace: Talks Delivered by Abdu'l-Baha during His Visit to the United States and Canada in 1912,* 33.

61. Shoghi Effendi, *The World Order of Bahá'u'lláh,* 202.

62. Stated another way, when asked for guidance on Baha'i law concerning a particular subject, the Universal House of Justice often leaves it up to individual conscience until such time as the Universal House of Justice may decide to legislate on the matter.

63. For an overview of Bahá'u'lláh's economic thought, see Graham, "The Bahá'í Faith and Economics: A Review and Synthesis," *Bahá'í Studies Review*, 7 (1997). http://bahai-library.org/ bsr/bsr07/712_graham_economics.htm.

64. 'Abdu'l-Bahá, *Selections from the Writings of 'Abdu'l-Bahá*, no. 202.3.

65. Shoghi Effendi, quoted in a letter dated October, 1985 from the Universal House of Justice to the peoples of the world (on file with author and available at https://www.bahai.org/library/authoritative-texts/the-universal-house-of-justice/messages/19851001_001/1#883867984), 170.

66. In relation to the United States and Canada, Shoghi Effendi focuses particularly on the virulent effects of racism. See Shoghi Effendi, *The Advent of Divine Justice*, ¶51–58.

67. Huntington, *The Clash of Civilizations and the Remaking of World Order*, 21.

68. Civilization has been defined in many different ways by international relations theorists. The somewhat static implications of the clash of civilizations thesis are contradicted by other definitions. A good example, which echoes the definition of Toynbee, is Robert Cox, who argues that civilization is "a product of collective human action, an amalgam of social forces and ideas that has achieved a certain coherence, but is continually changing and developing in response to challenges both from within and without." See Robert W. Cox & Michael G. Schechter, *The Political Economy of a Plural World: Critical Reflections on Power, Morals and Civilization*, 143.

69. Huntington, *The Clash of Civilizations and the Remaking of World Order*, 41–44.

70. Ibid., 21.

71. Ibid., 29.

72. Ibid., 216.

73. Ibid., 217.

74. Ibid., 310.

75. Ibid., 318. Exertion of such power could either be direct and force-based, or by more hidden means, such as the pervasive influence of globalization aided by computer and other technologies and backed by the knowledge that military might is always there to undergird it.

76. Ibid., 56–59.

77. Ibid., 318.
78. Ibid., 305.
79. Ibid.
80. Ibid., 306.
81. Shoghi Effendi, *The World Order of Bahá'u'lláh*, 170.
82. Bahá'u'lláh, *Tablets of Bahá'u'lláh*, 165.
83. Shoghi Effendi, *The World Order of Bahá'u'lláh*, 45.
84. Shoghi Effendi, *The World Order of Bahá'u'lláh*, 40, 203. For an overview of the uses of this various terminology, see Hatcher, *The Arc of Ascent*, 262–69.
85. Shoghi Effendi, *Bahá'í Administration*, 47.
86. For a statement of Robert Cox's approach to world order, see Cox, "Social Forces, States and World Orders: Beyond International Relations Theory," in Cox and Sinclair, *Approaches to World Order*, 85.
87. Similar observations have been made by other commentators. See Knight, "Challenging Established Ontology: Coexisting Civilizations in a Plural World," *International Studies Review* 5 (2003): 403–5.
88. Cox, "Towards a Posthegemonic Conceptualization of World Order: Reflections on the Relevancy of Ibn Khaldun," in Cox and Sinclair, *Approaches to World Order*, 144, 151–52.

7 / Some Reflections on Bahá'í Approaches to Social Change (coauthor Lex Musta)

1. Bahá'u'lláh, *Tablets of Bahá'u'lláh Revealed after the Kitáb-i-Aqdas*, 164, 172.
2. Universal House of Justice, *The Five Year Plan 2011–2016: Messages from the Universal House of Justice*, 20.
3. For a recent work that discusses Bahá'í approaches to social change, see Lample, *Revelation and Social Reality: Learning to Translate What is Written into Reality*.
4. Abizadeh, "Democratic Elections without Campaigns? Normative Foundations of National Bahá'í Elections," *World Order* 37, no. 1 (2005): 7–49.
5. Universal House of Justice, *The Five Year Plan 2011–2016: Messages from the Universal House of Justice*, 21.
6. Bahá'u'lláh, Epistle to the Son of the Wolf, 2.
7. Bahá'u'lláh, *Prayers and Meditations*, 178.3.

8. Bahá'u'lláh, *Tablets of Bahá'u'lláh Revealed after the Kitáb-i-Aqdas*, 87, 157.
9. 'Abdu'l-Bahá, *Selections from the Writings of 'Abdu'l-Bahá*, no. 15.6.
10. Bahá'u'lláh, Kitáb-i-Íqán, ¶170.
11. 'Abdu'l-Bahá, *The Promulgation of Universal Peace*, 33.
12. May, "The Bahá'í Principle of Religious Unity: A Dynamic Perspectivism," *Revisioning the Sacred: New Perspectives on a Bahá'í Theology*, vol. 8 in *Studies in the Bábí and Bahá'í Religions* series (Los Angeles: Kalimát, 1997): 8.
13. Bahá'u'lláh, quoted in Saiedi, *Logos and Civilization: Spirit, History, and Order in the Writings of Bahá'u'lláh*, 242.
14. Ibid., 243–47.
15. Bahá'u'lláh, The Kitáb-i-Aqdas, ¶73.
16. Saiedi, *Logos and Civilization: Spirit, History, and Order in the Writings of Bahá'u'lláh*, 243–44.
17. Bahá'u'lláh, *Tablets of Bahá'u'lláh Revealed after the Kitáb-i-Aqdas*, 85.
18. Shoghi Effendi, *The Advent of Divine Justice*, ¶53.
19. Letter dated July, 1925 from Shoghi Effendi to the Bahá'ís of Iran (copy on file with author).
20. Shoghi Effendi, *World Order of Bahá'u'lláh*, 202.
21. Bahá'í International Community, Office of Public Information, *The Prosperity of Humankind*, 3.
22. Lessig, "The Regulation of Social Meaning," *The University of Chicago Law Review* 62, no. 3 (1995): 951.
23. Ibid.
24. Ibid., 956.
25. Bahá'í International Community, Office of Public Information, *The Prosperity of Humankind*, 3.
26. Commissioned by the Universal House of Justice, *Century of Light*, 22.
27. Universal House of Justice, *The Promise of World Peace*, 1.
28. Ibid.
29. Ibid., 10.
30. For example, Shoghi Effendi writes:

We should—every one of us—remain aloof, in heart and in mind, in words and in deeds, from the political affairs and disputes of the Nations and of Governments. We should keep ourselves away from such thoughts. We should have no political connection with any of the parties and should join no faction of these different and warring sects. Absolute impartiality in the matter of political parties should be shown by words and by deeds, and the love of the whole humanity, whether a Government or a nation, which is the basic teaching of Bahá'u'lláh, should also be shown by words and by deeds. . . .

According to the exhortations of the Supreme Pen and the confirmatory explanations of the Covenant of God Bahá'ís are in no way allowed to enter into political affairs under any pretense of excuse; since such an action brings about disastrous results and ends in hurting the Cause of God and its intimate friends. (Shoghi Effendi, *Directives of the Guardian*, 56–57)

31. Saiedi discusses at some length Bahá'u'lláh's rejection of coercion in public and social life. See Saiedi, *Logos and Civilization: Spirit, History, and Order in the Writings of Bahá'u'lláh*, 362–70.
32. Shoghi Effendi, *World Order of Bahá'u'lláh*, 152.
33. For a good discussion of the new kind of politics imagined by the Bahá'í administrative order, see Ulrich Gollmer, Udo Schaefer, and Nicola Towfigh, *Making the Crooked Straight: A Contribution to Bahá'í Apologetics*, trans. Geraldine Schuckelt (Oxford: George Ronald, 2000).
34. Shoghi Effendi, *Call to the Nations*.
35. Bahá'u'lláh, Epistle to the Son of the Wolf, 25.
36. Universal House of Justice, *The Promise of World Peace*, 14.
37. Danesh, "Internationalism and Divine Law," *Journal of Law and Religion* 19.2 (2003–2004): 209–42.
38. Shoghi Effendi, quoted in the Universal House of Justice, *The Five Year Plan 2011–2016: Messages from the Universal House of Justice*, 38.
39. National Spiritual Assembly of the Bahá'ís of the United States, *The Vision of Race Unity: America's Most Challenging Issue*. https://bahai-library.com/nsa_race_unity.
40. Danesh, "Church and State in the Bahá'í Faith: An Epistemic Approach," *Journal of Law and Religion* 24, no. 1 (2008–2009): 21–63.
41. Letter from the Universal House of Justice dated April 27, 1995 to an individual believer. https://www.bahai.org/library/authoritative-texts/the-universal-house-of-justice/messages/19950427_001/1#985937741
42. Bahá'u'lláh, *Gleanings from the Writings of Bahá'u'lláh*, no. 117.1.

43. Universal House of Justice, *The Five Year Plan 2011–2016: Messages from the Universal House of Justice*, 21.
44. This is seen, for example, in the pattern of delay in the application of Bahá'u'lláh's laws. For a discussion of this theme, see Danesh, "The Politics of Delay—Social Meanings and the Historical Treatment of Bahá'í Law," *World Order* 35, no. 3 (2004): 33–45.
45. For example, see Shoghi Effendi's letter, "The Unfoldment of World Civilization," *The World Order of Bahá'u'lláh*, 161–206.
46. 'Abdu'l-Bahá, *The Promulgation of Universal Peace*, 182.

8 / Imagining Bahá'í Law

1. In relation to laws and ordinances, Bahá'u'lláh articulates different principles of interpretation than apply, for example, to allegorical passages. In relation to laws and ordinances Bahá'u'lláh emphasizes the importance of the evident or obvious meanings of the words.
2. As opposed to the authoritative interpretations of 'Abdu'l-Bahá and Shoghi Effendi, which are binding on both individual Bahá'ís and Bahá'í institutions.
3. A Latin term meaning to stand by what has been previously decided. In general terms, the principle of precedent—that earlier court decisions are binding on later courts faced with the same issue.
4. In Canada, for example, the legal definition of marriage was changed in 2005 to include two individuals of the same sex. It remains to be seen whether this and consequent changes in the law will interact with the role of state-mandated Bahá'í marriage officers, or other related issues to the legal recognition of Bahá'í institutions. This interaction will vary from jurisdiction to jurisdiction.
5. Schaefer, "An Introduction to Bahá'í Law: Doctrinal, Foundations, Principles, and Structures," 308.
6. Ibid., 317.
7. Ibid., 312–16.
8. Ibid., 317–23.
9. Ibid., 324–62.
10. Ibid., 319.
11. Ibid., 324.
12. For a review of the historical treatment of Bahá'í law, see Danesh, "The Politics of Delay—Social Meanings and the Historical Treatment of Bahá'í Law," *World Order*, 35, no. 3 (2004): 33–45.

NOTES

13. Bahá'u'lláh, The Kitáb-i-Aqdas, ¶7, 6.
14. Schaefer, "An Introduction to Bahá'í Law: Doctrinal, Foundations, Principles, and Structures," 321–23.
15. To be clear, the contingency of Bahá'í law on the construction of certain social conditions—and more generally claims about the relative nature of divine law—should not be construed as absolute. The Universal House of Justice's supplementary legislation cannot be in conflict with a law explicitly stated in the writings of Bahá'u'lláh (noting, however, that the definition of what constitutes a conflict remains unexamined). In other words, the laws of Bahá'u'lláh form a general framework or outline, and they are laws that are intended to be activated. These rules are expressions of divine will and give shape to the supplementary legislation that is expected to emerge in the future.
16. This is made explicit by 'Abdu'l-Bahá:

Those matters of major importance which constitute the foundation of the Law of God are explicitly recorded in the Text, but subsidiary laws are left to the House of Justice. The wisdom of this is that the times never remain the same, for change is a necessary quality and an essential attribute of this world, and of time and place. Therefore the House of Justice will take action accordingly . . .

Briefly, this is the wisdom of referring the laws of society to the House of Justice. In the religion of Islám, similarly, not every ordinance was explicitly revealed; nay not a tenth part of a tenth part was included in the Text; although all matters of major importance were specifically referred to, there were undoubtedly thousands of laws which were unspecified. These were devised by the divines of a later age according to the laws of Islamic jurisprudence, and individual divines made conflicting deductions from the original revealed ordinances. All these were enforced. Today this process of deduction is the right of the body of the House of Justice, and the deductions and conclusions of individual learned men have no authority, unless they are endorsed by the House of Justice. The difference is precisely this, that from the conclusions and endorsements of the body of the House of Justice whose members are elected by and known to the worldwide Bahá'í community, no differences will arise; whereas the conclusions of individual divines and scholars would definitely lead to differences, and result in schism, division, and dispersion. The oneness of the Word would be destroyed, the unity of the Faith

263

would disappear, and the edifice of the Faith of God would be shaken. ('Abdu'l-Bahá, quoted in Bahá'u'lláh, The Kitáb-i-Aqdas, 5–6)

17. The Universal House of Justice, on page 7 of its Introduction to the Kitáb-i-Aqdas emphasizes the principle of the "progressive application" of Bahá'í law and that the "number of laws binding on Bahá'ís is not increased by the publication of this translation." In this emphasis on aspects of the application of Bahá'í law, and that the "society for which certain of the laws of the Aqdas are designed will come only gradually into being" (page 6), the Universal House of Justice reflects the emphasis on method of use of the law of Bahá'u'lláh, 'Abdu'l-Bahá, and Shoghi Effendi. For a fuller discussion, see Danesh, "The Politics of Delay—Social Meanings and the Historical Treatment of Bahá'í Law," *World Order* 35, no. 3 (2004): 33–45.

18. For example, in Canada, a federation, only the federal government has the constitutional authority to pass criminal laws. The provinces, however, pass numerous laws on subject matter within their constitutional jurisdiction, and they include punishments in those laws (within limits) in order to ensure that the laws are taken seriously. Examples include punishments for a wide range of activities, such as certain traffic offenses, environmental offenses, hunting activity, forestry and resource extraction, etc. These provincial laws are not purely criminal but are regulatory or statutory in character.

19. Schaefer, "An Introduction to Bahá'í Law: Doctrinal, Foundations, Principles, and Structures," 324.

20. None of the words for *law* or *rule* in the Kitáb-i-Aqdas specifically implies a meaning of a criminal law or offense.

21. From a letter dated September 28, 1941 written on behalf of Shoghi Effendi to an individual believer, in *The Compilation of Compilations*, vol. 1.

22. From a letter dated May 21, 1954 written on behalf of Shoghi Effendi to an individual believer, published in *A Chaste and Holy Life*.

23. From a letter dated February 6, 1973 written by the Universal House of Justice to all National Spiritual Assemblies, published in *A Chaste and Holy Life*.

9 / Themes in the Study of Bahá'u'lláh's Kitáb-i-Aqdas: Emerging Approaches to Scholarship on Bahá'í Law

1. Bahá'u'lláh wrote in Persian and Arabic. Bahá'ís consider His writings to be the revealed word of God. The practice of the Bahá'í community is to translate Bahá'u'lláh's writings from their original language into English and then from English into other languages.

2. For discussion of the reasons for the delay in the translation and dissemination of the Kitáb-i-Aqdas see my article "The Politics of Delay: Social Meanings and the Historical Treatment of Bahá'í Law," *World Order* 35, no. 3 (2004): 33–45.

3. Universal House of Justice, Introduction, in Bahá'u'lláh, The Kitáb-i-Aqdas, 1.

4. Ibid., 3.

5. There is not a large number of laws in the Kitáb-i-Aqdas. While numbers may vary depending on what one considers a "law" to be, it is reasonable to conclude that there are fewer than a hundred of them in the book. Further, as is noted later, it has been argued that the Kitáb-i-Aqdas presents a very distinct concept of law.

6. Letter dated March 5, 1993 from the Universal House of Justice to the Bahá'ís of the World, in *Messages from the Universal House of Justice*, no. 150.

7. Ibid.

8. See Schweitz's "The Kitáb-i-Aqdas: Bahá'í Law, Legitimacy, and World Order," *Journal of Bahá'í Studies* 6, no. 1 (1994): 35–59, and John S. Hatcher's "Unsealing the Choice Wine at the Family Reunion," *Journal of Bahá'í Studies* 6, no. 3 (1994): 27–38. Both of these articles proceeded from this symposium.

9. See Walbridge's *Sacred Acts, Sacred Space, Sacred Time.*

10. See Baharieh Rouhani Ma'ani and Sovaida Ma'ani Ewing's *Laws of the Kitáb-i-Aqdas.*

11. See Bushrui's *The Style of the Kitáb-i-Aqdas: Aspects of the Sublime.*

12. See Saiedi's *Logos and Civilization: Spirit, History, and Order in the Writings of Bahá'u'lláh.*

13. See Schweitz's "The Kitáb-i-Aqdas: Bahá'í Law, Legitimacy, and World Order," *Journal of Bahá'í Studies* 6, no. 1 (1994): 35–59, and my essay "Some Reflections on the Concept of Law in the Bahá'í Faith," *Journal of Bahá'í Studies* 24, nos. 1–2 (2014).

14. See John S. Hatcher and William S. Hatcher's *The Law of Love Enshrined: Selected Essays*.

15. For example, the *Journal of Law and Religion* has published three articles on Bahá'í law: Schaefer's "An Introduction to Bahá'í Law: Doctrinal Foundations, Principles, and Structures" 18, no. 2 (2003): 308–69, my articles "Internationalism and Divine Law" 19, no. 2 (2003–4): 209–42, and "Church and State in the Bahá'í Faith: An Epistemic Approach," 24, no. 1 (2008): 21–63.

16. Universal House of Justice, Introduction, in Bahá'u'lláh, The Kitáb-i-Aqdas, 2–3.

17. See, for example, Walbridge's *Sacred Acts, Sacred Space, Sacred Time* and Ma'ani and Ma'ani Ewing's *Laws of the Kitáb-i-Aqdas*.

18. Examples of studies of gender equality in Bahá'í law include the following: Linda Walbridge and John Walbridge's "Bahá'í Laws and the Status of Men," *World Order* 19, no. 1–2: (1984–85): 25–36; Susan Stiles Maneck et al.'s "A Question of Gender: A Forum on the Status of Men in Bahá'í Law," *Dialogue* 2, no. 1, 1987, 14–34; John S. Hatcher's "The Equality of Women: The Bahá'í Principle of Complementarity," *Journal of Bahá'í Studies* 2, no. 3 (1990): 55–66; Schweitz's "Of Webs and Ladders: Gender Equality in Bahá'í Law" *World Order* 27, no. 1 (1995): 21–39; Bahiyyih Nakhjavani's "Exemption" *Bahá'í Studies Review* 3, no. 1 (1993): 75–78; Seena Fazel's "Inheritance," *Bahá'í Studies Review* 4, no. 1 (1994): 76–82; and Sen McGlinn's "Some Considerations Relating to Inheritance Laws," *Bahá'í Studies Review* 5, no. 1 (1995): 37–50.

19. Danesh, "Some Reflections on the Concept of Law in the Bahá'í Faith," *Journal of Bahá'í Studies* 24, nos. 1–2 (2014): 29–35, 39–44; Danesh, "Imagining Bahá'í Law," *Bahá'í Studies Review* 14, no. 1 (2007): 97–105.

20. Examples of connections to social and political theory can be seen in my article "Imagining Bahá'í Law," *Bahá'í Studies Review* 14, no. 1 (2007). For an example of the connection between ontology and law as a form of analysis, see William S. Hatcher's "The Kitáb-i-Aqdas: The Causality Principle in the World of Being," *Bahá'í World 1993–1994* (1994): 189–236.

21. Shoghi Effendi, quoted in the Universal House of Justice, Introduction, in Bahá'u'lláh, the Kitáb-i-Aqdas, 7.

22. Universal House of Justice, Introduction, in Bahá'u'lláh, The Kitáb-i-Aqdas, 7

23. An example of an area of law where Bahá'í institutions currently play an active role is the application of Bahá'í laws regarding marriage and divorce, such as the consent of parents for marriage and the need for a year of patience prior to divorce.

24. For instance, the Universal House Justice recently gave the following guidance on how Bahá'í institutions might apply Bahá'í laws regarding sexual ethics: "They [Bahá'í institutions] do not pry into the personal lives of individuals. Nor are they vindictive and judgemental, eager to punish those who fall short of the Bahá'í standard. Except in extreme cases of blatant and flagrant disregard for the law that could potentially harm the Cause and may require them to administer sanctions, their attention is focused on encouragement, assistance, counsel, and education" (Letter dated April 19, 2013, from the Universal House of Justice to an individual believer, at https://bahai-library.com/pdf/uhj/uhj_bahai_western_life.pdf).

25. Bahá'u'lláh, quoted in Shoghi Effendi, "A Description of the Kitáb-i-Aqdas by Shoghi Effendi," in Bahá'u'lláh, The Kitáb-i-Aqdas, 18.

26. See Ma'ani and Ma'ani Ewing's Laws of the Kitáb-i-Aqdas and Brian D. Lepard's Hope for a Global Ethic.

27. See John S. Hatcher's "Unsealing the Choice Wine at the Family Reunion," Journal of Bahá'í Studies 6, no. 3 (1994): 27–38.

28. See my essay entitled "Some Reflections on the Concept of Law in the Bahá'í Faith," Journal of Bahá'í Studies 24, nos. 1–2 (2014): 39–44.

29. For varying perspectives on this subject see Schaefer's "An Introduction to Bahá'í Law: Doctrinal Foundations, Principles, and Structures," Journal of Law and Religion 18, no. 2 (2003): 308–69, and my article "Imagining Bahá'í Law," Bahá'í Studies Review 14, no. 1 (2007): 97–105.

30. Shoghi Effendi, Unfolding Destiny, 453–54.

31. Walbridge, "Kitáb-i-Aqdas, the Most Holy Book." http://www.bahai-library.com/walbridge_encyclopedia_kitab_aqdas.

32. Bushrui has written and spoken much on this topic. Notes regarding his perspectives can be found at http://bahai-library.com/wilmette_kitab_aqdas_style. A fuller treatment of the subject is found in his book The Style of the Kitáb-i-Aqdas.

33. This is seen in a wide range of works. One example is Schaefer's "An Introduction to Bahá'í Law: Doctrinal Foundations, Principles, and Structures," *Journal of Law and Religion* 18, no. 2 (2003): 308–69.
34. Bahá'u'lláh, The Kitáb-i-Aqdas, ¶4–5.
35. Ibid., ¶6.
36. Ibid., viii.
37. See my article entitled "Some Reflections on the Concept of Law in the Bahá'í Faith," *Journal of Bahá'í Studies* 24, no. 1–2 (2014): 24–46.
38. In some respects, the more extensive commentary appears in works that are openly adversarial to the Bahá'í Faith, such as Francesco Ficicchia's *Der Bahá'ismus: Weltreligion der Zukunft? Geschichte, Lehre und Organisation in kritischer Anfrage* (Bahá'ism: World Religion of the Future? A Critical Inquiry into Its History, Teachings, and Organization), which drew highly critical conclusions about the dissemination of the Kitáb-i-Aqdas, the functioning of the Bahá'í administrative order, Bahá'í laws, and other topics. Ficicchia's assertions were soundly rebutted by Udo Schaefer, Nicola Towfigh, and Ulrich Gollmer in their volume *Desinformation als Methode* (published in English as *Making the Crooked Straight*).
39. See my article entitled "The Politics of Delay: Social Meanings and the Historical Treatment of Bahá'í Law," *World Order* 35, no. 3 (2004): 33–45.
40. Bahá'u'lláh, quoted in the Universal House of Justice, Introduction to Bahá'u'lláh, The Kitáb-i-Aqdas, 6.
41. Bahá'í laws on sexuality, which are applicable only to members of the Bahá'í community, emphasize that sexual relations should be between members of the opposite sex and within the institution of marriage. However, Bahá'ís are enjoined by the Universal House of Justice "not to attempt to impose these standards on society. To regard a person who has a homosexual orientation with prejudice or disdain is entirely against the spirit of the Faith" (letter dated May 9, 2014 from the Universal House of Justice to an individual believer, https://bahai-library.com/uhj_attitude_changes_homosexuality).
42. While gender equality is a cardinal principle of the Bahá'í Faith, and one for which it is quite well known, there are some apparent deviations from it—including, most notably, the restriction of the membership of the Universal House of Justice to men. At the same time, however,

gender equality is expressed at multiple levels and in different ways in both institutional and community Bahá'í life, and the principle of gender equality has been advocated for, including in several groundbreaking ways in nineteenth-century Iran, since the earliest days of the Faith.

43. The Kitáb-i-Aqdas contemplates capital punishment and lifetime incarceration as valid punishments for murder.

44. While there is substantial discussion on the Internet about the Bahá'í teachings on homosexuality, there are very few works published that look at the subject matter from a primarily theological and community practice perspective. There are some discussions of the topic in general works about Bahá'í law, but, with a few exceptions, detailed analyses of the legal aspects of Bahá'í teachings on the subject are still emerging.

45. See, for instance, Le Lievre's "The Death Penalty: Australian Legal Institutions vs. the Bahá'í Faith?" in *75 Years of the Bahá'í Faith in Australasia,* and Schaefer's "Crime and Punishment: Bahá'í Perspectives for a Future Criminal Law," In *Law and International Order, Proceedings of the First European Bahá'í Conference on Law and International Order,* 8–11.

46. In response to queries from individual Bahá'ís, the Universal House of Justice has written letters situating these laws within the broader understanding of Bahá'u'lláh's teachings. See, for example, the letter dated May 9, 2014, written on behalf of the Universal House of Justice that distances the discourse on homosexuality from the premises underlying current public debate. https://bahai-library.com/uhj_attitude_changes_homosexuality.

47. Universal House of Justice, Introduction in Baha'u'llah, The Kitab-i-Aqdas, 6 –7.

48. Ibid.

49. 2010 Ridván message from the Universal House of Justice to the Bahá'ís of the world.

50. Ibid.

Works Cited

Works by Bahá'u'lláh

The Call of the Divine Beloved: Selected Mystical Works of Bahá'u'lláh. Wilmette, IL: Bahá'í Publishing Trust, 2018.

Epistle to the Son of the Wolf. Wilmette, IL: Bahá'í Publishing Trust, 1988.

Gleanings from the Writings of Bahá'u'lláh. Wilmette, IL: Bahá'í Publishing, 2005.

The Kitáb-i-Aqdas: The Most Holy Book. Wilmette, IL: Bahá'í Publishing, 2019.

The Kitáb-i-Íqán: The Book of Certitude. Wilmette, IL: Bahá'í Publishing, 2019.

Prayers and Meditations. Wilmette, IL: Bahá'í Publishing, 2014.

Tablets of Bahá'u'lláh Revealed After the Kitáb-i-Aqdas. Compiled by the Research Department of the Universal House of Justice and translated by Habib Taherzadeh with the assistance of a Committee at the Bahá'í World Center. Wilmette, IL: Bahá'í Publishing Trust, 1988.

The Summons of the Lord of Hosts. Wilmette, IL: Bahá'í Publishing Trust, 2006.

Works of 'Abdu'l-Bahá

Foundations of World Unity. Wilmette, IL: Bahá'í Publishing Trust, 1979.

The Promulgation of Universal Peace. Wilmette, IL: Bahá'í Publishing Trust, 2007.

The Secret of Divine Civilization. Translated from the Persian by Marzieh Gail in consultation with Ali-Kuli-Khan. Wilmette, IL: Bahá'í Publishing Trust, 2015.

Selections from the Writings of 'Abdu'l-Bahá. Compiled by the Research Department of the Universal House of Justice. Translated by a Committee at the Bahá'í World Center and by Marzieh Gail. Wilmette, IL: Bahá'í Publishing, 2010.

Some Answered Questions. Wilmette, IL: Bahá'í Publishing, 2014.

A Traveller's Narrative Written to Illustrate the Episode of the Báb. Translated by E.G. Browne. Los Angeles: Kalimát Press, 2004.

Will and Testament of 'Abdu'l-Bahá. Wilmette, IL: Bahá'í Publishing Trust, 1944.

Works of Shoghi Effendi

The Advent of Divine Justice. Wilmette, IL: Bahá'í Publishing Trust, 2006.

Bahá'í Administration: Selected Messages 1922–1932. Wilmette, IL: Bahá'í Publishing Trust, 1974.

Call to the Nations. Wilmette, IL: Bahá'í Publishing, 2014.

Directives of the Guardian. Wilmette, IL: Bahá'í Publishing Trust, 1973.

God Passes By. Wilmette, IL: Bahá'í Publishing Trust, 2018.

Messages to the Bahá'í World, 1950–1957. Wilmette, IL: Bahá'í Publishing Trust, 1971.

Unfolding Destiny: The Messages from the Guardian of the Bahá'í Faith to the Bahá'ís of the British Isles. London: Bahá'í Publishing Trust, 1981.

The World Order of Bahá'u'lláh. Wilmette, IL: Bahá'í Publishing Trust, 1955.

Works of the Universal House of Justice

The Five Year Plan 2011–2016: Messages from the Universal House of Justice. West Palm Beach, FL: Palabra Publications, 2011.

Messages from the Universal House of Justice, 1963–1986. Compiled by Geoffry Marks. Bahá'í Publishing Trust, 1996.

The Promise of World Peace. Haifa: Bahá'í World Center, 1985.

Compilations

A Chaste and Holy Life. Compiled by the Research Department of the Universal House of Justice, at the Bahá'í World Center. London: Bahá'í Publishing Trust, 1988.

The Compilation of Compilations: Prepared by the Universal House of Justice 1963–1990, vol. 2. Australia: Bahá'í Publications Australia, 1991.

Official Statements and Commentaries

Century of Light. Prepared under the supervision of the Universal House of Justice. Haifa: Bahá'í World Center, 2001.

Other Works

Abizadeh, Arash. "Politics Beyond War: Ulrich Gollmer's Contribution to Bahá'í Political Thought." *World Order* 35, no. 3 (2004): 19–23.

———. "Democratic Elections Without Campaigns? Normative Bahá'í Foundations of National Bahá'í Elections." *World Order* 37 (2005): 7–49.

Alai, Cyrus. "Kitáb-i-Aqdas as Described and Glorified by Shoghi Effendi." *Lights of Irfan, Book 1*. Wilmette, IL: Irfan Colloquia, 2000, 21–30.

Amanat, Abbas. *Resurrection and Renewal: The Making of the Babi Movement in Iran, 1844–1850*. Ithaca, N.Y.: Cornell University Press, 1989.

Bahá'í International Community, Office of Public Information. *The Prosperity of Humankind*. Haifa: Bahá'í World Center, 1995.

Balyuzi, Hasan M. *'Abdu'l-Bahá: The Centre of the Covenant*. Oxford: George Ronald, 1971.

———. *The Báb: Herald of the Day of Days*. Oxford: George Ronald, 1973.

Berman, Harold J. *Law and Revolution: The Formation of the Western Legal Tradition*. Cambridge: Harvard University Press, 1983.

Browne, E. G. *Selections from the Writings of E. G. Browne on the Bábí and Bahá'í Religions*. Edited by Moojan Momen. Oxford: George Ronald, 1987.

Buck, Christopher. *Symbol and Secret: Qur'án Commentary in Bahá'u'lláh's Kitáb-i Íqán*. Los Angeles: Kalimát Press, 1995.

Bushrui, Suheil. *The Style of the Kitáb-i-Aqdas: Aspects of the Sublime*. Bethesda: University Press of Maryland, 1995.

Cole, Juan R. I. *The Concept of the Manifestation in the Bahá'í Writings*. Ottawa: Bahá'í Studies Publications, 1982.

———. *Modernity and the Millennium: The Genesis of the Bahá'í Faith in the Nineteenth-Century Middle East*. New York: Columbia University Press, 1998.

Coulson, Noel J. *A History of Islamic Law*. Edinburgh: Edinburgh University Press, 1964.

Cox, Robert and Timothy Sinclair, editors. *Approaches to World Order*. Cambridge: Cambridge University Press, 1996.

Cox, Robert W. & Michael G. Schechter. *The Political Economy of a Plural World: Critical Reflections on Power, Morals and Civilization*. Abingdon: Routledge, 2002.

Danesh, Roshan. "Church and State in the Bahá'í Faith: An Epistemic Approach." *Journal of Law and Religion* 24, no. 1: 21–64.

———. "Imagining Bahá'í Law." *Bahá'í Studies Review* 14, no. 1 (2007): 97–105.

———. "Internationalism and Divine Law." *Journal of Law and Religion* 19, no. 2 (2003–4): 209–42.

———. "The Politics of Delay—Social Meanings and the Historical Treatment of Bahá'í Law." *World Order* 35, no. 3 (2004): 33–45.

———. "Some Reflections on the Concept of Law in the Bahá'í Faith." *Journal of Bahá'í Studies* 24, no. 1–2 (March–June 2014): 27–46.

Donahue, Jr., Charles. "A Crisis of Law? Reflections on the Church and the Law over the Centuries." *The Jurist* 65 (2005): 1–30.

Fazel, Seena. "Inheritance." *Bahá'í Studies Review* 4, no. 1 (1994): 76–82.

Ficicchia, Francesco. *Der Bahaismus-Weltreligion der Zukunft? Geschichte, Lehre und Organisation in kritischer Anfrage.* Stuttgart: Evangelische Zentralstelle fur Weltanschauungsfragen, 1981.

Graham, Bryan. "The Bahá'í Faith and Economics: A Review and Synthesis." *Bahá'í Studies Review* 7 (1997): 15–38.

Hatcher, John S. *The Arc of Ascent: The Purpose of Physical Reality II.* Oxford: George Ronald, 1994.

———. "The Equality of Women: The Bahá'í Principle of Complementarity." *Journal of Bahá'í Studies* 2, no. 3 (1990).

———. "Unsealing the Choice Wine at the Family Reunion." *Journal of Bahá'í Studies* 6, no. 3 (1994).

Hatcher, John S., and William S. Hatcher. *The Law of Love Enshrined: Selected Essays by John Hatcher and William Hatcher.* Oxford: George Ronald, 1995.

Hatcher, William S. "The Kitáb-i-Aqdas: The Causality Principle in the World of Being." *The Bahá'í World: An International Record 1993–1994.* Haifa: Bahá'í World Center, 1994, 189–236.

———. "Reflections on Infallibility." *Journal of Bahá'í Studies* 17, no. 1–4 (2007).

Huntington, Samuel P. *The Clash of Civilizations and the Remaking of World Order.* New York: Touchstone, 1997.

"The Kitáb-i-Aqdas: its place in Bahá'í literature." *The Bahá'í World: An International Record 1992–1993.* Author unknown. Haifa: Bahá'í World Center, 1993, 105–117.

Knight, W. Andy. "Coexisting Civilizations in a Plural World." *International Studies Review* 5, no. 3 (2003): 403–5.

Lample, Paul. *Revelation and Social Reality: Learning to Translate What is Written into Reality.* West Palm Beach, FL: Palabra Publications, 2009.

Latimer, George. "The Social Teachings of the Bahai Movement." *Star of the West* 7 (1916): 133–139, 145–148.

Le Lievre, Roger. "The Death Penalty: Australian Legal Institutions vs. the Bahá'í Faith?" *75 Years of the Bahá'í Faith in Australasia.* Rosebery, Australia: Association for Bahá'í Studies Australia, 1996.

Lee, Anthony. *Choice Wine: The Kitáb-i-Aqdas and the Development of Bahá'í Law, Address at Fifth Annual Colloquium on Scriptural Studies.* Presentation by the author. Wilmette, IL: Bahá'í Studies Institute, 1995.

Lepard, Brian D. *Hope for a Global Ethic: Shared Principles in Religious Scriptures.* Wilmette, IL: Bahá'í Publishing Trust, 2005.

Lessig, Lawrence. "The Regulation of Social Meaning." *The University of Chicago Law Review* 62, no. 3 (1995): 943–1045.

Lewis, Bernard. *The Political Language of Islam.* Chicago: University of Chicago Press, 1995.

Ma'ani, Baharieh Rouhani, and Sovaida Ma'ani Ewing. *Laws of the Kitáb-i-Aqdas.* Oxford: George Ronald, 2004.

May, Dann J. "The Bahá'í Principle of Religious Unity: A Dynamic Perspectivism," in *Revisioning the Sacred: New Perspectives on a Bahá'í Theology,* edited by Jack McLean. Published in *Studies in the Bábí and Bahá'í Religions,* vol. 8. Los Angeles: Kalimát, 1997.

———. *The Bahá'í Principle of Religious Unity and the Challenge of Radical Pluralism.* Unpublished master's thesis in Interdisciplinary Studies, University of North Texas, 1993. http://bahai-library.com/theses/religious.unity/. Last accessed Sept. 17, 2008.

McGlinn, Sen. *Church and State: A Postmodern Political Theology, Book One.* Self-published, 2005.

———. "Church and State in the World Order of Bahá'u'lláh." Unpublished manuscript on file with the author.

———. "Some Considerations Relating to the Inheritance Laws of the Kitáb-i-Aqdas." *Bahá'í Studies Review* 5, no. 1 (1995): 37–50.

———. "Theocratic Ideas and Assumptions in Bahá'í Literature: An Inquiry." *Reason and Revelation: New Directions in Bahá'í Thought.* Edited by Seena Fazeel and John Danesh. Los Angeles: Kalimát Press, 2002, 39–82.

———. "A Theology of the State from the Bahá'í Teachings." *Journal of Church & State* 41 (1999): 697–724.

Modarressi Tabátabá'i, Hossein. *An Introduction to Shí'í Law: A Bibliographical Study*. London: Ithaca Press, 1984.

Nakhjavani, Bahiyyih. "Exemption." *Bahá'í Studies Review* 3, no. 1 (1993): 75–78.

National Spiritual Assembly of the Bahá'ís of the United States. *The Vision of Race Unity: America's Most Challenging Issue*. Wilmette, IL: Bahá'í Publishing Trust, 1991.

Ransom-Kehler, Keith. "A World at Peace: Bahá'i Administration as Presented to a Group of Free Thinkers." *The Bahá'í Magazine* 24, no. 7 (1933): 216.

Research Department at the Bahá'í World Center. "Memorandum to the Universal House of Justice. 14 August 1996," in Schaefer, Udo, *Bahá'í Ethics in Light of Scripture Vol. 2*. Oxford: George Ronald, 2009, 695–99.

———. "Monogamy, Sexual Equality, Marital Equality, and the Supreme Tribunal." Memorandum dated June 27, 1996 to the Universal House of Justice.

Robarts, John A. "A Few Reminiscences about Shoghi Effendi Taken from Pilgrim Notes of January 1955, from the Canadian National Spiritual Assembly Film Retrospective, and from Some Other Words of the Beloved Guardian." *The Vision of Shoghi Effendi*. Ottawa: Association for Bahá'í Studies, 1993.

Saiedi, Nader. "An Introduction to 'Abdu'l-Bahá's *The Secret of Divine Civilization*." *Converging Realities* 1, no. 1 (2000).

———. *Logos and Civilization: Spirit, History, and Order in the Writings of Bahá'u'lláh*. Bethesda, MD: University Press of Maryland, 2000.

Schacht, Joseph. *An Introduction to Islamic Law*. Oxford: Clarendon Press, 1964.

Schaefer, Udo. "Crime and Punishment: Bahá'í Perspectives for a Future Criminal Law." *Law and International Order, Proceedings of the First European Bahá'í Conference on Law and International Order*. Bahá'í Publishing Trust, 1996.

———. "Infallible Institutions?" *Bahá'í Studies Review* 9 (1999/2000): 17–45.

———. "An Introduction to Bahá'í Law: Doctrinal Foundations, Principles, and Structures." *Journal of Law and Religion* 18, no. 2 (2002–2003): 308–69.

Schaefer, Udo, Nicola Towfigh and Ulrich Gollmer. *Making the Crooked Straight: A Contribution to Bahá'í Apologetics.* Translated by Geraldine Schuckelt. Oxford: George Ronald, 2006.

Schweitz, Martha L. "The Kitáb-i-Aqdas: Bahá'í Law, Legitimacy, and World Order." *Journal of Bahá'í Studies* 6, no. 1 (1994): 35–59.

———. "Of Webs and Ladders: Gender Equality in Bahá'í Law." *World Order* 27, no. 1 (1995): 21–39.

Stiles Maneck, Susan, et al. "A Question of Gender: A Forum on the Status of Men in Bahá'í Law." *Dialogue* 2, no. 1 (1987): 14–34.

Stockman, Robert H. "Revelation, Interpretation, and Elucidation in the Bahá'í Writings." *Scripture and Revelation.* Edited by Moojan Momen. Oxford: George Ronald, 1997, 53–68.

Taherzadeh, Adib. *The Covenant of Bahá'u'lláh.* Oxford: George Ronald, 1992.

———. *The Revelation of Bahá'u'lláh: 'Akka, The Early Years 1868–77.* Volume 3. Oxford: George Ronald, 1983.

Vogel, Frank. *Islamic Law and Legal System: Studies of Saudi Arabia.* Leiden: Brill, 2000.

Walbridge, John. "Kitáb-i-Aqdas, the Most Holy Book." 1999. http://www.bahai-library.com/walbridge_encyclopedia_kitab_aqdas.

———. *Sacred Acts, Sacred Space, Sacred Time.* Oxford: George Ronald, 1996.

Walbridge, Linda, and John Walbridge. "Bahá'í Laws and the Status of Men." *World Order* 19, no. 1–2 (1984–85): 25–36.

Weiss, Bernard. *The Spirit of Islamic Law.* Athens: University of Georgia Press, 1998.

Index

A

'Abdu'l-Bahá
    articulation of world vision, 11–12
    explanation of the Universal House of Justice, 101–102
    injunction to avoid politics, 105
    love as the most great law, 17
    meaning of name, 79
    teaching on oneness, 110
    teaching on unity and diversity, 111
    teachings on truth, 110
    Will and Testament, 80
    writings considered authoritative interpretations of scripture, 60
acts of worship, 100
Administrative Order
    construction of, 80
    embryonic form of, 121
    future capacity of nucleus and pattern of new World Order, 74
    nucleus and pattern of World Order of Bahá'u'lláh, 121
    rooted in ethic of equality, 181
arcs of ascent and descent, 29–32

B

Báb, the
    establishment of Badí' calendar, 41
    expectation that own laws would be superceded, 137
    fulfillment of Islamic prophecies, 89–90
    rejection of, 92

279

Bábí community, 34, 89, 170
Bábí Faith, 43, 90, 126
Badí' calendar, 41
Bahá'í Faith
  founding of, 80
  Golden Age of, 86
  stages of, 82–83
Bahá'í law
  social and political dimension of, 48–55
Bahá'í theocracy, 73, 76, 105, 120–21
Bahá'u'lláh
  break with Shi'i context, 5, 11
  declaration of, 138
  explication of law, 10
  lawgiver, 137
  legal language, 12–17
  prohibition of conflict, 34
  Prophet-Founder of Bahá'í religion, 59, 60
  radicalism of, 7
  rationale for obedience to the law, 17–23
  request to 'Abdu'l-Bahá to write *The Secret of Divine Civilization*, 11
  revelation of Kitáb-i-Aqdas, 8, 31
  sovereignty of, 92
  station of purpose, 166
Bayán, 90, 133, 213

C

church and state
  epistemic approach to, 87–123
conferred infallibility, 103

D

disintegration, 149–54
dynamism, 65

E

Emperor Francis Joseph, 134

F

Faith of God, 37
flexibility, 202, 216
fragmentation, 149, 151–54
future society, 163, 224

H

hearts, 33–34, 69, 81, 88, 93, 104, 115, 121, 131, 138, 170, 176, 178, 182, 189
Houses of Justice, 79–80, 82, 144
humanity
    collective adolescence of, 65
    collective maturation of, 149

I

Imamate
    importance to Shi'i Islam, 6
    legal authority of in Shi'i Islam, 136
integration, 154–59
    economic and social, 63
    eternal soul and physical body, 65
    patterns of, 111

K

Kaiser William I, 134
King of Kings, 134
Kingdom of God, 60, 86–87, 106, 111–12
kings and rulers, 41, 115, 134, 155
Kitáb-i-Aqdas, the
    annotations of, 219

L

N

S

Secret of Divine Civilization, The, 11, 115
Shi'i
    imitation of a learned religious authority and, 9
    importance of obedience to attain salvation, 5
Shoghi Effendi
    appointment of as Guardian, 80
    authorized portions of the Kitáb-i-Aqdas and, 210
    conferred infallibility of, 103
    construction of administrative order and, 80
    description of City of God, 53
    description of humanity's collective adolescence, 65
    dissociation of the Faith from politics and, 105
    explanation of "new World Order," 61
    grandson of 'Abdu'l-Bahá, 80
    observation regarding emergence of federated system, 156–57
    passing of, 80, 145
    prediction of Administrative Order, 74
    successorship and authority of, 129
    theme of fragmentation, 151
sovereignty
    divine, 88–97
    Kitáb-i-Íqán and, 90, 94
Sultan 'Abdu'l-'Azíz, 134
Sunni
    importance of obedience to attain salvation, 5
    power of clerics, 100
sword, 169
    expressions of, 36
    prohibition of, 33–35, 37–39, 70–71, 113, 169–70, 182

T

tact, 22, 48, 73, 113, 139–40, 200, 221
twin duties of human beings, 13

U

uniformity, 168

unity, 112
    eye of, 112
    of God, 40, 91, 132
    of humanity, 126, 163, 167, 171, 183, 185–86, 188
    of nations and peoples of the world, 73, 110
    of reality, 112
    of religion, 163

Universal House of Justice, 101–102
    all matters of state to be referred to, 81
    conferred infallibility of, 103
    democratic institution, 101
    description of Kitábi-Aqdas, 211
    election of every five years, 144
    first election of in 1963, 80
    grant of legislative powers, 100
    preeminent institution of Bahá'í administrative system, 73
    relationship of between religious texts and legislative acts, 145–48
    supreme administrative body, 198

V

victory, 169

vision, 167

W

Will and Testament of 'Abdu'l-Bahá, 80, 144
    appointment of Shoghi Effendi as Guardian, 80
    creation of secondary houses of justice, 144

wisdom, 33, 48, 65, 90, 101–102, 113, 138–39, 144, 164, 168–69, 200, 221

World Order of Bahá'u'lláh, 121